Persuasion
Advances Through Meta-Analysis

Quantitative Methods in Communication

George A. Barnett, Editor

Persuasion: Advances Through Meta-Analysis
Mike Allen and Raymond W. Preiss, eds.

Network Models of the Diffusion of Innovations
Thomas W. Valente

forthcoming

The Zen of Empirical Research
William D. Richards

Persuasion
Advances Through Meta-Analysis

edited by

Mike Allen
University of Wisconsin-Milwaukee

Raymond W. Preiss
University of Puget Sound

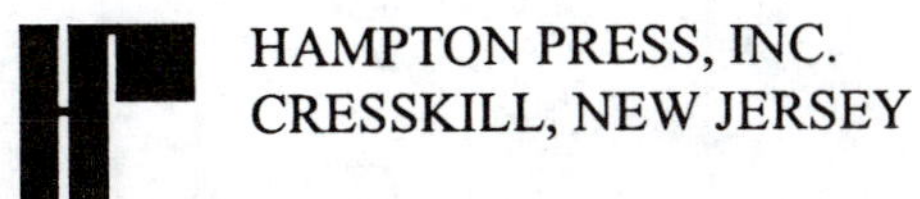
HAMPTON PRESS, INC.
CRESSKILL, NEW JERSEY

Printed in the United States of America

Library of Congress Cataloging-in-Publication Data

Persuasion : advances through meta-analysis / edited by Mike Allen, Raymond W. Preiss.

p. cm. -- (Quantitative methods in communication)

Includes bibliographical references and indexes.

ISBN 1-57273-066-8 (hardcover). -- ISBN 1-57273-067-6 (pbk.)

1. Persuasion (Psychology) I. Allen, Mike. II. Preiss, Raymond W. III. Series.

BF637.P4P42 1998

153.8'52--dc21 98-11061

CIP

Hampton Press Inc.
23 Broadway
Cresskill, NJ 07626

Contents

Contributors

Mike Allen is an associate professor at the University of Wisconsin-Milwaukee. His primary area of interest is the transmission of influence within interpersonal, public, and organizational settings. He has articles published in *Human Communication Research, Communication Monographs, Psychological Bulletin*, and *Communication Theory.*

William Benoit is an associate professor at the University of Missouri. His specialty is the analysis of public discourse. His work has been supported by federal grants and he has recently published a book on apologia as well as edited a book on argumentation.

David Buller is an associate professor at the University of Arizona. His work has been funded by federal grants. He concentrates on the issues of nonverbal communication. His research has appeared in *Human Communication Research, Journal of Nonverbal Behavior*, and *Communication Monographs.*

Nancy Burrell is an associate professor at the University of Wisconsin-Milwaukee. Her primary interests are the study of conflict and its resolution within the family. Her work has appeared in *Human Communication Research, Mediation Quarterly, Management Communication Quarterly*, and *Communication Monographs.*

Michael Cruz is an assistant professor at the University of Wisconsin-Madison. His focus on investigation involves issues in small group interaction and his research has appeared in *Communication Monographs.*

James Dillard is a professor at the University of Wisconsin-Madison. His area of research considers the issues of compliance gaining and social influence. His publications have appeared in *Personality and Social Psychology Bulletin, Human Communication Research,* and *Communication Monographs* as well as an edited book on compliance gaining.

Barbara Mae Gayle is an associate professor at the University of Portland. Her research specialty examines the issues surrounding gender and communication in society. Her current grant funded research examines issues of early 20th-century women's communication.

John Hall is a research associate at the University of Arizona. His research emphasis is on health-care communication issues.

Mark Hamilton is an associate professor at the University of Connecticut. His focus is on the issues surrounding the use and impact of various forms of language in social interaction and influence. He has published in *Communication Monographs, Human Communication Research, World Communication,* and *Communication Theory.*

John E. Hunter is a professor at Michigan State University. His focus is on methodology, personnel selection, and social influence. He has published two books on meta-analysis as well as a book on mathematical modeling of persuasion theories.

Randall Koper is an associate professor at the University of Pacific. His focus is on nonverbal communication. His research has appeared in *Human Communication Research* and the *Journal of Nonverbal Behavior.*

Paul Mongeau is an associate professor at the University of Miami. His interests include interpersonal communication. He has published in *Communication Yearbook, Communication Monographs,* and *Journal of Social Behavior and Personality.*

Raymond Preiss is an associate professor at the University of Puget Sound. His interests include the analysis of cognition and its relationship to communication. He has published in *Communication Education, Human Communication Research,* and *Communication Reports.*

John Reinard is a professor at California State University-Fullerton. His research program examines the impact of evidence on persuasion and argument. He has published a book on argumentation and articles for *Human Communication Research.*

James B. Stiff is an associate professor at Arizona State University. His research focuses on deception detection and jury selection. He has published two books as well as articles in the *Journal of Personality and Social Psychology* and *Communication Monographs.*

1

A Framework for Understanding: Meta-Analyses of the Persuasion Literature

Mark A. Hamilton
University of Connecticut

John E. Hunter
Michigan State University

As a technique for theory construction, meta-analysis is more than useful. It is a necessary tool. Artifacts at the level of individual studies often thwart efforts to draw correct theoretical inferences.

Many people know that meta-analysis is a good way to pull together findings across studies to more accurately assess treatment effects, basic correlations, and other facts. To test theories, you must have established facts. Because meta-analysis is a good way to accurately establish facts, it is indirectly a key part of theory testing. Fewer people are aware that the results of meta-analyses can differ in quality. Several factors influence the accuracy of meta-analytic findings. Some research domains are extensive, other scant. Some research domains are plagued by method artifacts, others are not. Researchers differ widely in their ability to correct for artifacts when they are present.

We begin this chapter by examining the objectives of meta-analysis. We identify the major study artifacts that often preclude researchers from drawing correct theoretical inferences, and explain why meta-analyses differ in terms of quality. In the second part of the chapter, we turn to a different agenda. We seek to integrate the findings in the various chapters of this book by relating all of the findings to a common theory and use information processing theory as a framework for explaining the meta-analytic findings in each of the substantive chapters.

THE GENERAL OBJECTIVES OF META-ANALYSIS

The purpose of meta-analysis is to use the data from multiple studies to generate a more accurate interpretation of findings than is possible by considering the studies one at a time. No study is perfect. The search for methods to improve the accuracy of scientific estimation and inference has been long. Some researchers now recognize that the way to improve the accuracy of their estimates is to identify and quantify study imperfections or "artifacts." Once a study artifact has been identified and quantified, it becomes possible to look for methods to correct for the impact of the artifact on study results.

At present, most researchers make no corrections for study imperfections. In part this is due to lack of knowledge and in part due to defensiveness produced by the virulence of current publication review practice. To correct for study imperfections, you must admit study imperfections. Many reviewers will seize on an admission that the study is not perfect as a reason for rejecting the study. As a result, current review practice causes researchers to pretend that their studies are perfect. The unfortunate fact is that there are no perfect studies. To pretend that there are perfect studies is to ignore the potential for correcting the effects of study imperfections.

Failure to correct for study imperfections means that study outcomes will be inaccurate. The larger the study imperfections, the larger the error produced when artifacts are not corrected. The same is true of meta-analysis. If a meta-analysis simply uses study outcome statistics without correcting for artifacts, the results of the meta-analysis will also be inaccurate. The probability of correction is much greater in meta-analytic reviews than in primary studies because the probability of sophisticated methodological knowledge is greater among meta-analysts. However, not all meta-analysts are sophisticated. Furthermore, there are many research domains where no primary researcher gathers the information necessary for the meta-analyst to make corrections.

Correction for Artifacts

Meta-analysis can solve problems that cannot be addressed within any one study. The most important artifact is sampling error. Meta-analysis can also be used to solve other problems related to study quality, such as the effects of error of measurement, imperfect construct validity, dichotomization of continuous variables, and restriction in the range of the dependent variable (Hunter & Schmidt, 1990, pp. 43-199, 231-339; Hunter & Rodgers, 1995).

Sampling Error. Surveys have consistently shown that current social scientists vastly underestimate the size of sampling error. Most researchers are shocked by the following facts. Suppose that we measure the size of an experimental treatment effect using the correlation between the treatment variable and the dependent variable. In order to have 95% confidence that the estimate of the correlation is accurate to two decimal places, the sample size needed is $N = 160{,}000$. Even if the typical study had a sample size of $N = 1000$, we would need the data from 160 studies to achieve that total sample size. In the experimental literature in the social sciences, the typical sample size is closer to $N = 100$ than to $N = 1000$. To get a total sample size of 160,000 with primary studies with N=100, you need the data from 1600 studies. Thus, the only way to solve the problem of sampling error is to combine the results across many studies. That is, meta-analysis is the only way to solve the problem of sampling error in contemporary research.

Measurement Error. When designing a study, most researchers use the best measurement procedure available to them. However, empirical studies consistently show that measurement is never perfect. In any process where measurement uses human responses, the randomness in human response process guarantees a large random element in measurement. This is random error of measurement or imperfect "reliability." Every instrument in the social sciences has been found to be imperfect. In most research domains, the average reliability is only modest (that is, within the range of .60 to .80), and there are some domains where the reliability is much lower. If no correction is made for random error of measurement, the correlation representing the treatment effect will be seriously understated.

Construct Validity. In most domains where human responses are part of the measurement process, there is slippage from perfect construct validity. The measurement is usually subject to at least minor systematic causal factors other than the construct that the researcher intends to measure. That is, in most domains there is at least some small measure of systematic error of measurement. In some domains, the construct validity of the measurement is only modest or even poor. If no correction is made for imperfect construct validity, the correlation representing the treatment effect may be seriously understated.

Dichotomizing Continuous Variables. In some studies, the researcher simplifies the data by using a binary nominal distinction to represent what is actually a quantitative variable. This artificial dichotomization diminishes the size of the treatment effect. Consider the case in which a researcher performs a median (50%–50%) split on continuously distributed variables. If the researcher conducts a median split on either the independent or dependent variable, the effect will only be .80 as large. If the researcher dichotomizes both variables, the effect size would be reduced by 36%. In more extreme splits of a distribution, such as a 90%–10% break, dichotomizing either the independent or dependent variable will result in an effect that is only .60 as large. If both independent and dependent variables are dichotomized with this extreme split, the effect size will be reduced by 64%. That is, in the case of extreme splits, the correlation would be only about one-third as large. If no correction is made for artificial dichotomization, the correlation representing the treatment effect will be seriously understated.

Restriction in Range. In some studies, the data available is for a population that is different from the desired reference population. The most common problem is that the data come from a restricted population, consisting of a subset of people selected from the reference population. This is called *range restriction*. The treatment effect will be reduced by range restriction. If the population is very severely restricted, the treatment effect can be reduced to near zero levels. If no correction is made for range restriction, the correlation representing the treatment effect will be seriously understated.

Conclusion as to Artifact. In every research domain yet studied, the studies have been found to be subject to sampling error and random error of measurement. Systematic error has been studied much less frequently, but has been found in all contexts where it could be studied. The occurrence of artificial dichotomization and range restriction is more sporadic. In every domain yet studied, meta-analysis is not only a convenient way to summarize multiple studies, it is required in order to generate correct estimates of actual treatment effects.

Variation in the Quality of Meta-Analyses

There are two reasons for the considerable variation in the quality and depth of current meta-analyses. First, research domains differ broadly in the amount of information available for computing effect sizes and adjusting for artifacts. Second, meta-analysts differ greatly in their methodological sophistication.

Study Limitations. There is immense variation in the extent to which researchers know statistical sampling theory, psychometric theory of measurement, and the other methods necessary to identify study imperfections and then correct for them. Hence, there is enormous variation in the extent to which primary research studies collect the information necessary to correct for study imperfections at the time of the primary study report. Meta-analysis provides an opportunity to correct for study imperfections at the point of reviewing the study.

In order to correct for study imperfections, it is not necessary that every researcher know enough to collect information about the effect of study imperfections. Rather, it would be enough if a representative sample of the studies in the domain collect the necessary information. Unfortunately, there are still many domains where *no* researcher collects the necessary information. In such domains, it is not possible for the meta-analyst to correct for those imperfections. That is, in very unsophisticated research domains, increased methodological sophistication on the part of the meta-analyst cannot make up for lack of sophistication on the part of the researchers.

Limitations in Reviewer Knowledge. It would be nice if all those who did meta-analysis were highly sophisticated in methodology, but that is not the case. The same variation in sophistication that is found among primary researchers is also found among those who review research, and hence among those who do meta-analysis. The result is that many meta-analysts make no effort to correct for certain study imperfections; they are unaware of a given problem, so it never occurs to them to correct for it.

Sophisticated methods of meta-analysis have been available since the inception of the technique. Even in their earliest methods, Schmidt and Hunter (1977, 1978) used psychometric theory to correct for the effects of sampling error, random error of measurement, and range restriction. By 1990, they had extended correction procedures to handle 11 different dimensions of study imperfection. However, many reviewers do not understand psychometric theory, so they do not understand the methods of meta-analysis that use sophisticated statistical procedures. These reviewers use more limited methods of meta-analysis.

When Glass (1976) coined the term *meta-analysis*, he was using a procedure of meta-analysis that made no correction for the effects of sampling error or other artifacts. It is not that Glass did not know of these study imperfections, he simply made a conscious decision to keep his methods simple enough so that even the most limited researchers could understand them. Glass used the same procedure that was used much earlier by people like Ghiselli (1966, 1973). That is, the meta-analyst converts results to a common statistical metric, then averages the values across studies. The most limited reviewers still use the original Glass procedure.

There is now a continuum of meta-analysis procedures that introduce the various corrections for artifacts, ranging from the Glass procedures that completely ignore study imperfections to the current Hunter and Schmidt procedures that can correct for as many as 11 dimensions of study imperfection. For example, many reviewers add a statistical test for "homogeneity" to the Glass procedure (Hunter & Schmidt, 1990, pp. 100-112). The null hypothesis for the significance test for homogeneity is the hypothesis that the population value of the outcome statistic is the same in all studies. That is, the null hypothesis is that sampling error might cause all of the observed variation in study results.

Hunter and Schmidt (1982) noted that the null hypothesis is very unrealistic; it ignores variation in study quality on all the other known dimensions of study imperfection. They recommend much more accurate procedures. However, the homogeneity test may be a rough approximation of real variation in some domains. In any case, a meta-analysis that tests for homogeneity is an improvement over a meta-analysis that ignores sampling error altogether.

The larger the number of dimensions of study imperfection that are corrected, the more accurate the estimates generated by the meta-analysis. However, even the simplest Glass procedure generates average results that have much smaller sampling error than is true of the results from single studies. That is, even the most unsophisticated meta-analysis improves considerably on the findings of single isolated studies.

INFORMATION PROCESSING THEORY AS AN ORGANIZATIONAL FRAMEWORK

One of the ways in which meta-analysis improves on the findings of single, isolated studies is that it allows researchers to observe patterns of results that are not visible at the level of primary studies. The results of single studies often appear to contradict one another because of sampling error and other study artifacts. The authors of single studies therefore find it hard to create meaningful theories. Because meta-analysis reduces the impact of sampling error and other study imperfections, the results of meta-analysis are less subject to false conflicts and false contradictions. This was true of the findings in this book. As we read the chapters of this book, we observed that nearly all the general findings were consistent with the information processing theory of persuasion. To show other readers the striking meaningfulness to results free of study artifacts, we share our observations.

In the sections that follow, we present a process model of attitude change, and then equations for predicting attitude change. We argue that information processing theory can explain as well as predict persuasion.

A Causal Process Model

In his process model of attitude change, McGuire (1968a, p. 179) proposed that receivers proceed through the following sequence of stages: exposure to the message, attention to the message, comprehension of the arguments and conclusions in the message, yielding to and being convinced by the arguments (acceptance), and retention of the content resulting from information integration. The belief change resulting from information integration would directly predict attitude change.

Overview

Consider a receiver listening to a message. During the message, the receiver can either focus on the message content or think about the source as a person, or switch back and forth between the two. The receiver may attend to neither, especially if the receiver is engaging in internal counterargument. The outcome is likely to depend on the relative time devoted to each focus of attention.

The receiver will not be affected by the message if the message is not perceived. Thus, the first key process is attention: To what extent does the receiver pay attention to the message? If the receiver pays no attention to the message, then it will have no effect at all. That is, completely effective distraction affords complete protection against attitude change. If the receiver pays only limited attention to the message while distracted by something else, the results can be complicated, as we note later in the discussion of the Buller and Hall chapter in this volume.

A key element in the effect of distraction on attitude change is the extent to which the receiver comprehends the message. Lowered attention to the message is likely to produce lower comprehension. For most messages, lower comprehension produces less change. However if a message has weak or disingenuous elements, lower comprehension may make the message more effective because the receiver fails to notice the weakness in the arguments. In particular, reduced attention to the message may reduce counterargument.

For messages that are at least minimally attended, there are differences in how the receiver will react to the various aspects of the message. In particular, the receiver can (a) focus on the message arguments, (b) focus on the source, or (c) focus on internal counterarguments. It is likely that the receiver will switch from one focus to another at different points in time during the persuasion event. The relative time spent on each focus is likely to produce different effects on both attitude change and source evaluations.

The Mediated Effects Model

In his two-factor model, McGuire (1968b) proposed that an individual difference variable such as distraction or anxiety would enter into the model as a predictor of message reception and yielding to the message. Attitude change would be a product of reception, yielding, and information integration, as shown in Figure 1.1.

The mediation principle states that reception depends on attention to, and comprehension of message content (McGuire, 1968b), with comprehension increasing attitude change. If the message contains weak arguments, comprehension might not increase persuasion, but in most experimental designs, the arguments contained in the message are strong and the message is coherent. The mediation principle also states that yielding depends on receivers' counterarguing of message content, and their ability to withstand disagreement with the source (McGuire, 1969). Yielding has been measured in very few studies, as has ability to withstand disagreement, whereas measures of counterarguing are much more common.

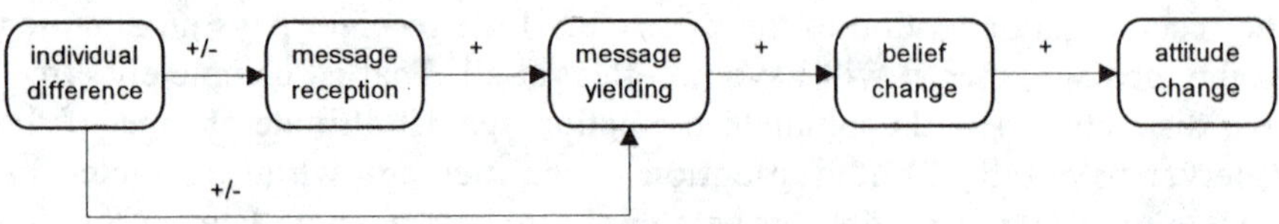

Figure 1.1

Heterogeneity Due to Mediated Effects

Unmeasured Mediating Variables. Some research designs measure only the antecedent individual difference variable and attitude change, and do not measure either of the important mediating variables such as comprehension or counterarguing. McGuire (1968b) pointed out that under such circumstances antagonistic effects in the model make it very hard to predict the outcome of the study. Each mediating process operates in opposite directions. Depending on which is stronger, the outcome could be increased change, reduced change, or no change if the two processes cancel each other out.

Situational Moderators. If the antecedent variable has a large negative effect on counterarguing and a small negative effect on comprehension, then the antecedent should enhance attitude change. Conversely, if the antecedent variable has a small negative effect on counterarguing and a large negative effect on comprehension, then the antecedent should have either no effect on attitude change or slightly inhibit it. McGuire (1968b) labeled this aspect of the model the *situational weighting* principle. Situational differences would make the correlation between the antecedent individual difference variable and attitude change appear heterogeneous.

The Threat of Confounds to the Model

It is possible that comprehension and yielding would appear to be dependent on the antecedent individual difference variable, although the correlations between the mediators and the individual difference variable were due to a common, exogenous antecedent variable. To alert readers to this possibility, McGuire (1968b, p. 1155) included the confounding assumption in his model.

The confound effect is most likely when an omitted exogenous variable is highly correlated with the antecedent individual difference in the model. One of the most likely candidates for such an exogenous variable would be the trait measure of a state variable included as the antecedent individual difference variable in the model. One of the examples McGuire (1968b) cited is that of anxiety. Based on the results of Millman's (1968) study, however, McGuire (1968a) concluded that trait anxiety was not a confounding exogenous antecedent for state anxiety.

Restriction in the Range of the Mediators

Variability in attention and comprehension scores depends on the situation. Variability in counterarguing also depends on the situation. As we noted earlier, restricting the range of a variable can dramatically reduce its correlation with other variables. When the message is repetitive or easy to process, there exists a restricted range of scores on the comprehension measure (McGuire, 1968a, p. 185). Under such circumstances, the correlation between comprehension and attitude change would be substantially reduced. It is also possible that the range of scores on the counterarguing measure would be restricted, leading to a reduced correlation between counterarguing and attitude change (McGuire, 1968b, p. 1149). The claim that the effect of the each of the mediators on attitude change will depend on its variability is McGuire's situational weighting assumption.

Comprehension. The correlation between comprehension and attitude change is usually small and positive. However, most studies of comprehension effects have been conducted in tightly controlled research laboratories. The researchers in most studies work hard to ensure that the message is easily comprehended. The researchers may even pretest messages to improve their comprehensibility. Moreover, the receivers in most laboratory studies are well educated and motivated to attend the message with the promise of extra credit.

In political debates that occur outside the laboratory, the effect of comprehension on attitude change should be much larger. Some messages may be hastily constructed and incoherent, whereas others may be painstakingly refined and very coherent. Receivers may have a tenuous grasp of the issue and possess only a slight interest in the topic, or they may have heard considerable debate on the topic because of its national importance. Thus, the effect of comprehension on attitude change could be much larger in political contexts than in tightly controlled laboratory studies. That is, the range of the correlation between comprehension and attitude change may have been severely restricted in past studies.

Counterarguing. The correlation between counterarguing and attitude change is usually large and negative. If counterargument were to be disrupted, yielding and attitude change should increase.

Principles Underlying the Prediction of Attitude Change

The Multiplicative Assumption. According to McGuire's *compensatory assumption*, an antecedent variable that has opposite effects on reception and yielding will have a nonmonotonic effect on attitude change, in the shape of an inverted U. His prediction of an inverted U function was based on his consideration of the combined effects of reception and yielding

(McGuire, 1969, pp. 243-244). For example, McGuire (1968a) claimed that the effect of intelligence on attitude change is nonmonotonic. For more intelligent receivers, reception would be high and yielding low, so attitude change would be constrained by yielding, resulting in minimal attitude change. For less intelligent receivers, reception would be low and yielding high, so attitude change would be constrained by reception, resulting in minimal attitude change. For moderately intelligent receivers, reception would be moderate as well as yielding, so neither factor would severely constrain attitude change, resulting in maximal attitude change.

The Additive Assumption. The prediction of a nonmonotonic effect of the individual difference variable on attitude change is based on the assumption that reception and yielding have a multiplicative effect on attitude change. In order to test the process model using correlational data, we made several simplifying assumptions. We assumed that the effects of comprehension on attitude and counterarguing on attitude are independent and additive. We also reduced the mediating variables down to two: comprehension and counterarguing.

In the additive model, the individual difference variable is antecedent to both comprehension and yielding. The antecedent individual difference variable can have two paths to attitude change within the model: The antecedent can influence comprehension (directly or mediated through attention), which will increase attitude change; or the antecedent can influence yielding, which will increase attitude change. The overall effect of a given antecedent variable on attitude change will depend on the two mediating processes shown in Figure 1.2.

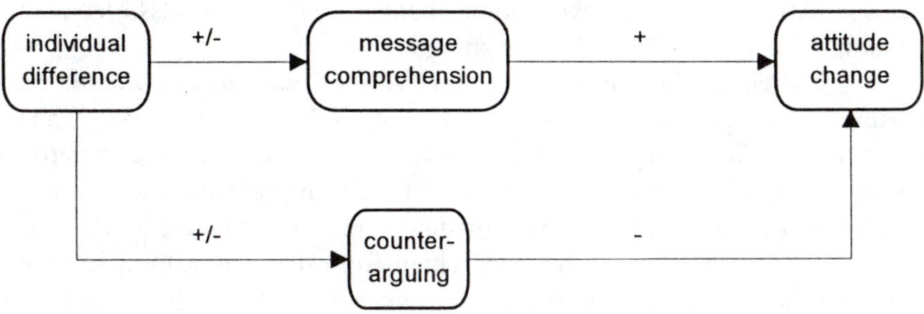

Figure 1.2.

Complementary Effects of the Mediators. Consider an antecedent variable such as forewarning that triggers counterarguing. Forewarning could cause counterarguing to begin even before the message starts. In this case, the receiver never pays full attention to the message and is thus likely to have little comprehension of it—this too would reduce attitude change. Thus forewarning would have two effects in the same direction: elicitation of counterarguing and reduced comprehension. That is, the two effects are in the same direction and hence complementary.

On the other hand, consider an antecedent variable such as source credibility. In the message-learning model (Hovland, Janis, & Kelly, 1953), credibility increases attention to message content (p. 37) while it increases the subjective probability that the arguments contained in the message are true (p. 73). By increasing attention, credibility should enhance comprehension; by increasing the subjective probability of an argument's truth, credibility should inhibit counterarguing. Thus credibility would have two effects in the same direction: decreased counterarguing and improved comprehension. That is, the two effects are in the same direction and hence complementary.

The more interesting antecedent variables in mediation model shown in Figure 1.2 are those that are supposed to increase reception and decrease yielding. That is, these antecedents increase both counterarguing and comprehension. McGuire (1969, p. 244) identifies intelligence, age, self-esteem, and anxiety as such antecedents. Although it is not listed among such antecedents,we believe that distraction should also belong to this category.

Distraction

If the receiver pays attention to a distracter, then comprehension of the message is reduced, which in turn reduces attitude change. However if the receiver pays attention to the distraction, counterarguing would also be reduced which would increase attitude change. That is, it is possible for distraction to have two effects that are antagonistic.

Buller and Hall (Chapter 8, this volume) use an information-processing theory approach to study the effect of distraction on attitude change. Buller (1986) found that the effect of distraction on attitudes was heterogeneous across type of distracters. He considered comprehension and counterarguing as mediators of the effect of distraction on attitudes. The *reduced comprehension* effect is the two-step chain from distraction to comprehension to attitude change. The *counterargument disruption* effect is the two-step chain from distraction to counterarguing to attitude change. If different types of distracters had different effects on comprehension and counterargument, we would expect that the effect of distraction on attitude would be heterogeneous across the different types of distracters. If different distracters have different relative effects on the two antagonistic processes, the final outcome could be in either direction. That is, the overall correlation between distraction and attitude change could be either positive or negative.

Vohs and Garrett (1968) believed that the intensity of the distraction would determine whether the reduced comprehension or counterargument disruption effects would dominate. Their hypothesis is a special case of the two-factor model shown in Figure 1.2. They sought to predict the relative size of the two mediating processes. Their theory predicts that for low-intensity distracters, distraction would have a large inhibiting effect on counterarguing and a small inhibiting effect on comprehension, whereas for high-intensity distracters, distraction would have a small inhibiting effect on counterarguing, and a large inhibiting effect on comprehension.

Based on his meta-analytic results, Buller (1986, p. 109) concluded that comprehension rather than counterargument was mediating the effect of distraction on attitude change. Our reexamination of the results of that meta-analysis reveals the counterargument mediated effect of distraction on attitude change is actually larger than the comprehension mediated effect of distraction on attitude change.

Buller (1986, Figure 2) plotted the correlation of distraction and comprehension against the correlation of distraction and attitude change. From this analysis he concluded that distraction did not have a nonmonotonic effect on attitudes. However, a test for quadratic nonlinearity requires primary data. Correlational results cannot be used to test the nonlinearity hypothesis.

The Buller meta-analysis did not test the additive two-factor model shown in Figure 1.2. In the next two sections, we develop a case for the process model of Figure 1.2 using Buller's meta-analytic results as evidence.

Counterarguing and Persuasion. Buller (1986) found that counterarguing had a large negative effect on attitude change ($r = -.50$, $N = 388$). The effect was homogeneous across studies. Buller dismissed the counterarguing correlation because some researchers think that counterarguing measures are invalid. There are many more researchers, however, that accept counterarguing measures as valid. We were thus willing to reconsider counterargument as a possible mediator variable. Distraction should decrease counterargument. For all but one of the distracter types (evaluation set), Buller found that distraction reduced counterarguing.

Comprehension and Persuasion. Buller found that comprehension had a very small positive effect on attitude change ($r = .06$, $N = 548$) and dismissed the small correlation between comprehension and attitude change because many distraction studies did not provide an estimate of that effect. Instead, the studies reported a negative effect of distraction on comprehension, and assumed a large positive effect of comprehension on attitude change.

This reasoning could be used to explain negative effects of distraction on attitude change. It has often been observed that there is only a small correlation between comprehension and attitude change (Hamilton, Hunter, & Boster, 1993; McGuire, 1985; Petty & Cacioppo, 1986). In most studies, however, the range of comprehension is restricted. Few studies in the distraction literature manipulated message comprehensibility. Receivers were rarely presented with incomprehensible messages. Instead, comprehension was restricted to a relatively high level. Hence, the correlation between comprehension and attitude change in most studies has been attenuated by restriction in range.

A number of studies that we are aware of have found a weak correlation between comprehension and attitude change: In Cruz, (Chapter 12, this volume), $r = .13$, $N = 169$; in Hamilton, Thompson, Daly and Kukunoor (1992), $r = .04$, $N = 280$; and in Hamilton, Zhao, and Kukunoor (in preparation, Experiment 2), $r = .13$, $N = 190$. The weighted average correlation across these studies is .09, $N = 639$, $k = 3$, $SD_\rho = 0$. This finding is consistent with the .06 reported by Buller. Even if we accept the larger .09 value as the correlation between comprehension and attitude change, its small size places a severe upper limit on the effect of distraction on attitude mediated by comprehension. Consider the overall comprehension-related findings of Buller (1986). Distraction reduced comprehension ($r = .23$), and comprehension increased attitude change ($r = .06$). The predicted effect of distraction on attitude mediate by comprehension would be the product of the two correlations—approximately zero ($r = -.01$).

The meta-analysis results from Buller (1986, Table 2) indicates that the effect of distraction on comprehension is in fact negative. Suppose that range restriction attenuates the correlation between comprehension and attitude change in the studies reviewed. Without range restriction, the correlation between the two variables might increase substantially. Hence, the negative effect of distraction on attitude mediated by comprehension could be much larger than -.01.

We think that it is wrong to assume that you must have either counterargument disruption *or* reduced comprehension. We think that distraction will produce *both* effects: Distraction will both disrupt counterargument *and* reduce comprehension. That is, distraction generates antagonistic effects; one effect that increases attitude change and another effect reduces attitude change. The net effect is the sum of the two opposite effects. The final outcome should vary from one type of distracter to another depending on how much counterarguing would occur with that particular distracter. This prediction is based on the two factor model shown in Figure 1.2.

Tests of the Two-Factor Model. We reexamined the effects of spoken verbal distracters and visual distracters (Buller, 1986, Table 6). Consider spoken verbal distracters first. These distracters reduced both counterarguing (r = -.22) and comprehension (r = -.28). Thus, distraction produced antagonistic effect of about the same size. The predicted change would be very small and this matches the result. There was little effect for distraction on attitude change (r = .03). The counterarguing mediated effect on attitude would be .11 (-.22* -.5), whereas the comprehension-mediated effect on attitude would be -.03 (-.28* .09), yielding a predicted correlation between distraction on attitude of .08. The difference between the predicted and obtained effect of distraction on attitude is small (error = .05).

Next, consider visual distracters. These distracters reduced counterarguing (r = -.28) and comprehension (r = -.52), and had a moderately small effect on attitude (r = .17). The counterarguing mediated effect on attitude would be .14 (-.28* -.5), whereas the comprehension mediated effect on attitude would be -.04 (-.52* .09), yielding a predicted correlation between distraction on attitude of .10. The difference between the predicted and obtained effect of distraction on attitude is again small (error = .07).

The results for heard verbal distracters (normal not delayed) reported by Buller (1986, Table 5) show that this distracter reduced counterarguing (r = -.21), and increased attitude change (r = .12). Unfortunately, no study in this subset of the literature measured comprehension and so we have no estimate of the path coefficient to measure the size of the diminished-comprehension effect due to this type of distracter. If the missing effect were assumed to be zero, the two-factor model shows excellent fit. The predicted effect of distraction on attitude, mediated by counterarguing, would be .10 (-.21* -.5). The difference between the predicted and obtained effect of distraction on attitude is trivial (error = .02).

The results for nonverbal distracters reported by Buller (1986, Table 5) show that this distracter reduced comprehension (r = -.32), and decreased attitude change (r = -.05). Unfortunately, no study in this literature measured counterarguing, and thus there is no estimate of the path coefficient for this type of distracter. If the missing diminished-counterarguing effect were assumed to be zero, the two-factor model shows excellent fit. The predicted effect of distraction on attitude, mediated by comprehension, would be -.03 (-.32* .09). The difference between the predicted and obtained effect of distraction on attitude is trivial (error = -.02).

Only one subset of distracters posed a problem for the two-factor model shown in Figure 1.2: the task-focus studies. These distracters reduced counterarguing (r = -.15) and comprehension (r = -.51), and had a moderately negative effect on attitude change (r = -.25). The counterarguing mediated effect on attitude change would be .08 (-.15* -.5), whereas the comprehension mediated effect on attitude would be -.04 (-.51* .09), yielding a predicted correlation between distraction on attitude of .04. The difference between the predicted and obtained effect of distraction on attitude is substantial (error = .29).

It is possible that the error in our path model is not due to its causal structure, but to our assumption that the effect of comprehension on change is approximately .09. If the comprehension effect is larger in the task-focus studies, then the path model would still fit results. Consider the value .66 for the effect of comprehension. With that value, the path model fits. This value is much larger than the .09 we observed across studies. However, the nature of the message is also quite different in the task focus studies than in the studies where the estimate of .09 was obtained. In task focus studies, people are considering real tasks. Because the message material is more complex, there may be a much larger range of comprehension in these studies than in the other studies which considered much simpler messages.

Speaker-Centered Set. Finally, the results in this set of studies showed evidence of a simple credibility effect (Hovland et al., 1953; McGuire, 1969). These source-relevant "distracters" reduced neither counterarguing (r = 0) nor comprehension (r = -.02). However, the label "distracter" seems inappropriate for these studies. If the source-relevant information did not effect counterarguing or comprehension, there is no basis for labeling it distraction.

Receivers who were instructed to focus on the credibility of the source were influenced by the premessage credibility of the source, whereas those who were instructed to focus on the message were not influenced by the source. That is, receivers who were in the source-focus condition attended to the source as the basis for their attitude, whereas received who were not in the source-focus condition attended to the message as the basis for their attitude.

For the source-focused receivers, the source with high premessage credibility was more persuasive than the source with low premessage credibility. These findings were consistent with a simple credibility effect as described by message-learning theory. We see no need to invoke additional concepts such as receiver expectations of source.

Conclusion Drawing

In Cruz (Chapter 12, this volume), the explicitness of the conclusion enhanced attitude change (r = .10). His causal model indicates that explicitness increases message comprehension (ρ = .55), which increases the perceived extremity of the position taken by the source (ρ = .65), which slightly increased persuasion (ρ = .06). The model, as specified, contains some sizable errors.

The path model shown in Figure 1.3 is based on our reanalysis of the Cruz data. Our path analysis indicated that premessage attitude effected both postmessage involvement (ρ = .26) and the position taken by the source (ρ = .17). Once these two effects are added to the model, the goodness of fit index soared from $p > .10$ to $p > .90$. More notably, the sizeable errors in the model disappear, such that the average error in the model is reduced to a respectable .07. Hence, the model actually fits better than the author thought.

The first of the two added paths reflects the fact that receivers with more extreme premessage attitudes also tend to be more involved with the attitude object after the message. In fact, the correlation between the two variables is probably attributable to their common antecedent, premessage involvement.

The positive effect of premessage attitude on perceived source position shown in Figure 1.3 is a simple assimilation effect. The more extreme a receiver's premessage attitude, the more consistent with that attitude the source's position is perceived to be. The position of the source is misperceived to be closer to the premessage position of the receiver.

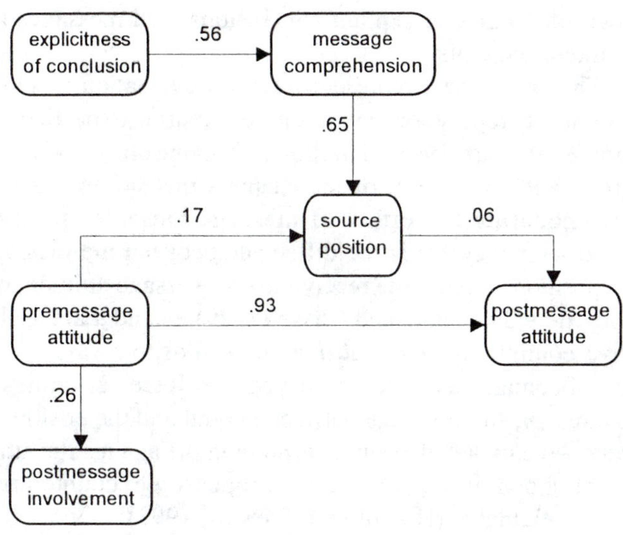

Figure 1.3.

The Mathematical Prediction Model

Information processing theory can be represented succinctly as a mathematical model of attitude change (Hunter, Danes, & Cohen, 1984). The attitude prediction model has recently been extended to include an explicit term for message strength (Hamilton et al., 1993; Hamilton, Hunter, & Burgoon, 1990; Hamilton & Stewart, 1993; Hamilton & Thompson, 1994). The prediction model shown in Equation 1 proposes that attitude change will be a multiplicative function of message strength (*ms*), evaluation of source (*s*), and message discrepancy (*d*) adjusted for counterarguing (*C*):

$$\Delta a = \alpha \frac{ms \cdot s \cdot d}{C} \qquad (1)$$

where Δa is attitude change from pre-message attitude to postmessage attitude. The alpha parameter reflects the affective impact of belief change on attitude change (see Hamilton & Thompson, 1994; Hunter et al., 1984 for a fuller discussion of this parameter).

The parameter *ms* is the strength of the message, a consequence of the verbal and nonverbal aspects of the presentation. The strength of an argument will depend on factors such as the perceived likelihood that the argument is true, and the evaluative consequences if it is true (see Hamilton, in press, for a review of these factors). Various determinants of message strength are studied in the chapters that follow: fear appeals, language intensity, powerful language, explicit conclusions, and messages that refute possible counterarguments.

The parameter *s* represents receiver evaluation of source. Depending on the context, receivers may focus on source expertise, bias, or liking (Hamilton & Stewart, 1993; Hamilton & Thompson, 1994; Hunter et al.,1984; McGuire, 1969). In several of the chapters that follow, source credibility is found to moderate the effect of message variables on attitude change. Message discrepancy (*d*) is the difference between the message value of the source's position (*m*) and the receiver's pre-message attitude toward topic (*a*). As proposed by Thurstone and Chave (1929), *m* and *a* are scaled on the same evaluative continuum such that $d = m - a$. Positive values of *d* indicate the direction of change advocated by the source. Receiver ratings of the position of the source, *m*, should range between neutral and the positive end of the attitude scale—even when the source is arguing the against the attitude object.

As shown in Equation 2, the propensity to counterargue *C* is a function of three elements (Hamilton & Stewart, 1993):

$$C = (1 + \beta d^2) \cdot (1 + \Gamma \mathrm{E}) \cdot (1 + \lambda \mathrm{I}) \qquad (2)]$$

Where β is the receiver's reaction to the extremity of the source's position and *d* is message discrepancy; Γ is a scaling parameter such that Γ is greater than or equal to 0, and *E* is the receiver's ego involvement; λ is a scaling parameter such that λ is greater than or equal to 0, and *I* is the receiver's accumulated information on the topic. Counterargument will be most easily discernable when the elements interact to inhibit attitude change.

Message Strength

Across the chapters, the pattern of results shows a moderately small positive effect of strength on attitude change. However, the size of these effects are underestimated in the meta-analyses that follow. In most of the studies included in the meta-analyses of this book, the reliability of the attitude measures were substantially less than perfect. Some studies even included single-item attitude measures. This unreliability in the attitude measure would seriously attenuate the correlation between the message strength variable and attitude change.

Three studies found that the strength of the manipulation moderated the effect of message strength on attitude change (Burrell & Koper, Chapter 11; Hamilton & Hunter, Chapter 6; Mongeau, Chapter 3—all,this volume). In these three meta-analyses, receiver perceptions were found to mediate the impact of the manipulated message strength variable on subsequent variables in the model. As the size of the manipulation effect diminished, so did the size of the correlation between manipulated message strength and attitude change. Despite attenuation due to measurement error and weak manipulations, the meta-analyses show a consistent pattern of results.

In Burrell and Koper (Chapter 11), powerful language enhanced persuasion ($r = .23$, $sd = .09$, $N = 413$). The heterogeneity in the effect of powerful language on credibility appears to be due to variance in the strength of the manipulation. Two studies by Bradac used very strong manipulations ($r = .58$, $sd = 0$, $N = 86$), whereas the other studies did not ($r = .19$, $sd = .04$, $N = 1304$). Three studies measured both perceived credibility and attitude. Across these studies ($N = 356$), powerful language enhanced credibility ($r = .29$), and to a lesser extent attitude change ($r = .21$). The correlations suggest a two-step model in which powerful language enhances perceived credibility ($\rho = .29$), and perceived credibility enhances attitude change (estimated $\rho = .72$).

In Allen (Chapter 4) two-sided messages that contained refutations of possible counterarguments were more persuasive than one-sided messages ($r = .08$), and one-sided messages were more persuasive than two-sided messages that mention possible counterarguments, but do not refute them (r = -.09). The three conditions represent levels of refutation that are low (two-sided, no refutation), moderate (one-sided), and high (two-sided, with refutation). As the refutation contained in the message increases, counterarguing by receivers should decrease. Consistent with the information processing model shown in Equation 2, the pattern of the correlations shows that as counterargument decreases, attitude change increases.

In Hamilton and Hunter (Chapter 6), intense language had no effect on attitude change when the message was attitude-congruent (r = 0); nor did intensity have an effect on attitude change for attitude-discrepant messages delivered by low-credibility sources (r = .03). That is, only when a high credibility source presented an attitude-discrepant message did intensity effect attitude change. The effect of attitude-discrepant messages on attitudes for high credibility sources depended on whether receivers were predisposed to counterargue or not. For the set of high-counterargument studies, intensity decreased attitude change (r = -.20). For the set of low-counterargument studies, intensity increased attitude change (r = .15).

Finally, Allen and Stiff (Chapter 9) found support for the discounting (dissociative) model of the sleeper effect. The discounting effect can be attributed to changes in message strength. More precisely, without any evidence to assess the subjective probability of a claim, receivers may decide that the probability is .50. Subjective probability should covary directly with source credibility. On the immediate attitude change measure, high-credibility sources should have a high subjective probability associated with their arguments, whereas low-credibility sources should have a low subjective probability associated with their arguments. As time elapses, receivers may forget the subjective probability associated with a given argument because the do not remember the source. However, they do remember their evaluation of the message. Hence, at the point of the delayed attitude measure, the formerly high probability associated with the high-credibility source will decrease toward .50, and the formerly low probability associated with the low-credibility source will increase toward .50. The longer the time elapsed, the greater the convergence of the two probabilities toward .50.

Message Discrepancy and Counterarguing

When receivers are confronted with a discrepant message, the degree to which they end up accepting the conclusion will depend on the amount of counterarguing they do. Gayle, Allen and Preiss (Chapter 10, this volume) reviewed studies on the effect of using rhetorical questions in the persuasive message. They found that the directness of the question moderates its effect on persuasion. Studies compared messages with particular types of rhetorical questions to messages without such questions. Attitude change was increased by the presence of indirect questions (r = .13, SD = .04, N = 630), as compared to no indirect questions. Attitude change was also increased by the presence of mixed questions (r = .09, SD = .05, N = 560), as compared to no mixed questions. Finally, attitude change was slightly reduced by the presence of direct questions (r = -.04, SD = 0, N = 760), as compared to no direct questions. Thus, the direct form of rhetorical question was less persuasive than the indirect form, or when the two forms were mixed.

This is consistent with the predictions from information-processing theory. Interrogatives or questions from a source should elicit more thought from receivers, because conversational norms oblige receivers to answer questioning sources. The more direct the question, the more thought it should elicit. When rhetorical questions are included in a discrepant message, receivers' thoughts are likely to be counterarguments. The more direct the question, the greater the counterarguing in answer to the question.

As with language intensity, the effect of fear appeals on attitude change should depend on the discrepancy of the message and receiver counterarguing (see Equations 1 and 2). Mongeau (Chapter 3, this volume) found that the higher the manipulated fear, the greater the attitude change (r = .19), and the greater the behavior change (r = .12). These results suggest a three-step causal model from manipulated fear to perceived fear (ρ = .35), from perceived fear to attitude (ρ = .54), and from attitude to (ρ = .63) behavior.

The effect of manipulated fear on attitude change and behavior change was attenuated due to measurement error and restriction in range. Mongeau also found that the size of the effects increased substantially with the strength of the fear appeal manipulation. He found substantial variance around the average fear-attitude-change correlation (SD_ρ= .17) and the fear-behavior-change correlation (SD_ρ= .19). Some of that variance in these effects should be due to the three artifacts mentioned. Suppose these artifacts had been corrected for. We would still expect substantial variance around the average correlations. A portion of this variance should be due to message discrepancy and counterarguing. When message discrepancy is low, the effect of the fear manipulation on attitude change and behavior change should be small or nonexistent. When message discrepancy is high, the effect of fear on attitude change and behavior change could be either negative (if receivers are counterarguing the message) or positive (if receivers are counterarguing the message).

Message Sidedness

We would expect that message discrepancy and counterarguing would moderate the effect of message-sidedness on attitude change. In their meta-analyses of the sidedness literature, both Allen (1991) and O'Keefe (1993) found that two-sided messages containing refutations were more persuasive than one-sided messages. If the message happens to refute a receiver's own counterarguments, this should enhance attitude change. Even if the receiver had not thought of any of the counterarguments refuted in the message, observing the source effectively blunt attacks on the position advocated should bolster receiver confidence in the source's credibility. Greater post-message credibility should increase attitude change. Thus, it is not surprising that the two-sided refutational message is more persuasive than the one-sided message.

The Nonrefutational Message Dispute. Allen (1991, 1993) concluded that two-sided messages which mentioned opposing arguments but did not refute them were less persuasive than one-sided messages. Consider the two-sided nonrefutational message: The source presents one or more arguments for the position advocated, then undermines that position by offering counterarguments that go unrebutted. Receivers will judge the message to be uncompelling or even incompetent. The nonrefutational two-sided messages should therefore result in little if any attitude change. On the other hand, most messages are one sided, and many of these are persuasive. So the one-sided message should result in more attitude change than the two-sided nonrefutational message; yet O'Keefe (1993) disputed the Allen conclusion.

O'Keefe's main critique of Allen's meta-analysis was that it misclassified two-sided "nonrefutational" messages as "refutational." The dispute between the two meta-analysts can be resolved by coding two-sided messages as eliciting either high or low counterargument. Two-sided messages that contain strong evidence for the position advocated by the source plus weak evidence against the position advocated would be placed in the low counterargument condition. Conversely, two-sided messages that contain weak evidence for the position advocated plus strong evidence against would be placed in the high counterargument condition.

Counterargument as Moderator. Consider three types of two-sided messages. Two-sided refutational messages contain supporting arguments, a few counterarguments, and rebuttals of the counterarguments. Hence, they would be classified as low counterargument messages. Typical two-sided nonrefutational messages contain supporting arguments with a few counterarguments. Hence they would be classified as high counterargument messages. The classification of these two types should be noncontroversial.

The type of two-sided message disputed by Allen (1993) and O'Keefe was atypical in that it contained supporting arguments, a few counterarguments, then supportive material unrelated to the counterarguments (for example, Hovland, Lumsdaine, & Sheffield, 1949). Although O'Keefe is correct in labeling these messages as "nonrefutational," they are most likely low counterarguing messages. Hence, Allen (1991, 1993) was correct in grouping them with the two-sided "refutational" messages to achieve homogeneity in what we would call the "low-counterargument" group.

Message Discrepancy as Moderator. Allen (1991, Table 3) examined whether message discrepancy moderated the effect of message sidedness on persuasion. His test was inconclusive, however, given the small number of studies in the low discrepancy (favorable audience) and high-discrepancy (unfavorable audience) conditions. Allen (Chapter 5, this volume) had twice the number of studies in the "refutational" and "nonrefutational" conditions as Allen (1991). However, Allen -this volume- did not test the discrepancy moderator hypothesis with all the relevant studies. Instead, he used only those studies that allowed an estimate of both low and high discrepancy.

As in Allen (1991), the discrepancy moderator test of Allen (this volume) had very low power. In Chapter 5 here, Allen reported chi-square homogeneity tests and percent variance explained by the refutation moderator. In the nonrefutation condition, only 8% of the variance could be explained by message discrepancy. However, in the refutational condition, up to 24% of the variance could be explained by message discrepancy. Subsequent meta-analyses of the sidedness literature should fully explore discrepancy as a moderator, particularly in the comparison of one-sided messages to two-sided refutational messages.

Forewarning

In Benoit (Chapter 7, this volume), forewarning receivers of a source's impending message inhibited attitude change ($r = -.17$, $SD = 0$, $N = 1359$). This inhibiting effect occurred regardless of whether the forewarning was of the source's intent to persuade or the position the source was going to take. The forewarning effect was not influenced by the amount of time given to the receiver to consider the forewarning before receipt of the message.

The probability of counterarguing increases with message discrepancy (see Equation 2). Receivers forewarned that the message will be discrepant will have the opportunity to begin counterarguing before the message starts. This could greatly reduce attention to the message.

Counterattitudinal Advocacy

Preiss and Allen (Chapter 13, this volume) consider studies in which the participant is asked to write an essay arguing for a position that is opposite to their own position. From the point of view of information-procession theory, the important feature of such a task is that the essay writer reviews counterattitudinal arguments during message construction. Thus the writer would be predicted to change in the direction of the arguments and therefore change in the direction opposite to their initial position. This is what is found in these studies, although it is tangential to the interest of these researchers. In the studies reviewed by Preiss and Allen, the central issue is the incentive offered by the researcher for participation; typically, some amount of money. The question that they ask is this : Is there more change if you offer a large incentive or a small incentive?

There is a huge moderator variable for these studies : (a) studies where participation is voluntary versus (b) studies where all subjects are asked to participate with no choice offered (called "coerced" participation by Preiss & Allen). If participation is voluntary, then the finding is that there is more change for low incentive than for high incentive ($k = 23$, $r = -.30$). On the other hand, if all subjects are required to participate, then there is more change for high incentive than for low incentive ($k = 5$, $r = +.33$).

Voluntary Participation. Consider the studies with voluntary participation. Most of these studies are post-only designs. Thus the findings cumulated in the meta-analysis are comparisons between the post-average attitudes of those who get high incentive and those who get a low incentive. The average computed will be the mean attitude for those who participated. It seems likely that participation will be easiest for those subjects whose initial attitude is closest to the position advocated. Thus it is likely that participation is a biased sampling procedure: Those with highest discrepancy are least likely to participate. However, the linear discrepancy model for change predicts that postmessage attitudes will still have the same rank order as premessage attitudes, so those who participate will be those with attitudes closer to the position advocated.

What is the likely effect of differences in incentive? The classic finding is that the more you offer, the larger the number who choose to participate. Thus if you offer little, only those with attitudes very close to the advocated position will agree to participate. If you offer a lot, then many more people will participate; which means that you will get people whose initial position is farther from the position advocated. Thus the higher the incentive, the lower the mean initial attitude among participants and thus the lower the postmessage attitude among the participants. Therefore, information-processing theory predicts that the correlation between incentive and "persuasion" will be negative. This matches the finding of the Preiss and Allen meta-analysis.

Uniform Participation. If all subjects participate, then differences in incentive do not cause differences in the makeup of the participant population; all participate in both the high- and low-incentive conditions. On the other hand, "participation" need not mean the same thing in different conditions.

Information-processing theory predicts that the extent of change will be primarily determined by the number of arguments considered. Consider two writers who start at the same initial level. The writer who can remember and review more arguments will be more influenced than the writer who remembers and reviews few arguments. Thus information-processing theory predicts that high-quality essays will cause more change than low-quality essays.

Consider, then, the effect of different levels of incentive. Assume that the group which is paid more feels a higher obligation to work hard. High incentive will thus induce a longer and more intense search through memory for relevant arguments. Thus the high incentive group will work harder to produce higher quality essays that will have a larger number of arguments. The high-incentive group will thus change by more and finish with a higher postmessage attitude.

Information-processing theory therefore predicts that with universal participation, high incentive will cause higher change than low incentive. That is, information processing theory predicts a positive correlation between incentive and outcome which is just what Preiss and Allen found.

Summary on Counterattitudinal Advocacy. Most of the research on incentives and counterattitudinal advocacy was done by either those who at that time believed in cognitive dissonance theory or those who were attacking dissonance theory. Therefore, almost all authors thought in terms of elaborate motivational arguments for the results. Preiss and Allen follow this tradition by discussing their findings in terms of those theories. However, information-processing theory explains these findings without any new or convoluted theories of motivation. This is just as well because both dissonance theory and the antidissonance theories considered in the incentive literature have long since been disconfirmed by studies done in other areas.

Source Credibility

Source credibility should act as a multiplier of message discrepancy effects, as shown in Equation 1. Consistent with this prediction, Hamilton and Hunter (Chapter 6, this volume) found that source credibility enhanced attitude change when the message was discrepant, but not when the message was attitude congruent (see Figure 6.3). In Reinard (Chapter 4, this volume), testimonial assertions from sources enhanced attitude change ($r = .25$, $SD = .06$, $N = 1762$). When such source expertise effects prevail, this suggests that receivers were using source expertise as a premise for accepting the message claim (Chaiken, 1980).

Source credibility did not moderate the effect of fear appeals on attitude change (Mongeau, 1983). It may be that the messages in most fear appeal studies are easy to understand. If receivers can fully understand the arguments, there is no need to defer to the opinions of authority figures.

CONCLUSIONS

We began this chapter by identifying artifacts that reduce the accuracy of meta-analytic conclusions. Corrections for such artifacts depend on the amount of information available in primary studies, but it also depends on the knowledge of the meta-analyst.

The problems with single sample studies is clear in the persuasion literature. Sampling error causes deviations in results from population values. If a theory is correct, the population values will follow the pattern predicted by the theory but the sample values may not. This problem is made much worse by the use of the significance test, which falsely suggests that you can trust the labels "significant" and "not significant". The persuasion literature has been a hotbed of claims and counterclaims caused largely by sampling error. When meta-analysis is used to reduce the influence of sampling error, the underlying pattern is much clearer. What we showed in the chapter above, is that all of the results in the meta-analyses below fit into one theoretical framework: information-processing theory. Even the strong advocates of that theory never made this claim. They kept trying to deal with the sampling error in single small sample studies. There were many small-sample studies that seemed to have results that disconfirmed the overall theory.

Those who review isolated small-sample studies have noted that the overall pattern of results favored information-processing theory, but they were puzzled at findings that seemed to contradict the theory. Furthermore, there was no pattern to the deviant studies. This is no surprise from the point of view of meta-analysis. There is no pattern to sampling error!

REFERENCES

Allen, M. (1991). Meta-analysis comparing the effectiveness of one- and two-sided messages. *Western Journal of Speech Communication, 55*, 390–404.

Allen, M. (1993). Determining the persuasiveness of message sidedness: A prudent note about utilizing research summaries. *Western Journal of Communication, 57*, 98-103.

Buller, D. (1986). Distraction during persuasive communication: A meta-analytic review. *Communication Monographs, 53*, 91-114.

Chaiken, S. (1980). Heuristic versus systematic information processing and the use of source versus message cues in persuasion. *Journal of Personality and Social Psychology, 39*, 752-766.

Ghiselli, E. (1966). *The validity of occupational aptitude tests.* New York: Wiley.

Ghiselli, E. (1973). The validity of aptitude tests in personnel selection. *Personnel Psychology, 26*, 461-477.

Glass, G. (1976). Primary, secondary, and meta-analysis of research. *Review of Research in Education, 5*, 351-378.

Hamilton, M.A., Hunter, J.E., & Boster, F.J. (1993). The elaboration likelihood model as a theory of attitude formation: A mathematical analysis. *Communication Theory, 3*, 50–65.

Hamilton, M., Hunter, J., & Burgoon, M. (1990). An empirical investigation of an axiomatic model of the effect of language intensity on attitude change. *Journal of Language and Social Psychology, 9*, 235-255.

Hamilton, M., & Stewart, B. (1993). Extending an information processing model of language intensity effects. *Communication Quarterly, 41*, 231-246.

Hamilton, M. A., & Thompson, W. L. (1994). Testing an information processing model of message intensity effects. *World Communication, 23*, 1-14.

Hamilton, M. A., Thompson, W. L., Daly, T., & Kukunoor, K. (May, 1992). *Language intensity and attitude change on significant social issues: An information processing model.* Paper presented to the International Communication Association Convention, Chicago, IL.

Hamilton, M.A., Zhao, H.Y., & Kukunoor, K. (in preparation). A comparison of two message processing models.

Hovland, C., Janis, I., & Kelly, H. (1953). *Communication and persuasion.* New Haven, CT: Yale University Press.

Hovland, C.L., Lumsdaine, A., & Sheffield, F. (1949). *Experiments on mass communication*. Princeton, NJ: Princeton University Press.

Hunter, J., Danes, J., & Cohen, S. (1984). *Mathematical models of attitude change* (Vol. 1). New York: Academic Press.

Hunter, J.E., & Rogers, R. (1995). Flawed theories about study flaws. In W.A. Pasmore & R.W. Woodman (Eds.), *Research in organizational change and development* (Vol. 8, pp. 297–335). Greenwich, CT: JAI.

Hunter, J., & Schmidt, F. (1982). Ability tests: Economic benefits versus the issue of fairness. *Industrial Relations, 21*(3), 293-308.

Hunter, J. E., & Schmidt, F. L. (1990). *Methods of meta-analysis: Correcting error and bias in research findings*. Newbury Park, CA: Sage.

McGuire, W. J. (1968a). Personality and attitude change: An information-processing theory. In A. Greenwald, T. Brock, & T. Ostrom (Eds.), *Psychological foundations of attitudes*. New York: Academic Press.

McGuire, W. J. (1968b). Personality and social influence. In E. Borgatta & W. Lambert (Eds.), *Handbook of social psychology* (2nd ed., pp. 136-314). Reading, MA: Addison-Wesley.

McGuire, W. (1969). The nature of attitudes and attitude change. In G. Lindzey & E. Aronson (Eds.), *The handbook of social psychology* (2nd ed., Vol. 3, pp. 136-314). Reading, MA: Addison-Wesley.

McGuire, W.J. (1985). Attitudes and attitude change. In G. Lindzey & E. Aronson (Eds.), *Handbook of social psychology* (3rd ed., Vol. 2, pp. 233–346). New York: Random House.

Millman, S. (1968). Anxiety, comprehension, and susceptibility to social influence. *Journal of Personality and Social Psychology, 9*, 251–256.

Mongeau, P. (1983). *Fear appeals and persuasion: A meta-analysis*. Unpublished master's thesis, Arizona State University, Tempe, AZ.

O'Keefe, D. (1993). The persuasive effects of message sidedness variations: A cautionary note concerning Allen's (1991) meta-analysis. *Western Journal of Communication, 57*, 87-97.

Petty, R.E., & Cacioppo, J.T. (1986). *Communication and persuasion*. New York: Springer-Verlag.

Schmidt, F.L., & Hunter, J.E. (1977). Development of a general solution to the problem of validity generalization. *Journal of Applied Psychology, 65*, 643-661.

Schmidt, F.L., & Hunter, J.E. (1978). Moderator research and the law of small numbers. *Personnel Psychology, 31*, 215–232.

Thurstone, L. L., & Chave, S. (1929). Theory of attitude measurement. *Psychological Review, 36*, 222-241.

Vohs, J.L., & Garrett, R.L. (1968). Resistance to persuasion: An integrative framework. *Public Opinion Quarterly, 32*, 445-452.

2

Meta-Analysis of Controlled Message Designs

John E. Hunter
Michigan State University

Mark A. Hamilton
University of Connecticut

Critics of meta-analysis have attacked it on many grounds. Sometimes the target of the attack centers on the data in the meta-analysis. These attacks attempt to show that the underlying studies on which the meta-analysis contain flaws. The essence of this criticism is captured by the familiar expression "garbage in, garbage out." Other times, the target of the attack is meta-analysis as a method. These attacks attempt to show inadequacies in particular meta-analytic procedures. The use of meta-analysis to study persuasion has been attacked on both grounds.

Recent attacks on meta-analyses of the persuasion literature reject almost the entire mass of persuasion research as methodologically flawed. If all the studies that contain this alleged flaw must be rejected, then the meta-analyses reported in this book are useless. Not just these meta-analyses would be useless, however. All current narrative reviews of the literature use this same database of studies. If these past studies contain fundamental flaws, then all attempts to gain knowledge from past studies would be pointless. In this chapter, we present the case for making empirical generalizations based on meta-analyses of past persuasion studies.

Many communication variables are defined in terms of variation in the nature of the message presented. For example, the studies analyzed in the chapter on language intensity effects contrast messages of identical logical content which differ in the intensity of the lexical markers used in the message. In these studies, one kernel message is created, and then manipulated to form a high-intensity version and a low-intensity version. The study then compares the persuasiveness of the two versions of the message. Designate this research design as the controlled message design. If it were true that the nature of the treatment effect depended on the particular message used, no individual study would discover this. However, it would show up in other studies because each study usually uses a different message as its kernel.

Our position argues that the controlled message study can contribute to persuasion theory, even when using only one message in the design. Most of the literature in persuasion consists of single, controlled-message designs. Jackson and Jacobs (1983) and O'Keefe (1990) described this literature as fundamentally flawed because the studies do not employ multiple messages. They argued that the vast majority of existing studies have virtually no value.[1] We know people who interpret the Jackson and Jacobs article to show that almost all past research in persuasion should be ignored because of design flaws. They accept that persuasion theory must start from scratch. For these people, all the effort of past researchers has been lost. Moreover, they believe that the Jackson and Jacobs article showed that single, controlled message studies should not be published in the future. Indeed, we know of many studies that have been rejected specifically on the basis of the Jackson and Jacobs design principles. There exist reviewers who reject articles because they deviate from these design principles. Acceptance of the multiple message requirement greatly reduces the number of studies that could be done because a multiple message design demands far greater resources than a single message design. This in turn would have a chilling effect on meta-analysis in the short run and persuasion theory in the long run.

---

[1]The literature in communication in general, as well as social psychology and education, also consists largely of single, controlled-message design. Thus, the Jackson and Jacobs criticism extends to these other domains.

GENERALIZING TO MESSAGE POPULATIONS

The rationale for this bold, frontal assault on the persuasion and communication literature came from the assumption that the single, controlled message design could not provide a means of generalizing to message populations. Jackson and Jacobs (1983) offered a solution to the alleged generalizability problem. They argued for randomly selecting many messages from a natural population of messages. Variables that might be confounded with the experimental treatment would be controlled by using a great many messages nested within experimental conditions.

The claim that only multiple message designs should be used was refuted. Hunter, Hamilton, and Allen (1989) explained: (a) how experimenter control provides a much stronger method of controlling potential confounding variables than a design in which many naturalistic messages are nested within experimental condition, (b) that the Jackson and Jacobs distinction between naturalistic and controlled messages stemmed from false assumptions concerning message construction in the real world, and (c) that meta-analysis could be used to address concerns about message generalizability. Subsequent work by Jackson and O'Keefe (Jackson, O'Keefe & Jacobs, 1988; Jackson, O'Keefe, Jacobs & Brashers, 1989; O'Keefe, Jackson, & Jacobs, 1988) dropped the recommendation that naturalistic messages be nested within experimental condition. Instead, they argued that multiple message designs would provide a more powerful means of assessing message effects than meta-analyses of single message designs, launching a fusillade of arguments against meta-analysis.

This chapter serves three purposes. First, we argue that the past persuasion literature is still very much worth analyzing. The fact is that meta-analysis solves the generalizability problem alleged by Jackson and O'Keefe. Second, we show that multiple-message designs have never uncovered a substantively meaningful moderator variable in persuasion. The multiple-message design has not contributed to persuasion theory. Finally, we defend meta-analysis against the attacks of Jackson and her associates. Meta-analysis can be used to detect unknown moderator variables that might qualify conclusions regarding message treatment effects.

POTENTIAL HETEROGENEOUS INTERACTIONS

There is a potential drawback to the single message design. If there exists an interaction between the treatment variable and message content, then the results researchers obtain depends on which particular messages they use.

This potential weakness has been known for many years, and is the foundation of the position taken by Jackson and Jacobs (1983) and O'Keefe (1990). We illustrate this argument with a hypothetical example. Suppose that intense language were more persuasive when used by a football coach giving a locker room pep talk to his team, but less persuasive when used by a politician giving a campaign stop pep talk to his supporters. The authors of a study using a sports message would conclude that intense language is more persuasive. The authors of a study using a political message would conclude just the opposite. There would be no way that this message by topic interaction could be detected within a single message study. In an early round of debate on message design, Hunter, Hamilton, and Allen (1987) showed that this problem could be solved by meta-analysis. Jackson et al. (Jackson & Jacobs, 1987; Jackson et al., 1988) responded by attacking meta-analysis. Those attacks are rebutted in this chapter.

We call the message treatment by message content interaction a *potential* problem for the single message design because no such interaction has yet been replicated in the persuasion literature, as we show later in the chapter. Jackson and Jacobs (1983) originally argued that these interactions would be so ubiquitous that they would mar every domain of communication. Hence, there would be no point in doing single message designs.

Assume there were a message treatment by content interaction. A comparison of results across studies should, in principle, show that different authors obtained different results, leading the author of a review article to conclude that message treatment interacts with an unspecified variable. The reviewer could then compare the studies that obtained one result with studies that obtained another to identify the nature of the interaction. The fly in the ointment of the review study is sampling error. Some authors will get deviant results not because of an interaction, but because of sampling error. Indeed, there are many research domains where bitter arguments have long raged that turn out to be caused by only sampling error.[2] There are many domains where all of the reported differences in study results have been

---

[2]For example, Stogdill (1948) and Mann (1959) wrote narrative reviews of the literature on the personality traits of leadership and found apparently contradictory results for every trait studied. They concluded that there are no personality traits consistently linked to leadership. On the other hand, theoretical analyses of leadership behavior in one leadership setting after another kept pointing to certain traits such as intelligence. A meta-analysis by Lord, DeVader, and Alliger (1986) showed that the inconsistency in past results was largely due to sampling error; the residual variance is small for four of the six traits studied. Other meta-analyses on leadership have also found stable results across studies once the effect of sampling error is eliminated (see the review in Hunter & Hirsh, 1987).

shown to be due to sampling error. The solution to the problem of sampling error is meta-analysis, as noted in the preceding chapter of this volume.

If there is no message treatment by content interaction, then meta-analysis will show that differences in study conclusions were caused by sampling error. On the other hand, suppose that someday a domain is found in which there is a heterogeneous interaction. Imagine that a review of existing studies has suggested a variable which is thought to moderate the effect. The studies can then be sorted according to that hypothesis. Meta-analysis will determine whether or not the interaction exists and will also show whether there is any further interaction to be sought.

Evaluating the Single Message Design

The early work of Jackson et al. (Jackson, 1984; Jackson & Jacobs, 1983) boldly claimed that only multiple message studies are valid. Their later work (Jackson et al., 1988; Jackson et al., 1989) would disappoint many of the readers who were thrilled by the provocativeness of the early statements. Jackson et al. (1989) no longer argue that naturalistic messages are required and use illustrations with the controlled message design. They no longer argue for nested designs and use crossed designs as illustrations. Although Jackson et al. (1989) have tacitly abandoned their more extreme position, they have never repudiated it in print. Finally, they continue to argue that the single message design must be rejected.

The Original Argument for Multiple Message Designs

Why did Jackson and Jacobs (1983) demand multiple message studies? Their demand did not start with an argument for the use of multiple messages. Rather, they cited what they believed to be inconsistencies in the persuasion literature, and argued that such research domains are fundamentally flawed by the fact that investigators use experimental messages created by scientists. They believed that real messages by real people would show entirely different results and they claimed that only research done with naturalistic messages would be valid. The original paper alleged that the moderator "natural versus contrived" would be a heterogeneous moderator across research domains. Shortly after original paper was published, it became clear that there was no empirical support for this claim (see the subsequent review showing the lack of such interactions). Subsequent papers by Jackson et al. quietly abandoned the recommendation that only natural messages be used, although their original claims were never explicitly recanted. Consider their original claim (Jackson & Jacobs,1983, Jackson et al. 1988), that researchers should rely on natural variation in the treatment variable rather than experimental control. They suggested that "messages be chosen so as to maximize their naturalness" (Jackson & Jacobs, 1983, p. 177), so that pretesting and possible experimenter manipulation of content could be avoided. Message content (including topic) would vary from one treatment condition to another. This is an example of a nested design.

Imagine that only natural messages give valid results. Consider the implications for study design, using language intensity as an example. We start by seeking our high- and low-intensity messages in the "real" world. That is, we focus our attention on the population of natural high-intensity messages and the population of natural low-intensity messages. If a randomly chosen high- and a randomly chosen low-intensity natural message are to be compared, then there will be no matching on logical content and there may not even be matching as to message object. The high-intensity messages will be entirely separate and independent from the low-intensity messages. In the language of analysis of variance, this means that messages are "nested" within treatment conditions. To choose just one message at random from each set would typically result in using messages that differ from each other along many irrelevant dimensions. The classic answer to this is to use a sample of messages. That is, the study would use a random sample of messages from each treatment condition message population—in the same way that receivers are sampled in the typical study. The larger the number of messages used, the better the random counterbalancing of the irrelevant dimensions, and hence the better the estimate of the treatment effect.

Note that if Jackson and Jacobs (1983) had been right about the need for only natural message designs, they would have been right about the need for multiple messages. That is, the original argument for multiple message designs remain subsidiary to the argument for only natural message studies. However, even though they have abandoned the claim that only nested, natural message designs are valid (they now espouse crossed message designs); they still cling to the requirement of multiple message designs even though that requirement no longer flows logically from the substantive arguments.

Hunter et al. (1989) refuted each of the Jackson et al. arguments for the naturalistic, nested message design, identifying errors in reasoning, philosophy of science, and interpretation of empirical findings. We review the two most important of these criticisms, that the Jackson et al. argument contain logical inconsistencies, and that Jackson et al. confuse confounding with interaction.

The multiple message, nested design can only be used if there exists *no* message interaction (Winer, 1971). The nested design cannot work if there is an interaction even when studies are compiled using meta-analysis. Only crossed designs can detect and identify interactions. If message content is to be crossed with the treatment variable, then the messages are necessarily contrived.

The problem with the nested, multiple message design is that it is vulnerable to confounding. Jackson et al. (Jackson, 1984; Jackson & Jacobs, 1983; Jackson et al., 1988; Jackson et al., 1989; O'Keefe, et al., 1988) claimed that messages differ in an infinite number of ways, such that an experimenter could not hope to control all possible variables that might interact with a treatment effect. They asserted that the traditional design cannot detect all possible treatment by message content interactions. If there were such an interaction, then it is true that one study could not detect it. However, that interaction could be detected across a set of single message studies. On the other hand, consider the implications of what they say for the nested design. If two natural messages differ in infinitely many relevant ways, then the treatment variable is confounded with each of those extraneous variables. There is no way to know if the results for any given message stem from the treatment variable or from one of the other characteristics of that message. This is precisely what lead to the development and use of the crossed design in which the same kernel message is used in both treatment conditions.

The substance of the Jackson et al., argument actually denies the validity of the nested multiple message design, especially if there is an interaction. It is important to note that even in their most recent papers, they still do not acknowledge the fact that the nested design requires the assumption that there be no interaction. They still do not acknowledge the extremely low power known to be unavoidable in the nested design.

The Current Argument for Multiple Message Designs

In an effort to rescue the central argument of their original paper that only multiple message studies are valid, and that single message studies should be abandoned, Jackson and her associates have generated a new set of arguments. Jackson et al. (1989) argued that multiple message designs are necessary because unknown content variables interact with treatment variables. If this were true, then the nested design would be invalid. Although Jackson et al. do not acknowledge this, their recent papers present only examples in which the same kernel message is manipulated to meet the treatment conditions.

Jackson has consistently recommended a large number of message replications per study. Jackson (1984) advised 20 messages per experimental condition, and Jackson (1990) advised 20 to 30 messages per condition. Given that current persuasion studies have between 20 and 30 subjects per condition, this means that each subject in a condition receives a different message. If each subject per condition receives a different message, then message is completely confounded with subject (see, for example, B.J. O'Keefe & McCornack, 1987). Jackson has consistently recommended the completely confounded design (Jackson & Jacobs, 1983; Jackson et al., 1988, p. 131). The basis for this claim is the premise that if there is a message treatment by content interaction, then power to detect the treatment main effect in a multiple message design increases with the number of messages (Hunter et al., 1989; Jackson & Jacobs, 1983; Jackson, et al., 1988; Morley, 1988). As Morley (1988) noted, however, researchers are not likely to be inclined to generate 20 to 30 long messages per study, guaranteeing less than optimal performance for the detection of main effects in the multiple message design.

Hunter et al. (1989) pointed out a more serious problem for the completely confounded design—it cannot detect a message treatment by content interaction. Jackson et al. (1989) responded to this criticism by making a full reversal from their earlier position: They now claim that they are interested in message treatment main effects but not in detecting treatment by message interactions.

O'Keefe (1990) offered an additional criticism of the single message design. He asserts that the single message design is flawed because an experimental manipulation can be described in any number of ways. To illustrate his point, he cited the opinionated language literature, in which several researchers use different conceptual definitions for the same operational definition. Variation in conceptual definition among these authors is not surprising, given that they were coming from different theoretical orientations. Note, however, that this problem can occur just as easily with multiple message designs. This potential problem disappears at the level of meta-analysis. Regardless of the label applied to a variable by an author, the meta-analyst can combine studies using the same operationalization to determine the effect of the variable on the dependent variable of interest.

THE SEARCH FOR MESSAGE TREATMENT BY CONTENT INTERACTIONS

Despite empirical evidence to the contrary, Jackson et al. maintain that message by treatment interactions are ubiquitous. This belief appears to stem from a confusion about what constitutes an interaction. Jackson and Jacobs (1983) attempted to illustrate the complexity of determining message effects by considering the impact of speech introduction types (a question, a joke, or a startling statement) and speech functions (attention getting and rapport creating) on persuasiveness. Most persuasion theories would predict that both attention and rapport increase attitude change. If a particular study does not vary either attention or rapport, then usually the message will be created so as to maximize both attention and rapport. Jackson and Jacobs correctly stated that current theory does not guarantee choosing an optimal message. However, this lack of knowledge represents uncertainty and is not an interaction. Thus their illustration of the ubiquitous interaction is not actually an interaction. Jackson et al. continue to argue that message content interacts with treatment in many unknown ways. We believe this position underestimates the current level of theory about message effects, particularly in an area as well developed as persuasion. If researchers are so incompetent as to not be able to guess at large interactions, then meta-analyses in the persuasion domain would find evidence of unknown interactions. The following section presents our search for message by treatment interactions. Our continuing search over a 5-year period has yet to yield a replicable example.

Evidence From Meta-Analysis

Jackson and Jacobs (1983) claimed that most researchers assume that such interactions exist, and that those who assume otherwise are "naive" (Jackson, 1984; Jackson & Jacobs, 1987). However, they presented no survey evidence to back up the claim that "most researchers" believe in such interactions. They present no list of meta-analyses showing that such interactions exist.

Jackson and Jacobs (1983) cited only one example of an interaction, the literature concerning the impact of language intensity on attitude change. They pointed out that across studies the variables language intensity and attitude change have sometimes correlated positively, sometimes correlated negatively, and sometimes not correlated at all. Unfortunately, the authors failed to note the effect sizes in these studies. As a meta-analysis of language intensity effects shows, most study differences were due to sampling error. There were moderators, but they were homogeneous interactions predicted by traditional theories. There was no evidence of unpredictable, capricious message effects.

Jackson (1984) cited an example of an interaction, the one-sided versus two-sided argumentation literature. The meta-analysis of the sidedness literature, however, showed that there is no such interaction. Table 2.1 contains the results of other meta-analyses. These findings are stable across studies. Jackson et al. (1989) cited the results of the fear appeal and sidedness meta-analyses as evidence that such variables must interact with message treatments in other studies. This assumes, of course, that content such

Table 2.1. Results of Meta-Analyses.

finding	*k*	*N*	*r*	*SD*
forewarning reduces attitude change	12	1359	.18	.04
evidence enhances attitude change	16	2800	.19	.10
powerful language increases credibility	16	1390	.22	.01
powerful language increases attitude change	6	463	.25	.01
manipulated fear increases perceived fear	12	3322	.34	.02
manipulated fear increases attitude change	13	1914	.21	.03
manipulated fear increases behavior change	6	1757	.17	.05

as fear appeals and message-sidedness will go unnoticed by researchers when they are designing their experiments. The fact that no meta-analysis has uncovered a fear-appeal or message-sidedness moderator indicates that researchers have effectively avoided such confounds in their designs.

Evidence From Multiple Message Studies

Although Jackson et al. (1989) did not claim to have found evidence of replicated established interactions—we cannot find any—they did claim to have found individual studies with treatment by message replication interactions. They identified 19 studies that have used multiple message designs. Of the 19 studies, 8 did not provide sufficient information to determine if message content by treatment interactions exist. Of the remaining 11 studies, Jackson et al. (1989) claimed that 7 found evidence of a message content by treatment interaction. In three of the seven studies cited by Jackson et al. (Bradac & Mulac, 1984; Doelger, Hewes, & Graham, 1986; Tracy, 1983), post hoc inspection of the results by the authors led them to conclude that the treatment by message replication interaction was so insubstantial that they could make an unqualified interpretation of the treatment effects. Thus there are only four studies that can be claimed to have found a substantively significant interaction. We examine these four studies next.

Jackson et al. (1988) cited a study by Rogers and Mewborn (1976) as evidence of a treatment by message replication interaction. This study reported different fear appeal effects across topic. However, after reviewing 23 studies, and a total of 3,693 subjects for a meta-analysis on fear-appeal effects, Boster and Mongeau (1984) concluded that, "While there are not many studies per topic, the available evidence suggests that the fear manipulation-attitude correlation does not vary substantially across topic" (p. 56).

Jackson et al. (1988) also cited a study by Hample and Dallinger (1987), which found a situation by message (compliance strategy) interaction. As Boster (1985) and Hunter and Boster (1987) have shown, compliance gaining strategies such as those used in the Hample and Dallinger study are arrayed along a single underlying dimension of endorsement. Hample and Dallinger noted that an analysis using this underlying dimension eliminates the situation effect.

The treatment by message replication interaction in the other two studies cited by Jackson et al. (1988) was due to methodological artifacts. In Tracy (1982), on one of the four topics a coherence confound occurred. Results on this topic differed from those on the three topics where there was no coherence confound. The result was that the ANOVA falsely indicated a treatment by message replication interaction. In Housel (1985), a treatment by message replication interaction was reported on two of four dependent measures. Housel included two measures of comprehension. On the measure of "content comprehension," the traditional comprehension item, Housel found no interaction. He did find an interaction on the "personal comprehension" measure. However, analysis of the substantive nature of the interaction shows it should have been found on content comprehension as well. The fact that this interaction was not found on the content comprehension measure is conceptually a failure to replicate the finding. The failure to replicate the finding indicates that it was likely due to sampling error. Housel also found an interaction on recall accuracy, but post hoc inspection by the author showed that this interaction was not substantively meaningful.

To summarize the empirical literature on treatment by message interactions, meta-analyses have not found heterogeneous interactions of the kind claimed to be ubiquitous by Jackson and Jacobs (1983) and by Jackson et al. (1989). Multiple message designs such as those by Allen et al. (1990) have not found substantive moderator variables despite extremely high power. Furthermore, there is no evidence for such an interaction in the specific studies cited by Jackson et al. (1989). Thus the evidence suggests that such interactions are actually quite rare.

IN DEFENSE OF META-ANALYSIS

Suppose that Jackson and Jacobs (1983) are correct. Suppose that there exist many message by treatment interactions in the persuasion literature. Is the multiple message design the only alternative? The most frequently used alternative in persuasion (and other communication domains) is the meta-analysis of single message studies. In meta-analysis, the message by treatment interaction represents a special case of a moderator variable that causes true study results to differ from one study to the next. Every method of meta-analysis focuses on potential moderator variables. There are two steps: (a) to see if there are such differences and (b) the identification the moderator variables if there are any. Thus, meta-analysis of single message study results will both detect and identify a treatment by message interaction if there is one.

Jackson (1984) and Jackson et al. (1988) have criticized meta-analysis. Their arguments proceeded along two lines. First, they denied that meta-analysis can fulfill its basic function, that is, to determine effect sizes across studies. Jackson (1984) asserted that researchers are "delusional" if they prefer meta-analysis to multiple message designs, because there will be too few replications to establish a stable effect size estimate, or differences in design will prevent comparison across studies. We show here that meta-analysis is less susceptible to a lack of replication than other review procedures, and that Jackson et al. overstated problems associated with conducting meta-analyses. Second, they asserted that the moderator tests of meta-analysis cannot identify message treatment by replication interactions. Originally, Jackson (1984) insisted that the meta-analytic procedures of Hunter, Schmidt, and Jackson (1982) would not allow analysis using two sources of sampling error—people and messages. Hunter et al., (1989) noted that messages replications can be easily handled as a potential moderator variable. Jackson et al. (1989) redirected their criticism of moderator tests in meta-analysis to argue that the reuse of messages by researchers and correction for artifacts obscures the detection of message content by treatment interactions. We show that the reuse of messages is rare, and not a problem for meta-analysis when it does occur.

Estimating Mean Effect Size

The estimation of effect sizes and their variation is much more accurate if there are many studies than if there are few studies in a research domain. That is, the power of meta-analysis is greatest in areas where studies are widely replicated. Jackson et al. (1988) worried that if few replications exist in a particular domain, then meta-analysis will have insufficient power to detect a main effect for the variable of interest.

The power of any review of the literature depends on the quality of that literature, and the number of studies in the domain is a critical dimension of quality in that domain. Meta-analysis is no more dependent on wide replication than any other form of cumulative review. In fact, because meta-analysis makes more efficient use of statistical information than is true in narrative reviews, narrative reviews are more dependent on replication than are meta-analyses. The sampling error in unreplicated studies has a larger effect on nonquantitative reviews than on quantitative reviews, because nonquantitative reviews make no effort to place confidence intervals about their conclusions. Nonetheless, in the next sections we show that Jackson et al. have overstated the problems associated with (a) lack of replication, (b) obtaining existing studies, and (c) calculating effect sizes across studies.

Adequate Replication

Consider the argument that a lack of replication prevents meta-analysis. It seems to us that if a line of research is salient to the field of persuasion, particularly one theoretically important, it will be both replicated and extended. If a study is not replicated or extended, then it probably is not significant to the field. In the usual meta-analysis, studies are intended as "replications" only in the broad scientific sense of the word: Each study measures the same independent variable and the same dependent variable. Identical replications are useful in meta-analysis because they permit the elimination of sampling error by aggregating the identical replications before starting to examine the extent of homogeneity of results across studies that are not identical replications. Unfortunately, only a few "identical replications" are likely to be found in any area. A more likely find is a replication and extension of research findings that allows a retesting of a message treatment effect while examining some other aspect of its impact. Bradac (1986) has made this same point. He cited a study by Kelly, Chase, and Tucker (1979), who reviewed *Human Communication Research and Communication Monographs* over a 5-year period and found that one of five studies constitutes at least a partial replication.

Meta-analysis does not require exactly the same results across conceptual replications. Instead, meta-analysis can test whether or not a set of studies claimed as conceptual replications are actually replications. Meta-analysis tests whether or not a set of studies claimed to be heterogeneous actually show heterogeneous results.

The key idea for comparing studies using meta-analysis is the concept of homogeneity. Studies are perfectly homogeneous if the true effect sizes are uniform across the studies. First, consider identical replications. If all the studies in a set constitute identical replications, then the true effect sizes are uniform by definition. Meta-analysis finds that all differences in study results are due to sampling error. Thus if the studies are designed to have perfect replication, meta-analysis will demonstrate perfect homogeneity.

In research domains such as persuasion, studies thought to bear on the same question are only conceptual replications. There is a theoretical reason to believe that the studies have the same independent and the same dependent variable, although the actual variables are not identical. Usually, a theory predicts roughly the same results across studies. That is, the expectation stemming from conceptual replication is homogeneity of effect sizes, despite differences in the specific content of the study. Meta-analysis tests for homogeneity across studies. If meta-analysis finds that effect size differs from study to study, then meta-analysis can test for potential moderator variables to see if the moderator explains some portion of the variation in results. Even if no such moderator variables are found, the meta-analysis can estimate the extent of generalization of results in that domain. If results are not homogeneous, then meta-analysis can provide a quantitative measure of the amount of variation across studies.

Obtaining Existing Studies

Jackson et al. (Jackson, 1984; Jackson et al., 1988) claimed that meta-analysis will be rendered useless by "publication bias." They claim that small effect sizes will be underrepresented because statistical significance tests cause only large effect sizes to be published. This claim is called the "file drawer" problem (Rosenthal, 1979) and has been both discussed and studied for many years. Many recent meta-analyses have compared published and unpublished studies (see Hunter and Schmidt, 1990, pp. 506-516, for a review). Rosenthal (1984) reviewed 12 meta-analyses in education and found virtually no difference between published and unpublished effect sizes. In personnel selection, there is no difference between published and unpublished results across a very wide selection of topics. Publication bias has not been discovered in any meta-analysis to date. It should be noted that if there were a file drawer problem, it is not a problem with meta-analysis per se. Rather, it would indict the entire database for persuasion. If published studies have incorrect results, then there is no review process that can draw correct inferences from cumulated research. All attempts at science would be wasted. Fortunately, empirical evidence suggests that there is actually no file drawer problem.

It should be noted that the multiple message study is not exempt from the file drawer criticism. Study sample size is determined by author resources, not by design principles. Thus, multiple message designs would have the same statistical properties as single message designs. If there were a file drawer problem, then the multiple message design would go down the drain with the rest of science.

Jackson et al. (1988) made a related criticism of meta-analysis, arguing that some studies are difficult to obtain, so researchers will not include them in a meta-analysis. But is this a problem? If only a random sampling of studies were lost, this would weaken the meta-analysis because the total sample size would be smaller. However,if there are enough studies available, the fact that certain studies were lost would have no effect on the outcome. Lost studies are only a problem if the lost studies systematically differ from available studies. If available studies are unrepresentative, however, this creates a disaster for any approach to science, not just meta-analysis. No scientist can review a lost study. The lost study criticism becomes really a criticism of all review articles—including narrative reviews as well as meta-analysis. Fortunately, researchers have a wealth of resources to resolve this difficulty should it arise: interlibrary loan services, contacting the author (or institution) by mail (electronic or conventional) or telephone.

Calculating Estimates Across Studies

Jackson (1984) and Jackson et al. (1988) cited a number of "practical difficulties" with conducting meta-analyses on message effects. They pointed to "widely varying research designs" limiting the comparison of results from one study to another. Those who have conducted meta-analyses know that this is seldom a problem. The relevant effect sizes can almost always be extracted, regardless of the design (Glass, McGaw, & Smith, 1981; Hunter & Schmidt, 1990). They also claim that "specific message cases get confounded with all sorts of other variables" from study to study. Specifically, they claimed that effect sizes might vary due to other moderator variables in a design, such as different dependent measures, different sample characteristics and different research contexts. Allen et al. (1990) showed that this concern over different dependent measures was unfounded. Results from meta-analyses indicate that worries about sample characteristics and research contexts are likewise not a problem. Even when such differences exist, the effects are small.

Jackson et al. (1988) argued that meta-analysis is plagued by the inadequate reporting of results. However, this claim ignores the well-established editorial policies of the major journals in communication regarding adequate reporting of results. They present neither arguments nor published examples to suggest that these standards have suddenly eroded.

Moderator Tests

In claiming that meta-analysis does not allow inference from samples to populations, Jackson (1984) did not distinguish the various goals of different methods of meta-analysis. Glass et al. (1981) defined their objective to be estimation of the mean observed effect size across studies. Hunter et al. (1982), on the other hand, sought out the true effect size free of artifactual distortions such as imperfect measurement and sampling error. As a result, Jackson (1984) failed to distinguish between methods that focus solely on mean effect size (e.g., Glass et al.) and those that estimate variance across studies (e.g., Hunter et al.).

The sampling assumptions for Glass et al. do not apply to Hunter et al., and the detection of moderator variables is much more powerful in variance-centered methods. Monte Carlo tests (Spector & Levine, 1987) show that the Hunter et al. procedure is a powerful tool for detecting moderator variables. If the Hunter et al. technique errs, it is likely to be in the direction of Type I, rather than Type II errors. In other words, the Hunter et al. procedure is a liberal test for moderator variables. Jackson et al. (1988) and O'Keefe (1990) vaguely alluded to critics of meta-analytic moderator tests (Hedges & Olkin, 1986; Osburn, Callendar, Greener and Ashworth, 1983; Sacket, Harris, & Orr, 1986; Spector & Levine, 1987), who have alleged that moderator tests to detect heterogeneity across studies possess unresolved defects. Hunter and Schmidt (1990) provided an extended rebuttal of these criticisms.

Jackson et al. claim that heterogeneity across studies has been underestimated because researchers have (a) reused messages, and (b) corrected for artifacts such as sampling error and measurement error before conducting heterogeneity tests.

The Reuse of Messages

Jackson and Jacobs (1983), Jackson et al. (1988) and O'Keefe (1990) asserted that the practice of reusing experimental messages is rampant, and that this leads to an underestimation of heterogeneity across studies. We note first that the mathematical logic of the argument is wrong. Suppose we have a set of numbers X1, X2, . . . , Xn. They will have a variance Vx. Suppose that each number is duplicated so that we have 2n numbers : X1, X1, X2, X2, . . . , Xn, Xn. The new variance will be identical to the old variance.

Mere replication of numbers does not systematically reduce variance. Thus, reusing experimental messages does not cause an underestimation of heterogeneity. In any case, the critics provide no evidence for widespread reuse of messages. They cite only three examples. Kelly et al. (1979) reviewed a large number of communication studies for evidence of replication. They found that only one study in five was even a partial replication of a previous study. Thus, message reuse occurs so infrequently as to have negligible impact.

There may be a domain in which one odd message has been reused by a school of researchers so many times that they appear to have established and replicated some phenomenon that is not there for other messages. A meta-analysis would identify this subset of studies as a moderator variable and show them to be deviant. A case somewhat like this was identified by Johnson and Eagly (1989). Their meta-analysis uncovered the problem.

We would like to argue for message reuse. Consideration of sampling error shows that any component of identical replication can be quite useful. Studies with identical replication can be cumulated before the meta-analysis across conceptual replications to generate larger effect sizes for single studies. This would greatly improve the likelihood of identifying the moderator variable when finding a treatment interaction. Consider the hypothetical case of the deviant message. Reuse of that message makes the deviant message visible. If the message were used in only one small sample study, it would contribute to variance but it might not be identified as the problem study.

One area of persuasion that has seen extensive reuse of the same message across studies concerns the effect of argument quality on attitude change at various levels of involvement. Johnson and Eagly (1989) found that researchers affiliated with Ohio State University could produce empirical evidence supporting the Elaboration Likelihood Model (Petty & Cacioppo, 1981, 1986), but that unaffiliated researchers could not. The Johnson and Eagly finding demonstrates that meta-analysis detects results biased by the reuse of messages.

Correction for Artifacts

It is important to distinguish between true differences in study results and apparent or artificial differences between study results due to sampling error, measurement error, weak manipulations, differences in construct validity, and the like. Correction for artifacts is recommended by most current methods of meta-analysis, although both sampling error and error of measurement were ignored in the early work by Glass et al. (1981).

Surprisingly, Jackson et al. (1989) continue to criticize current meta-analytic procedures based on the outdated reasoning of Glass et al. Jackson et al. (1989) asserted that meta-analysts who employ such procedures are being "creative," implying that the researchers are fabricating results in order to suppress ubiquitous message treatment by content interactions. Jackson et al. also believe that subsetting procedures, like those used by Dillard, Hunter, and Burgoon (1984) to uncover moderator variables, obscure the ubiquitous message content interactions.

The fact is that subsetting is the accepted method of identifying interactions not only in meta-analysis, but in analysis of variance as well (where it is called "post hoc analysis"). They provide no rationale for believing that subsetting works within analysis of variance but does not work within meta-analysis. How else do we test a hypothesis such as, "High intensity is more persuasive in sports messages but is less persuasive in scientific messages"? Subsetting is the standard method of identifying interactions throughout statistics. We know of not one article anywhere in statistics arguing that subsetting is wrong. Jackson et al. offer no argument to show that it is wrong, only the allegation.

CONCLUSION

We started this chapter by reviewing the genesis of the Jackson et al. multiple messages argument. We showed that the multiple messages argument was subsidiary to a more provocative proposition: in their original article, Jackson and Jacobs (1983) vigorously argued that the message effects literature was worthless because it was primarily based on studies which used contrived messages. They argued that the desire to use the single message, controlled message design had caused researchers to use artificial and unrealistic messages instead of natural messages. To solve this problem, they prescribed the use of designs employing multiple, naturalistic messages nested within treatment conditions.

Each of the arguments for the naturalistic and nested design made by Jackson et al. were refuted by Hunter et al. (1989). In subsequent papers, Jackson and coworkers argued a less dramatic position. Jackson et al. (1989) ceased to argue for nested designs, or for natural messages. Indeed, their hypothetical examples are all of crossed designs using contrived variations from the same kernel message. However, they still prescribe multiple message designs and proscribe single message designs.

These critics (Jackson & Jacobs, 1983; Jackson et al., 1989) have argued for the completely confounded design in which each receiver gets a different messages. This suggestion runs counter not only to meta-analytic thinking, but to the convention of analysis of variance. If only one subject is used per message, then there is a perfect confounding between individual differences, error of measurement, and the treatment by message interaction (if any). Edwards (1960) noted that the interaction can only be separately identified if there is replication within treatment by message combinations. That is, Edwards has shown that detection of the interaction requires multiple receivers within each treatment by message combination.

Hunter et al. (1990) noted further problems with the multiple message design if only a small number of receiver are used for each message (where "small" means 100 or so). They noted that if an interaction is detected, then further data is needed to identify the interaction. In order to figure out what study feature is causing the interaction, it is necessary to know which message had which effect; that is, it is necessary to know which particular messages showed large effects and which showed small effects. For this purpose, it is optimal to maximize the number of receivers for each message. For purposes of identifying treatment by message interactions, the ideal design is the single message design. Unexpected interactions are then detected and identified at the level of the review study, where meta-analysis is an ideal tool for such analysis.

In a later article, Jackson et al. (1989) abandoned interest in identifying treatment by message content interactions. Instead, they argued that the most important tasks are to detect the "treatment main effect" and detect the interaction. If this is true, then the multiple message design is still effective (although analysis of variance requires at least two subjects per message or else the interaction is assumed to be nonexistent).

This argument is backwards. They are proposing radically different research objectives in order to justify the designer analysis they prefer. Effective design requires the opposite: using the best design and analysis in order to achieve the objectives set by substantive analysis. The persuasion literature is unambiguous: Theoretical articles and research reviews are dominated by an interest in identifying interactions where they are found. To use a design that obscures the process of identifying interactions is to use a design that is directly opposite to the objectives of current theory building.

There are also mathematical problems with failing to identify an interaction if present. If there is an interaction, then it is a misnomer to talk of "the treatment effect," as Jackson et al. (1989) have: "the" treatment effect does not exist; rather, there are many treatment effects. What Jackson et al. have done is to identify "the treatment effect" with what in analysis of variance is called the "treatment main effect." In analysis of variance, however, there is the consistent warning that if an interaction exists, then the treatment main effect can be meaningless. If half the studies show intensity as having a positive effect whereas the other half of the studies show intensity as having a negative effect, then the treatment main effect is 0, which describes no study at all.

The conceptual problem of the treatment by message interaction is handled correctly by meta-analysis. If there is an interaction, then meta-analysis refers to the treatment main effect as "the average effect size was aaa." Advanced meta-analytic studies always follow this statement with the phrase, "with a standard deviation of sss." Thus, in meta-analysis there is never the confusion between the treatment main effect and a nonexistent "treatment effect."

We come finally to the catch-22 for the multiple message design. Analysis of variance shows that if there is no treatment by message interaction, then the multiple message design has noticeably lower power than the single message design. That is, the multiple message design is never optimal unless there is an interaction. On the other hand, if there is an interaction, then the treatment effect differs for different messages and understanding of treatment effects requires the identification of the rules that cause one message to show a different effect than another. Analysis of variance shows that in order for this post hoc analysis to have optimal power, the number of receivers for each message should be as high as possible. If there is an interaction, then for any fixed sample size the number of messages should be as small as possible. This means that the multiple message design is never optimal.

Traditionally, researchers have opted to use the single message design at the individual study level, and to identify treatment by message interactions (if any) at the level of the review study. The traditional review study was narrative, but meta-analysis makes possible a quantitative analysis comparing study results. From a statistical point of view, meta-analysis is the logical extension of analysis of variance to handle multiple messages gathered using instruments with different units of analysis, different populations, and so on. Meta-analysis can be viewed as the quantitative completion of the single message design process.

Jackson (1992) has recently sought to pit analysis of variance against meta-analysis as if they were competing analyses. The fact is that analysis of variance is a special case of meta-analysis in which all the homogeneity assumptions of exact replication are assumed. There is no competition—meta-analysis simply works much better if the restrictive assumptions of analysis of variance are met Jackson and colleagues have argued that meta-analysis is a poor technique because it aggregates across studies, but the multiple message design also aggregates. If analysis of variance is used as they suggest, the results for single messages are never even computed or examined. This is a severe aggregation process. The issue is not whether to aggregate or not; the need is to aggregate in a conceptually clear manner. Meta-analysis always considers messages individually and describes interactive treatment effects with phrases such as "the average treatment effect." Meta-analysis is therefore much clearer than the multiple message methodology advocated in Jackson et al. (1989). If there is an interaction, then meta-analysis of single message studies is also massively more powerful for the identification of the interaction.

In order to defend the multiple message design, Jackson and colleagues have attacked meta-analysis (Jackson et al., 1988; Jackson et al., 1989; O'Keefe et al., 1988) O'Keefe, Jacobs & Brashers, 1989). Most of these criticisms were shown to be mathematical errors. The most devastating criticism, if true, is the file drawer problem. If it really were true that published studies represented a drastically unrepresentative set of results (in comparison to the hypothesized massive representative database in the file drawers), then it is true that meta-analysis based on only published studies would be correspondingly biased. Most meta-analysts, however, make a concerted effort to include unpublished results if they can find them. Comparison of published and unpublished results has so far shown no difference in results. Actual data to date has found no evidence for a file drawer problem. In any case, if published studies cannot be trusted, this is a problem for all scientific review and reasoning, not just for meta-analysis.

Finally, it should be noted that the attacks made on meta-analysis do not support use of multiple message studies. First, because multiple message studies are also small sample studies, the results of individual studies do not become scientifically sound until they are combined to eliminate the effect of sampling error. That is, the cumulative analysis of multiple message studies requires the use of meta-analysis. Second, if there were a file drawer problem, it would be just as bad for multiple message studies as for single message studies. The principles of Type I and Type II sampling error apply just as much to multiple message studies as to single message studies. If there were a file drawer problem, then the published multiple message studies would be an unrepresentative sample of multiple message studies.

In conclusion, Jackson and colleagues have argued strongly to reject the traditional persuasion design in which a single kernel message is manipulated to form contrived messages that embody desired treatment effects. Most of their early arguments were abandoned, but they still cling to the claim that only multiple message designs should be used. They could only defend the multiple message design requirement by attacking meta-analysis, because the meta-analysis of single message studies has been shown to be mathematically optimal. We have shown that their attacks on meta-analysis are both mathematically and substantively unsound. Even if multiple message studies are done, meta-analysis is needed to combine results across the multiple message studies so as to escape the effects of sampling error. Until some utopian society provides funds for studies to be done with a minimum sample size of 5,000, results of individual studies will always have considerable error. Until that time, solid scientific inference in persuasion research will require the combination of results across studies. Meta-analysis is currently the best known method of cumulating results across studies.

REFERENCES

Allen, M., Hale, J., Mongeau, P., Berkowitz-Stafford, S., Stafford, S., Shanahan, W., Agee, P., Dillon, K., Jackson, R., & Ray, C. (1990). Testing a model of message sidedness: Three Replications. *Communication Monograph, 57*, 275-291.

Boster, F. J. (1985). Argumentation, interpersonal communication, persuasion, and the process(es) of compliance gaining message use. In J. R. Cox, M. O. Sillars, & G. B. Walker (Eds.), *Argument and social practice: Proceedings of the fourth SCA/AFA conference on argumentation* (pp. 578-591). Annandale, VA: Speech Communication Association.

Boster, F. J., & Mongeau, P. (1984). Fear-arousing persuasive messages. In R. N. Bostrom (Ed.), *Communication Yearbook 8* (pp. 330-375). Beverly Hills, CA: Sage.

Bradac, J. J. (1986). Threats to generalization in the use of elicited, purloined, and contrived messages in human communication research. *Communication Quarterly, 34*, 55–65.

Bradac, J. J., & Mulac, A. (1984). A molecular view of powerful and powerless speech styles: Attributional consequences of specific language features and communicator intentions. *Communication Monographs, 51*, 307-319.

Dillard, J. P., Hunter, J. E., & Burgoon, M. (1984). Sequential request persuasive strategies: Meta-analysis of foot-in-the-door and door-in-the-face. *Human Communication Research, 10*, 464-488.

Doelger, J.A., Hewes, D.E., & Graham, M. (1986). Knowing when to "second-guess": The mindful analysis of messages. *Human Communication Research, 12*, 301-338.

Edwards, A. E. (1960). *Experimental design in psychological research*. New York: Holt, Rinehart & Winston.

Glass, G. V., McGaw, B., & Smith, M. L. (1981). *Meta-analysis in social research*. Beverly Hills, CA: Sage.

Hample, D., & Dallinger, J. M. (1987). Individual differences in cognitive editing standards. *Human Communication Research, 14*, 123-144.

Hedges, L. V. & Olkin, I. (1985). *Statistical methods for meta-analysis*. Orlando, FL: Academic Press.

Housel, T. J. (1985). Conversational themes and attention focussing strategies: Predicting comprehension and recall. *Communication Quarterly, 33*, 236-253.

Hunter, J. E., & Boster, F. J. (1987). A model of compliance-gaining message selection. *Communication Monographs, 54*, 63-84.

Hunter, J. E., Hamilton, M. A., & Allen, M. (1987, May). *The design and analysis of language experiments in communication*. Paper presented to the International Communication Association, Montreal, Canada.

Hunter, J. E., Hamilton, M. A., & Allen, M. (1989). The design and analysis of language experiments in communication. *Communication Monographs, 56*, 341-363.

Hunter, J. E., & Hirsh, H. R. (1987). Applications of meta-analysis. In C. L. Cooper & I. T. Robertson (Eds.), *Review of industrial psychology* (Vol. 2). New York: Wiley.

Hunter, J. E., & Schmidt, F. L. (1990). *Methods of meta-analysis: Correcting error and bias in research findings*. Newbury Park, CA: Sage.

Hunter, J. E., Schmidt, F. L., & Jackson, G. B. (1982). *Meta-analysis: Cumulating research findings across studies*. Beverly Hills, CA: Sage.

Jackson, S. (1984). *Meta-analysis and generalization in communication research*. Paper presented at the annual meeting of the Central States Speech Association, Chicago, IL.

Jackson, S., & Jacobs, S. (1983). Generalizing about messages: Suggestions for design and analysis of experiments. *Human Communication Research, 9*, 169-181.

Jackson, S., & Jacobs, S. (1987, May). *The search for systematic message effects: Contributions of meta-analysis and better design*. Paper presented at the meeting of the International Communication Association, Montreal, Canada.

Jackson, S., O'Keefe, D. J., & Jacobs, S. (1988). The search for reliable generalizations about messages: A comparison of research strategies. *Human Communication Research, 15*, 127–142.

Jackson, S., O'Keefe, D. J., Jacobs, S., & Brashers, D. E. (1989). Messages as replications: Toward a message-centered design strategy. *Communication Monographs, 56*, 364-384.

Johnson, B. T., & Eagly, A. H. (1989). Effects of involvement on persuasion: A meta-analysis. *Psychological Bulletin, 106*, 290-314.

Kelly, C., Chase, L., & Tucker, R. (1979). Replication in experimental communication research: An analysis. *Human Communication Research, 5*, 338-342.

Lord, R. G., DeVader, C. L., & Alliger, G. M. (1986). A meta-analysis of the relation between personality traits and leadership perceptions: An application of validity generalization procedures. *Journal of Applied Psychology, 71*, 402-410.

Mann, R. D. (!959). A review of the relationships between personality and performance in small groups. *Psychological Bulletin, 56,* 241-270.

Morley, D. D. (1988). Meta-analysis techniques: When generalizing to message populations is not possible. *Human Communication Research, 15,* 112-126.

O'Keefe, D. (1990). *Persuasion: Theory and research.* Newbury Park, CA: Sage.

O'Keefe, B. J., & McCornack, S. A. (1987). Message design logic and message goal structure: Effects on perception of message quality in regulative communication situations. *Human Communication Research, 14,* 68-92.

O'Keefe, D. D., Jackson, S., & Jacobs, S. (1988). Reply to Morely. *Human Communication Research, 15,* 148-151,

Osburn, H. G., Callendar, J. C., Greener, J. M., & Ashworth, S. (1983). Statistical power of tests of the situational specificity hypothesis in validity generalization studies: A cautionary note. *Journal of Applied Psychology, 68,* 115-122.

Petty, R. E., & Cacioppo, J. T. (1981). *Attitudes and persuasion: Classic and contemporary approaches.* Dubuque, IA: Brown.

Petty, R. E., & Cacioppo, J. T. (1986). *Communication and persuasion.* New York: Springer-Verlag.

Rogers, R. W., & Mewborn, C. R. (1976). Fear appeals and attitude change: Effects of a threats noxiousness, probability of occurrence, and the efficacy of coping responses. *Journal of Personality and Social Psychology, 34,* 54-61.

Rosenthal, R. (1979). The "file drawer problem" and tolerance for null results. *Psychological Bulletin, 86,* 638-641.

Rosenthal, R. (1984). *Meta-analytic procedures for social research.* Newbury Park, CA: Sage.

Sacket, P. R., Harris, M. M., & Orr, J. M. (1986). On seeking moderator variables in the analysis of correlational data: A Monte Carlo investigation of statistical power and resistance to Type I error. *Journal of Applied Psychology, 71,* 302-310.

Specter, P. E., & Levine, E. L. (1987). Meta-analysis for integrating study outcomes: A Monte Carlo study of its susceptibility to type I and type II errors. *Journal of Applied Psychology, 72,* 3-9.

Stogdill, R. M. (1948). Personal factors associated with leadership: A survey of the literature. *Journal of Applied Psychology, 69,* 673-686.

Tracy, K. (1982). On getting the point: Distinguishing "issue" from "events": An aspect of conversational coherence. In M. Burgoon (Ed.), *Communication yearbook 5* (pp. 279-301). Beverly Hills, CA: Sage.

Tracy, K. (1983). The issue-event distinction: A rule of conversation and its scope condition. *Human Communication Research, 9,* 320-334.

Winer, B. (1971). *Statistical principles in experimental design* (2nd ed.). New York: McGraw-Hill.

3

Another Look at Fear-Arousing Persuasive Appeals

Paul A. Mongeau
Miami University

Persuasion practitioners have long used fear when attempting to change attitudes and behaviors. From the pulpit to the televised commercial, fear remains a favorite persuasive tool. The primary question in this meta-analysis is to what extent does increasing the amount of fear-arousing material in a message influence perceived fear, attitudes, behavioral intentions, and behaviors?

A fear-arousing persuasive appeal (or, more simply, a fear appeal) describes a threat. Second, the appeal indicates that message recipients are likely to experience that threat. Third, fear appeals indicate that one way of avoiding that threat is to perform the change in attitudes and/or behaviors recommended by the message source (Boster & Mongeau, 1984; O'Keefe, 1990).

The primary goal of this chapter is to extend the Boster and Mongeau (1984) meta-analysis investigating the impact of fear appeals on perceived fear, attitudes, and behaviors. The previous meta-analysis is extended in two ways. First, the previous meta-analysis is updated through the addition of recent research. Second, studies investigating the impact of fear appeals on behavioral intentions (a dependent variable not considered in Boster & Mongeau) is analyzed. In analyzing the impacts of fear on behavioral intention, attention is focused exclusively on tests of the Protection Motivation Explanation (Rogers, 1975, 1983).

RESEARCH AND THEORY ON FEAR APPEALS

Research performed on the persuasive of impact of fear appeals yields inconsistent results. Some studies report that increasing fear decreased persuasion (e.g., Goldstein, 1959; Janis & Feshbach, 1953). Several studies report the opposite; that is, increasing fear increases persuasion (e.g., Hewgill & Miller, 1966). Finally, some studies indicate that increasing the amount of fear in a message has no impact on persuasion (e.g., Kohn, Goodstadt, Cook, Sheppard, & Chan, 1982). Over the years, several attempts at *explaining* these conflicting results have been advanced.[1]

Drive Models

Early explanations for the impact of fear appeals center on the drive-producing and reducing qualities of fear appeals (for a fuller explication of drive models, see Boster & Mongeau, 1984; Leventhal, 1970; Sutton, 1982). Early drive models posit that strong fear appeals create fear within audience members. Fear acts as a drive, which audience members must reduce. Although there are many methods of drive reduction, early explanations posit that audience members reduce drive by adopting the attitude and/or behavior advocated in the message. Because the reduction of the unpleasant drive is rewarding, the initial drive models predict that the greater the fear produced by the message the greater the attitude change.

> Hypothesis 1: The original drive model predicts positive and linear relationships between fear and perceived fear, attitudes, and behaviors.

[1]More complete reviews of models explicating the impacts of fear appeals can be found in Beck and Frankel (1981), Boster & Mongeau (1984), and Rogers (1983).

Initial drive explanations fail to adequately account for conflicting findings relating fear to persuasion until extended by Janis (1967; Janis & Leventhal, 1968). Specifically, Janis argued that fear can either enhance or inhibit the effectiveness of a persuasive message. Specifically, when messages present low levels of fear, recipients are unlikely to be concerned about the threat. Very strong levels of fear, on the other hand, are likely to generate defensive avoidance. Defensive avoidance is characterized by "preoccupation with hypervigilant speculations and ruminations which generate defensive maneuvers . . . that interfere with acceptance of the safety measures recommended by the communicator" (Janis & Leventhal, 1968, p. 1056). In other words, the recommended coping response (e.g., change in attitudes and/or behaviors) is inadequate to reduce the drive produced by the strong fear appeal.

According to the revised drive model, optimal conditions for attitude change are created by inducing a moderate amount of fear within audience members. Moderate fear heightens awareness of the threat but does not create so much fear as to generate defensive avoidance (Janis, 1967). In sum, the revised drive model posits that the impact of fear on attitudes follows an inverted U-shaped pattern. Attitude and behavior change becomes greater under conditions of moderate fear than either low or high fear. For this explanation to fit the inconsistent data, Janis argued that those studies which found inverse relations between fear and persuasion spanned the moderate to high portion of the fear continuum, whereas those studies that found positive relationships between fear and persuasion spanned the low to moderate levels of the fear continuum.

> Hypothesis 2: The revised drive explanation predicts positive and linear relationships between fear and perceived fear. Relationships between fear and attitudes and fear and behaviors will be curvilinear (i.e., inverted U-shaped).

Parallel Response Model

Leventhal's (1970, 1971) Parallel Response Model (PRM) posits that persuasion combines emotional and cognitive processes. Specifically, the PRM presumes that exposure to a fear-appeal creates one of two primary coping processes: (a) fear control (an emotional process), or (b) danger control (a cognitive process). Fear control "is an emotional coping process in which listeners strive to reduce the fear generated by the persuasive message" (Boster & Mongeau, 1984, p. 335). When engaging in fear control, recipients concentrate on their own emotional reaction rather than the message.

As a consequence, recipients are unlikely to concentrate on, let alone heed, message recommendations.

Danger control, on the other hand, represents "a problem-solving process in which the listener scans the external environment for information pertinent to dealing with the threat presented in the persuasive message" (Boster & Mongeau, 1984, p. 335). When engaging in danger control, recipients concentrate on the threat depicted by the message and, as a consequence, focus on message recommendations as a means of controlling the threat.

The relationship between fear and persuasion predicted by the PRM depends on whether fear control or danger control processes are operative. When fear control processes are generated exclusively, fear remains inversely related to persuasion. When danger control processes are exclusively generated, fear is positively related to persuasion. The PRM can predict an inverted U-shaped function. Sternthal and Craig (1974) argued that "it is predicted that incremental increases in emotional material ultimately lead to disruption of danger control resulting in a non-monotonic relationship between fear and persuasion" (p. 26).

The PRM is noteworthy by defining persuasion as both an emotional and a cognitive process. The addition of the cognitive component provides a more complete explanation of responses to fear appeals. The PRM is incomplete, however, because it does not properly identify the conditions under which fear control and/or danger control operative. Therefore, it is unclear when the PRM predicts that fear should inhibit persuasion and when fear should facilitate persuasion. As a consequence, the PRM may be invoked to *explain* nearly any set of outcomes between fear and persuasion, although is unable to *predict* when these outcomes should occur. As such, this explanation is unfalsifiable.

Protection Motivation Explanation

The study of persuasion through the 1980s and into the 1990s strongly emphasized cognitive processes (Eagly & Chaiken, 1984). It should come as no surprise, then, that the most recent attempt to explain the impact of fear appeals also strongly emphasizes cognition. In the most recent version of the Protection Motivation Explanation (PME; Rogers, 1983; see also Rogers, 1975) a fear appeal is described as being composed of four components: (a) The noxiousness of the threat presented, (b) the probability that the threat will strike if no preventive action is taken, (c) the efficacy of the recommended coping response, and (d) the receiver's ability to enact that coping response. These components are predicted to combine to create protection motivation. Protection motivation acts as a traditional motive as "It arouses, sustains, and directs activity" (Rogers, 1975, p. 158).

In the revised PME, Rogers (1983) predicted that protection motivation should be a positive function of: (a) severity of the threat, (b) the threat's likelihood of occurrence, (c) the efficacy of the recommended coping response, and (d) the recipients' perception that they are able to perform that coping response. Protection motivation will vary inversely with: (a) response costs and (b) reinforcements associated with maladaptive responses.

Moreover, Rogers (1983) predicted that these variables may interact to influence protection motivation. Specifically, "If response efficacy (or self-efficacy) is high, severity and/or vulnerability will have a simple main effect on intentions; if response efficacy is low, increments in severity and/or vulnerability will either have no effect or a boomerang" (p. 170).[2]

The PME (unlike other explanations) does not consider perceived fear to be an important determinant of persuasion. In the revised PME, (see Rippetoe & Rogers, 1987; Rogers, 1983), perceived fear is predicted to be a function of perceived severity and perceived probability of the threat. Perceived fear, in turn, is not predicted to have an impact on other, important, persuasion variables (e.g., attitudes, behaviors, or behavioral intentions).

> Hypothesis 3: The Protection Motivation Explanation predicts that either severity or probability of the threat will interact with either response efficacy or self-efficacy to influence behavioral intentions.

In sum, four explanations for the impact of fear on persuasion have been discussed; (a) the original drive model, (b) the revised drive model, (c) the Parallel Response Model, and (d) the Protection Motivation Explanation. These explanations differ in the predicted relationships between fear, perceived fear, attitudes, behavioral intentions, and behaviors. The meta-analytic data should provide evidence of the relative validity of each of these explanations.

---

[2]This prediction is imprecise. Any of four interaction effects are predicted and each interaction can have either of two functional forms and still be consistent with the PME. When each interaction might occur (and in which form) is not detailed.

METHODS[3]

The Data

Data for this meta-analysis are comprised of study statistics and information concerning characteristics from studies investigating the impact of fear on perceived fear, attitudes, behavioral intentions, and behaviors. Study statistics included linear correlations and quadratic coefficients between fear and perceived fear, attitudes, behaviors, and behavioral intentions. Study characteristics included sample size; type of experimental design; year of publication, topic of the fear appeal; whether the subjects were volunteers or non-volunteers; and the number of items and intervals comprising each dependent measure (see Boster & Mongeau, 1984).

These data were obtained from published reports investigating the impact of fear on perceived fear, attitudes, behavioral intentions, and behaviors. Searches using electronic databases (e.g., ERIC, PSYCHLIT) were chosen for their comprehensiveness and availability. In addition, each study's reference list was inspected for additional articles.

Criteria for Inclusion

In order to be included, studies had to meet several criteria (see Boster & Mongeau, 1984). Studies must (a) present original data, (b) manipulate fear (or noxiousness; i.e., present messages that vary in fear-arousing content), (c) measure perceived fear, attitudes, behaviors, or behavioral intentions and (d) present sufficient statistical information to compute relevant effects sizes.

RESULTS

Summary statistics comparing the impact of fear on perceived fear, attitudes, and behaviors are presented in Table 3.1. In all three cases, the effect sizes are very similar to those reported by Boster and Mongeau (1984).

---

[3]Methods used in this meta-analysis mirror those outlined by Boster & Mongeau (1984). Thus, a complete discussion of the methods can be found in the earlier report.

Table 3.1. Summary Statistics Indicating the Impact of Fear on Perceived Fear, Attitudes, and Behaviors.

	Type of dependent variable		
		Perceived	
	Fear	Attitudes	Behaviors
Mean linear effect size	.351	.190	.118
[# studies, # subjects]	[45, 7645]	[29, 4311]	[19, 3445]
Weighted variance	.019	.035	.040
Variance expected by sampling error alone	.005	.006	.005
$\chi 2$ (df)	188.89 (44)	162.40 (28)	141.72 (18)
Mean quadratic effect size	.075	.089	.062
[# studies, # subjects]	[13, 3516]	[15, 2135]	[9, 2081]

Perceived Fear

Data relevant the relationship between fear and perceived fear were obtained from 45 studies including a total sample size of 7645. The mean fear-perceived fear correlation (weighted by sample size) was moderate and positive (r = .35). This is neither significantly nor substantially different from the effect size reported by Boster and Mongeau (r = .36). The weighted (by sample size) variance among correlations (s^2 = .019) was substantially larger than the amount of variation expected by sampling error (s^2 = .005). Put another way, there is significantly greater variation in the distribution of correlations than would be expected by sampling error $\chi 2(44)$ = 188.89, $p < .001$.

Boster and Mongeau (1984) reported little data to indicate the presence of moderator variables. In the present analyses, none of the study characteristics were significantly nor substantially correlated with the fear-perceived fear effect size.

The impact of fear manipulations on perceived fear is linear. The quadratic effect could be estimated from 13 studies including 3516 subjects. The average quadratic effect size (weighted by sample size) is trivial (r = .08). Given an average sample size of 270, the mean quadratic effect size is not statistically significant and substantially smaller than the average linear effect size. The quadratic effect size reported here is very similar to that presented by Boster & Mongeau (r = .07).

Attitude

Data relevant to the relationship between fear manipulations and attitudes were obtained from 29 studies using a total sample size of 4,311. The mean (weighted by sample size) fear–attitude correlations was positive, yet rather small ($r = .19$). The weighted (by sample size) variance in correlations ($s^2 = .035$) is substantially larger than that expected by sampling error ($s^2 = .006$). There is significantly more variation in the distribution of correlations than would be expected by sampling error $\chi 2(28) = 162.40, p < .001$).

The impact of fear on attitudes is linear. The quadratic effect could be estimated from 15 studies including 2135 subjects. The average quadratic effect size (weighted by sample size) is positive, yet trivial ($r = .09$). Given an average sample size of 147, the mean quadratic effect size is not statistically significant and substantially smaller than the mean linear effect size. These effect sizes are very similar to those presented by Boster & Mongeau (1984; linear $r = .21$, quadratic $r = .09$).

There is evidence that methodological factors influence the size of the fear–attitude correlation. The number of levels of the independent variable (r (27) = .39; p = .03), number of items measuring attitudes (r (24) = .43; $p = .03$), and the number of intervals on attitude measures (r (21) = . 38; $p = 0.52$) were all significantly correlated with the fear–attitude linear correlation. These data suggest that the fear–attitude correlations may be attenuated by both range restriction and measurement error. Studies with more levels of fear have greater variation in the independent variable and, consequently, less range restriction. Studies using more attitude measurement items, all other things being equal, are likely to be more reliable (see Boster and Mongeau, 1984). Because both unreliability of measurement and range restrictions attenuate correlations, the effect sizes reported here are likely to be underestimates.

The fear–attitude effect size is probably moderated by the fear–perceived fear effect size. Boster and Mongeau (1984) presented data suggesting that studies with larger fear–perceived fear correlations also tended to exhibit larger fear–attitude correlations. The present data also suggest such a pattern. The correlation between the fear–perceived fear correlation and fear–attitude correlations is significant and substantial (r (16) = .51; $p < .05$). These data suggest that the fear attitude relationship is moderated by perceived fear.

Boster & Mongeau (1984) confirmed that age interacts with fear to influence attitudes. Although no study added to earlier data set directly investigated this question, the estimated age of participants correlated strongly and positively with the size of the fear–attitude correlation (r (27) =

.36; $p < .053$). Specifically, studies where subjects are relatively old (e.g., non-college-student adults) tended to generate stronger fear-attitude correlations than did studies with relatively younger subjects (e.g., junior high school students).

Boster and Mongeau (1984) found that fear interacted with trait anxiety to influence attitudes. They claimed that:

> For low-anxiety participants there is either no correlation between manipulated fear and attitude or a small positive correlation between manipulated fear and attitude. For high anxiety participants there is either no correlation between manipulated fear and attitude or a small negative correlation between manipulated fear and attitude. (p. 353)

No study in this revised meta-analysis investigated the fear by anxiety interaction effect on attitudes.

Behavior

Data relevant to the relationship between fear and behaviors were obtained from 19 studies including a total sample size of 3,445. The mean fear–behavior correlation (weighted by sample size) was positive and rather small ($r = .12$). The weighted (by sample size) variance among correlations ($s^2 = .040$) is considerably larger than the variation expected by sampling error ($s^2 = .005$). There is significantly more variation in the distribution of fear–behavior correlations than would be expected by sampling error $\chi 2(18) = 141.72, p < .001$.

The impact of fear on behavior is linear. The quadratic effect could be estimated from 9 studies including 2,081 subjects. The average quadratic effect size (weighted by sample size) is positive yet trivial ($r = .06$). Given an average sample size of 231, the mean quadratic effect size is not statistically significant and smaller than the average linear effect size. Again, these effect sizes are very similar to those reported by Boster and Mongeau (1984; linear $r = .10$, quadratic $r = .03$).

There is evidence that methodological factors moderate the fear–behavior correlation. Specifically, the number of behavioral measures was significantly correlated with the fear–behavior effect size ($r\ (14) = .52$, $p < .03$). Strong fear–behavior correlations tend to be found in those studies with multiple, as opposed to single, behavioral measures. Again, this indicates that the fear–behavior correlations may be attenuated by measurement error.

The fear–behavior relationship may be mediated by the fear–perceived fear relationship. That is, the strength of the fear–behavior relationship may be limited by the size of the fear–perceived fear relationship. In the present data, the fear–perceived fear effect size is strongly correlated with the fear–behavior effect size (r (14) = .67; $p < .01$). This implies that one reason for variation in fear-behavior correlations may be the differential strength of the fear manipulations.

As was true with attitudes, Boster and Mongeau (1984) reported that both anxiety and age interact with fear to influence behavior. They suggest that the fear by anxiety interaction on behaviors is similar to that uncovered on attitudes. Specifically, they reported that fear has no impact on behaviors for high-anxiety subjects, whereas fear has a positive impact on behaviors for low-anxiety subjects. No study added to the meta-analysis investigated this relationship.

Boster and Mongeau reported that the form of the fear by age interaction on behavior is exactly opposite of these variables' impact on attitude. Specifically, Boster and Mongeau (1984) reported that as the age of participants increased, fear–behavior correlations became smaller. In the present data, approximate age of subjects was not significantly correlated with the fear–behavior effect size (r (17) = -.16; $p = .50$). This value is substantially smaller than that reported in the earlier meta-analysis. The earlier value may have been an anomaly.

Behavioral Intentions: Testing the Protection Motivation Explanation

The key to testing the PME is the analysis of the interaction effects predicted by Rogers (1983). Rogers predicted that there may be four interaction effects which influence behavioral intentions (i.e., noxiousness by self-efficacy, noxiousness by response efficacy, vulnerability by self-efficacy, and vulnerability by response efficacy). Four studies contained data relevant to the interactions with response efficacy and three studies are relevant to the interactions involving self-efficacy.[4]

Two studies report significant vulnerability by response efficacy interactions. These interactions are relatively robust (mean η weighted by sample size = .31). Rogers (1985) found that vulnerability had a substantial

---

[4]Each of the PME's four independent variables have been manipulated successfully. Mean correlations (weighted for sample size) for the noxiousness–perceived noxiousness relationship, (r = .66), the vulnerability–perceived vulnerability relationship (r = .58), the response efficacy–perceived response efficacy relationship (r = .67), and the self–efficacy – perceived self-efficacy relationship (r = .50) all indicate strong manipulations. There is, however, more variation in all these distributions than would be expected by sampling error alone. Too few studies exist at this time to allow for a meaningful search for moderator variables.

positive impact on behavioral intentions under conditions of high, but not low, response efficacy. Rogers and Mewborn (1976; in only one of three message-topic conditions), found that vulnerability generated a negative impact on intentions when self-efficacy was low, but a positive impact when response efficacy was high.

Two studies (Rogers, 1985; Rogers & Mewborn, 1975) reported significant noxiousness by response efficacy interactions (mean weighted $\eta = .24$). Both these interactions take the same form. Noxiousness produced a positive impact on behavioral intentions under conditions of high response efficacy, but not under conditions of low response efficacy.

None of the studies reported significant noxiousness by self-efficacy or vulnerability by self-efficacy interactions. Although not predicted in the PME, both Wurtele and Maddux (1987) and Maddux and Rogers (1983) reported significant vulnerability by response efficacy by self-efficacy interactions. In the Maddux and Rogers investigation, respondents reported strong behavioral intentions when at least two of the independent variables were high. When fewer than two of the independent variables were high, respondents reported lower levels of behavioral intentions. In the Wurtele and Maddux study, the impact of self-efficacy on intentions depended on both vulnerability and response efficacy. When vulnerability information was not included in the message, self-efficacy influenced intentions only when response efficacy information was also excluded. When vulnerability was high, self-efficacy influenced intentions only when response efficacy information was included as well.

There is evidence of nonadditivity in the data testing the PME. Robberson and Rogers (1988) found that fear and topic of the persuasive appeal interacted to influence attitudes. Robberson and Rogers compared the effectiveness of positive and negative fear appeals on exercise. Messages either described the health benefits of exercising or the impact of exercise on one's self-esteem.

When Robberson and Rogers' (1988) messages emphasized the physical health benefits of exercise, negative fear appeals were found to be superior to positive appeals. On the other hand, when the message emphasized the influence of exercise on self-esteem, positive fear appeals were found to be more effective in producing behavioral intentions than negative appeals.

These data indicate that fear-arousing messages may be most effective when they advocate changes in attitudes and/or behavior that result in improvement of one's physical health (rather than mental or economic health). The present meta-analytic data could test the potential moderating impact of message topic, however, only four studies used non-health-related topic. Because so few studies investigated non-health-related topics, such a comparison would be of dubious utility.

DISCUSSION

Theoretical Considerations

These meta-analytic data are relevant to the various models of fear appeals discussed earlier. The meta-analytic data are inconsistent with each of the models. The original drive model predicts positive correlations between fear and perceived fear, attitudes, and behaviors. These data are inconsistent with this model because several negative correlations between fear and attitudes and behaviors are found. The revised drive model predicted an inverted-U-shaped relationship between fear and perceived fear and persuasion. These data are inconsistent with this explanation because the impact of fear on perceived fear, attitudes, and behaviors is consistent with a linear rather than quadratic function. The parallel response model is not falsifiable (Boster & Mongeau, 1984). Any pattern of data is potentially consistent with this model's predictions. The PRM is able to explain any set of outcomes, but not able to predict when each outcome should occur. Finally, these data are also inconsistent with the protection motivation explanation. The PME predicts any of four interaction effects between components of the model and behavioral intentions. Across five studies, only two of these interactions were found to be significant. In addition, the PME is unable to account for the fear by age and fear by anxiety interactions uncovered by Boster and Mongeau.

Practical Considerations

These meta-analytic results provide persuasion practitioners with considerable food for thought. First and foremost, adding additional fear-arousing content to a persuasive message is likely to generate greater levels of persuasion. Specifically, no evidence exists that generating extremely strong levels of fear produces defensive avoidance processes and a corresponding decrease in persuasion. The impact of fear on perceived fear, attitudes, behaviors, and behavioral intentions is linear.

Critics assert that the lack of a stronger curvilinear effect is due to ethical constraints placed on experimenters. These critics argue that defensive avoidance (and the corresponding reduction in persuasion) occurs only at very high levels of fear which are unattainable in the laboratory because exposure to such strong fear may pose unreasonable risk to research participants. This position is tenable in that there are levels of perceived fear beyond the researcher's ethical reach. There are ethical considerations that attenuate the *practitioner's* ability to produce extremely strong levels of fear as well. There are many examples of advertisements that were discontinued after only a few showings because viewers found them to be overly disturbing. One example is the infamous "daisy" advertisement used by Johnson against Goldwater in the 1964 presidential campaign. The ad depicted a young child plucking the petals off a daisy. As she counted down the number of remaining petals her voice was replaced with the mechanical voice of a missile countdown. As the countdown reached zero, the ad cut to a nuclear explosion (implying that Goldwater would be quick to "push the button" and throw the United States into a nuclear conflict). The ad was shown very few times because of negative viewer feedback. In sum, the range of fear aroused in naturalistic fear appeals is likely to be similar to the levels of fear aroused in the laboratory.

The fear–attitude and fear–behavior correlations reported both here and in the Boster and Mongeau (1984) are relatively low. Given these relatively low correlations, practitioners may doubt the utility of using fear appeals. This notion is mistaken for two reasons. First, the amount of fear-arousing persuasive content in a message is unlikely to be a direct determinant of persuasion outcomes. Boster and Mongeau argued that the relationship between fear and attitudes and between fear and behaviors is moderated by perceived fear. This is important because these data suggest the relationship between fear and perceived fear is not strong (i.e., manipulations are not strong). This weak relationship between fear and perceived fear is likely to limit the strength of the fear–attitude and fear–behavior correlations.

The second reason that practitioners should not doubt the utility of fear appeals is that the size of the correlations reported here are likely underestimates of the true relationships between variables. Several study characteristics (e.g., number of attitude or behavior items, number of levels of the independent variables) were significantly correlated with fear effect sizes, indicating that fear correlations with perceived fear, attitudes, and behaviors may be attenuated by both range restriction and measurement error. Put another way, the true relationship between fear and the dependent variables are likely to be somewhat larger than reported here.

Overall, increasing the amount of fear-arousing content in a persuasive message is likely to generate greater attitude and behavior change. The extent of that change, however, depends, in part, on the nature of the audience. Boster and Mongeau (1984) presented data consistent with both a fear by age interaction on attitudes and behaviors and a fear by anxiety interaction on attitudes and behaviors.

The fear by anxiety interaction is clear. Increasing fear is likely to lead to greater persuasion for low-anxiety respondents. Increasing fear is likely to have no persuasive impact for high-anxiety subjects. High-anxiety individuals may be less willing and/or able to cognitively process the recommendations provided in the fear appeal.

The present data suggest that fear and age interact to influence attitudes. Fear exerts a stronger impact on attitudes when subjects in the studies are older (i.e., adults) than when subjects are younger (i.e., high school or junior high school students). Fear may be more effective in influencing older individuals because the topics of the messages may be more relevant (or involving) to them (most topics dealt with health topics). Adults may be more cognizant and concerned with their own health and aware of the financial burden caused by health problems.

Therefore, the effectiveness of a fear appeal is likely to be determined in part by the nature of the audience. Importantly, in nearly all cases, the impact of fear on attitudes is linear and positive. For some people (i.e., older individuals, low trait anxiety) the impact of fear on attitudes and behaviors is likely to be stronger than on other individuals (particularly those high in trait anxiety).

Constructing a Fear Appeal

The effectiveness of a fear appeal is determined, in large part, by the nature of the message. A successful fear appeal is likely to be composed of several parts as highlighted by the PME. Specifically, Rogers (1983) asserted that a fear appeal is a combination of four components: (a) the noxiousness or severity of the depicted threat, (b) the probability of the threat's occurrence, (c) the efficacy of the recommended coping response, and (d) the ability of audience members to enact the recommended coping response.

In order to be effective, a fear appeal must present a threat that is both noxious and real. First, the threat depicted must represent a severe threat to audience members' well being. Second, the threat must be depicted as one that is likely to strike audience members. A fear appeal must do more, however, than simply describe a noxious and imminent threat; that is, a fear appeal must present an adequate means of controlling or eliminating the threat as well. In particular, persuaders should concentrate on the *efficacy* of the coping response. The means of avoiding the threat must be *effective* (i.e., high response efficacy) and within the audience members' behavioral repertoire (i.e., high self-efficacy). Without all components the effectiveness of a fear appeal is likely to be attenuated (Rogers, 1983).

In sum, fear appeals should highlight the threat and the recommended means of avoiding the threat. The importance of these components is highlighted by Aristotle (trans. 1932), who argued:

> If there is to be the anguish of uncertainty, there must be some lurking hope of deliverance; and that this is so would appear from the fact that fear sets men deliberating—but no one deliberates about things that are hopeless. (p. 138)

REFERENCES

Aristotle (1932). *The rhetoric of Aristotle* (L. Cooper, trans.). Englewood Cliffs, NJ: Prentice-Hall.

Beck, K. H., & Frankel, A. (1981). A conceptualization of threat communications and preventative health behavior. *Social Psychology Quarterly, 44*, 207–214.

Boster, F. J., & Mongeau, P. (1984). Fear-arousing persuasive messages. In R. Bostrom (Ed.), *Communication yearbook 8* (pp. 330–375). Newbury Park, CA: Sage.

Eagly, A. H., & Chaiken, S. (1984). Cognitive theories in persuasion. In L. Berkowitz (Ed.), *Advances in experimental social psychology* (Vol. 17, pp. 267–359). New York: Academic Press.

Goldstein, M. J. (1959). The relationship between coping and avoiding behavior and response to fear arousing propaganda. *Journal of Abnormal and Social Psychology, 58*, 247–252.

Hewgill, M. A., & Miller, G. R. (1966). Source credibility and response to fear-arousing communications. *Speech Monographs, 32*, 95–101.

Janis, I. L. (1967). Effects of fear arousal on attitude change: Recent developments in theory and research. In L. Berkowitz (Ed.), *Advances in experimental social psychology* (Vol. 3, pp. 166–224). New York: Academic Press.

Janis, I. L., & Feshbach, S. (1953). Effects of fear-arousing communications. *Journal of Abnormal and Social Psychology, 48*, 78–92.

Janis, I. L., & Leventhal, H. (1968). Human reaction to stress. In E. Borgatta & W. Lambert (Eds.), *Handbook of personality theory and research* (pp. 1041–1085). Chicago: Rand-McNally.

Kohn, P. M., Goodstadt, M. S., Cook, G. M., Sheppard, M., & Chan, G. (1982). Ineffectiveness of threat appeals about drinking and driving. *Accident Analysis and Prevention, 14*, 457–464.

Leventhal, H. (1970). Findings and theory in the study of fear communications. In L. Berkowitz (Ed.), *Advances in experimental social psychology* (Vol. 5, pp. 119–186). New York: Academic Press.

Leventhal, H. (1971). Fear appeals and persuasion: The differentiation of a motivational construct. *American Journal of Public Health, 61*, 1205–1224.

Maddus, J. E., & Rogers, R. W. (1983). Protection motivation and self-efficacy: A revised theory of fear appeals and attitude change. *Journal of Experimental Social Psychology, 19*, 469–479.

O'Keefe, D. J. (1990). *Persuasion: Theory and research.* Newbury Park, CA: Sage.

Rippetoe, P. A., & Rogers, R. W. (1987). Effects of components of protection-motivation theory on adaptive and maladaptive coping with a health threat. *Journal of Personality and Social Psychology, 52*, 596–604.

Robberson, R. R., & Rogers, R. W. (1988). Beyond fear appeals: Negative and positive appeals to health and self-esteem. *Journal of Applied Social Psychology, 18*, 277–288.

Rogers, R. W. (1975). A protection motivation theory of fear appeals and attitude change. *Journal of Psychology, 91*, 93–114.

Rogers, R. W. (1983). Cognitive and psychological process in fear appeals and attitude change: A revised theory of protection motivation. In J. Cacioppo & R. Petty (Eds.), *Social psychophysiology: A sourcebook* (pp. 153–176). New York: Guilford.

Rogers, R. W. (1985). Attitude change and information integration in fear appeals. *Psychological Reports, 56*, 179–182.

Rogers, R. W., & Mewborn, C. R. (1976). Fear appeals and attitude change: Effects of a threat's noxiousness, probability of occurrence, and the efficacy of coping responses. *Journal of Personality and Social Psychology, 34*, 54–61.

Sternthal, F., & Craig, C. (1974). Fear appeals: Revisited and revised. *Journal of Consumer Research, 7*, 22–34.

Sutton, S. R. (1982). Fear-arousing communications: A critical examination of theory and research. In J. R. Eisner (Ed.), *Social psychology and behavioral medicine* (pp. 303–337). New York: Wiley.

Wurtele, S. K., & Maddux, J. E. (1987). Relative contributions of protection motivation theory components in predicting exercise intentions and behavior. *Health Psychology, 6*, 453–466.

4

The Persuasive Effects of Testimonial Assertion Evidence

John C. Reinard
California State University, Fullerton

Although at one time scholars opined that research on the persuasive effects of evidence was in conflict (see Bostrom, 1983; Kellermann, 1980), detailed examinations of the literature reported great consistency when comparing experimental conditions and effects (Reinard, 1988; Reynolds & Burgoon, 1983). In fact, concluding a review of over 50 years of research into the subject, Reinard stated:

> If one looks not at the conclusions researchers have drawn, but examines the operational definitions used and the results obtained, there is surprising consistency in the research. Indeed, even including studies that are methodologically troubled, there actually may be more consistency in evidence research than can be found in almost any other area

> of persuasion. Evidence appears to produce general persuasive effects that appear surprisingly stable. Even so, there are situations in which the persuasive effects of evidence may be enhanced or reduced. (p. 46)

Experiments using very different types of evidence (testimonial assertions, reports, statistics, and the like) produced different results, although within each evidence category findings were highly consistent. Furthermore, the failure of many studies to include a true control condition (no evidence included in messages) led those researchers to conclude erroneously that evidence use did not enhance influence (Gilkinson, Paulson, & Sikkink, 1954; Whitehead, 1971). When properly classified by operational definitions, alleged differences in evidence effects have been shown to be illusory.[1] The research reveals that testimonial assertion evidence (sometimes combined with other evidence forms) is persuasive when the sources are identified and their qualifications briefly explained. Although providing additional argument development by presenting the evidence without indicating any sources enhances persuasion, greatest influence occurs when full citations are indicated by the advocate.

Nevertheless, the *extent* of the evidence relationship with persuasion remains unknown. Although evidence affects persuasion, the size of the impact constitutes a matter of some natural interest for scholars and practitioners alike. This research project was completed to determine the magnitude of effects of testimonial assertion evidence on attitude change. This chapter is divided into sections dealing with defining the problem area, the methods for the meta-analysis, the analysis of results, and the conclusions.

DEFINING THE PROBLEM

Starting with a recognition that testimonial assertion evidence increases the persuasiveness and perceptions of credibility of communication sources,[2] the

---

[1]A review of evidence research literature is beyond the scope of this chapter and interested readers may examine the Reinard (1988) summary review for specific summary findings. This meta-analysis may be considered a companion to that article.

[2]Originally, data were collected for source credibility dimensions as well. Although not reported in the text of the paper, it was observed that the average effect size for the character dimension of credibility was .253 (unweighted mean) and .251 (weighted mean). The sample size across studies was 762 based on 7 studies, with a standard deviation of r = .127 (both unweighted and weighted mean r). For the competence dimension, the average effect size was .327 (unweighted mean) and .319 (weighted mean). The sample size across studies was 641 based on 5 studies, with a standard

major research problem was: How large is the effect of evidence on attitude change? Evidence becomes defined as "factual statements originating from a source other than the speaker, objects not created by the speaker, and opinions of persons other than the speaker that are offered in support of the speaker's claims" (McCroskey, 1969, p. 171). This definition is critical because some studies merely substitute evidentiary material (Toba, 1975) or "base rate information" (Borgida & Nisbett, 1977) for evidence used by a source. Hample (1977) argued that evidence is always present since receivers "fill in" evidence of their own when the source provides no specific data. Even so, for this meta-analysis it was decided operationally to restrict evidence to situations in which a source introduced material from an outside source in an effort to support a position. Studies of general information processing were not relevant to this discussion and, hence, were omitted.

Furthermore, studies dealing with contrasts of amounts of evidence, relevance of evidence, quality of evidence, credibility of evidence sources, strength of evidence, and factors external to the evidence (such as topic and speaker characteristics) were excluded from this meta-analysis. Similarly, although studies of outcomes other than attitudes have been completed, this project limits itself to attitude change as an archetype of persuasion.

METHOD

Given the concern for determining effect sizes, meta-analysis was applied to testimonial assertion studies. The methods for retrieving research studies, coding studies, and assessing effect sizes are discussed.

Identifying Studies

Research into the persuasive effects of evidence began in earnest in 1935 with work completed by Chen in the heyday of public opinion and propaganda research. Even so, most of the serious inquiry into the subject did not blossom until the 1950s. Fortunately, evidence effects were the object of occasional literature reviews, including one by the author that brought the subject current through 1988. This literature review served as the basis for extracting studies for examination in this meta-analysis. In the quest for relevant research, *Dissertation Abstracts*, as well as journals in communication,

---

deviation of r = .164 (unweighted mean r) and .159 (weighted mean). The diffuse comparison of r for heterogeneity produced insignificant chi square values of 5.88, df - 4 (unweighted mean r) and 5.433, df = 4 (weighted mean r).

speech, and psychology, were reviewed. Tables of contents for conventions in communication were reviewed for the years extending from 1969 through 1988 to extract additional unpublished research. It appears that there has been no great blossoming of research in evidence during the years after 1988.

Thus, the use of primary (but not exclusively) testimonial evidence was the chief object of inquiry. Other criteria also had to be satisfied for a study to become part of the "data set:"

1. The study had to contain experimental research into the persuasive effects of evidence. No conceptual "think pieces," status surveys, or historical analyses were included.
2. Studies must have featured a true control condition. As previously noted, the absence of "no evidence" condition in many past studies made their conclusions uninterpretable. Thus, studies by Gilkinson et al. (1954) and by Whitehead (1971) were deleted. In both cases, the authors had mistakenly claimed to have a "no evidence" condition and asserted that evidence had insignificant effects.
3. No more than three data collections per reported study were permitted for inclusion. In the one case (McCroskey 1967c) in which three studies were selected, the studies themselves were carried out at different times and were reported in a detailed review of 13 experiments. Aside from the McCroskey study and the Reinard (1984) study in which two experiments were reported, only one data collection per reported study was used.
4. Information necessary for computation of effect sizes was required for inclusion of a study. In studies reviewed, only the experiments by Florence (1975), Reinard, Charles, and Crawford (1974), Reinard and Reynolds (1976), and Reinard (1984) explicitly computed effect sizes. In many studies, enough data were available to permit computation of effect sizes. When information proved unavailable through direct examination of materials, dissertations and theses on which the works were based were referenced when the opportunity to do so existed. For instance, in the case of studies by McCroskey (1967a), McCroskey and Dunham (1966), and Holzman (1966), it was possible to reference the extended summary report written by McCroskey (1967c) or the relevant dissertation respectively. When this method still produced a difficulty, other estimation options were explored and their impact assessed.
5. Studies were included if they could be examined to compare two groups—a full experimental group (full use of evidence complete with source citations and qualifications) and a control group

(exposed to no evidence). When data were drawn from a multi-level factorial design, only the comparisons between the two conditions described here were used. In some cases it was not possible to reconstruct these two conditions alone from the available data.[3] Similarly, included studies were limited to main effect results only. Interactions that could not be decomposed suggested complex relations beyond the scope of this meta-analysis.

6. Only studies of short-term effects were included. Although evidence appears to enhance long-term persuasion (Reynolds & Burgoon, 1983, pp. 93-94) for highly and lowly credible sources, this meta-analysis was limited to short-term effects only.
7. Only studies of attitude change were included. Thus, the Fleshler, Ilardo, and Demoretcky (1974) and Smith (1972) studies were excluded because they employed nonattitude measures of response.
8. Studies included were by Babich (1971/1972), Cathcart (1955), Florence (1975), Holtzman (1966), Krusemark (1974), McCroskey (1966/1967a), McCroskey studies 4-6 (1967c), McCroskey and Dunham (1966), Reinard et al. (1974), Reinard and Reynolds (1976), and Reinard studies 1-2 (1984). For the McCroskey (1966/1967a) study, only the effects for the federal aid to education topic were included since McCroskey had observed that the other topic (capital punishment) was confounded with excessive levels of prior familiarity among subjects, which led them to reject the topic out of hand. In the McCroskey studies 4 through 6, only the effects of low-credibility sources were involved, because the studies were primarily dedicated to contrasting effects for highly and lowly credible sources and ceiling effects had plagued the results of previous studies involving highly credible speakers. In the Holtzman (1966) study, the unfamiliar sponsor condition was used, because familiarity of the sponsor (especially a highly credible one) was taken as a confounding of credibility with influence-related dependent variables.

---

[3]Interestingly enough, the 1955 article by Cathcart based on his 1953 dissertation included four groups, but used a series of t tests for each comparison. Of course, therefore, with each significance test at the .05 level, the true alpha risk for the experiment would be .26 based on the formula: experimentwide alpha risk = 1 - (1 - testwise alpha)^{k} where k is the number of significance tests completed (Bonferroni inequality < .30). Had Cathcart used the preferred ANOVA to compare the means of the four treatment groups (one of which was a true control), the overall F would not have been statistically significant at alpha = .05.

Other studies were excluded from the potential list of experiments (see Reinard, 1988, p. 11) because they possessed qualities that made them incomparable with other work in this area. The 1935 study by Chen was excluded because the messages were very long pro- and anti-Chinese propaganda lectures that were not akin to any manipulations found in remaining studies (see Stiff, 1986 for similar exclusion). Confounding in two master's theses troubled their execution, and thus the theses were excluded from this listing. In particular, the thesis by Anderson (1958) had been criticized (McCroskey, 1967b, 1967c) for its use of a message topic (censorship) that was banal and, therefore, produced artificially suppressed evidence effects. Furthermore, the study was attacked for its potential confounding of evidence with speaker credibility. In another master's thesis, none of the independent variables (ego-involvement, evidence types) appeared to make a significant difference despite a strong research tradition for each (Fisher, 1972). This latter study seemed to self-destruct and the author provided thoughtful criticism of the work. Although criticisms of these theses have appeared in print (McCroskey, 1967b, 1969; Reinard, 1988), to date there have been no published efforts to defend them against any criticisms. Interestingly enough, Rosenthal (1984b) found that master's theses typically presented noticeably weaker effects than journal articles, unpublished research papers, or studies published in scholarly books. The excluded studies were qualitatively different from other remaining in this study because their manipulations were confounded with other influential sources of variation. To be on the conservative side, one might consider the these to be examples of "file drawer" research.

There was insufficient information to compute effect sizes for the study completed by Bostrom and Tucker (1969). Thus, two strategies were followed in the analyses. In the first case, a minimum effect size was estimated for this study using the formula for constructing a confidence interval about *r* (Glass & Hopkins, 1984, pp. 305-306). In the second case, all meta-analysis computations were completed with this study deleted. Other strategies are available, of course (Mullen & Miller, 1991, p. 437), and this technique is consistent with the conservative estimate of a significant *p*.

Studies that involved the use of evidence during small-group deliberations originally were included (Cronin, 1972/1973; McCroskey, Young, & Scott, 1972). These studies were eventually deleted for their obvious difference in kind.

Coding Studies and Assessing Effect Sizes

Studies were coded in five ways for subsequent comparisons. First, those studies in which a deliberating group was exposed to evidence were identified and distinguished from studies in which evidence was not introduced into a group deliberation. Second, the studies were coded for the number of independent variables they contained. The increasing number of predictor variables reflects a reduction in the observed effect sizes (both r and standardized difference scores d). The consistent presence of such a pattern could indicate the potential role of moderator variables on evidence effects. Observation of the studies producing such differences could lead to the development of limitations and potentially useful rules regarding the impact of evidence on persuasion. Third, the dates on the studies also were used to test effect size differences across time. Fourth, studies were coded according to whether they used a live speaker or employed written messages for the evidence induction.

Finally, the quality of the experiments was evaluated by a group of four raters (not including the author). The raters were professional colleagues who had taught research methods in communication at least once at the upper division level. After a review of detailed summaries of the studies, raters assessed the quality of the experiments on a scale ranging from 0 to 10, with 10 defined as "A study with very strong internal and external validity" and 0 defined as "A study with truly weak internal and external validity." Because the ratings later were subjected to a rank ordering for fitting of orthogonal polynomials, it was decided to check the internal consistency of the expert judges' rankings by use of Kendall's coefficient of concordance. The observed W was .74, a rating that was deemed acceptance for this analysis.

Assessing Effect Sizes

Because it already was known that a significant evidence effect existed, the primary matter at hand involved determining its size. The magnitude of effect was indexed by the metric r. Because two groups (control without evidence and experimental with evidence complete with source qualifications) were compared consistently in the included studies, it was possible to rely on standard formulae to convert test data to r (Wolf, 1986, p. 35). Correlations were transformed by taking each one's inverse hyperbolic tangent (Fisher's Z). The standardization or linearization of r obtained by this transformation served as the basis for other analyses. When appropriate, other formula were used to find Z for data distributed as d, the difference between means divided by the standard deviation, or as p, for the Z corresponding to probability values p. Significance testing was done with alpha risk set at .05.

RESULTS

As Table 4.1 shows, data considered studies that either did nor did not involve group deliberations. In addition, findings were classified according to whether or not the studies included the minimum estimate of effect size for the study by Bostrom and Tucker (1969) (see Table 4.2). The results clearly revealed that effect sizes showed great heterogeneity when the group studies were included, as indicated by significant chi square values for the diffuse tests of homogeneity. Yet, when studies involving group deliberations were excluded, the assumption of homogeneous effect sizes could not be rejected. When a focused comparison was made of the effect size differences of the studies with and without group deliberations, the linear contrast was statistically significant ($z = 3.63$). This permitted the deletion of studies involving group deliberations and focus only on those evidence experiments involving traditional messages of advocacy.

Table 4.1. Effects on Attitude Change Including Estimated Minimum Effect Sizes.

Results	Group interaction included	Without group interaction studies
n across studies	2800	1920
number of studies	16	14
mean *r* (unweighted mean)	.234	.252
mean *r* (weighted mean)	.185	.234
range of *r*	.326	.19
largest *r*	.346	.346
smallest *r*	.02	.156
sd (unweighted mean *r*)	.11	.065
sd (weighted mean *r*)	.098	.061
heterogeneity of *r*		
chi-square unweighted mean *r*	33.5 df = 15 p < .05	7.93 df = 13 p > .05
chi-square weighted mean *r*	26.581 df = 15 p < .05 cv = 24.996	7.17 df = 13 p > .05 cv = 22.362

Table 4.2. Effects on Attitude Change Excluding Estimated Minimum Effect Sizes.

Results	Group interaction included	Without group interaction studies
n across studies	2642	1762
number of studies	15	13
mean *r* (unweighted mean)	.236	.258
mean *r* (weighted mean)	.186	.24
range of *r*	.326	.178
largest *r*	.346	.346
smallest *r*	.02	.168
sd of *r* (unweighted mean *r*)	.114	.062
sd of r *(*weighted mean *r)*	.10	.059
heterogeneity of *r*		
chi-square unweighted mean *r*	33.931 df = 14 p < .05	6.828 df = 12 p > .05
chi-square weighted mean *r*	26.446 df = 14 p < .05 cv = 23.685	6.095 df = 12 p > .05 cv = 21.026

Among nongroup studies, the observed effects were stable and surprisingly comparable. There is some controversy regarding the desirability of weighting studies according to their sample sizes.[4] For this meta-analysis both methods of calculation were reported. The average effect sizes for the weighted means of the two conditions (with and without the estimated minimum effect size from the Bostrom and Tucker, 1969, study) differed by only .006 for both the unweighted and weighted means, with the weighted mean slightly lower than the unweighted mean. The mean r found in this study ranged from .234 to .258. Not surprisingly, the mean effect size increased

[4]Some submit that weighting of *Zs* for sample size is preferred because it avoids distorting results based on "small or unrepresentative samples of subjects" (Wolf, 1986, p. 39). Others contend that because researchers in one theoretic domain tend to produce much operationally duplicative research, "weighted by sample size, however, will simultaneously differentially weight a paradigm when ordinarily, there is no priori rationale for weighting one more heavily than the next" (Mullen & Miller, 1991, p. 442).

when the estimated minimum effect size was deleted. The standard deviation of r also was modest, as indicated by the test of homogeneous effect sizes and the observed standard deviations of *r*.

Examining Alternative Interpretations of Effects

Aside from the contrasting of group and nongroup studies, other focused comparisons of effect sizes aided in the interpretation of results. The first comparison contrasted effect sizes for studies with differing numbers of independent variables. If increasing the number of independent variables appreciably changed the effect sizes for evidence, this condition could suggest an important role served by other forces moderating the effects of evidence use. The *z* for the contrast involving studies including the estimated effect size value was -3.39, and without the estimated effect size was -3.48. In each case these results were significant. The negative coefficient indicated that effect sizes tended to decline as the number of independent variables in an experiment increased. It appears that other independent variables may moderate evidence effects, suggesting the value of variable cause screening studies to find common sets of moderator variables that dominate in evidence effects.

No other focused tests produced significant effects. When studies were contrasted by date of publication, no significant trend in effect sizes was found for either the data set with estimated effect sizes included (z = .52) or when the estimated effect size was deleted (z = .63). The contrast by study quality also showed no significant differences for either the data that included estimated effect size (z = 1.31) or the data that excluded estimated effect sizes (z = 1.25). Thus, quality differences did not have a significant impact on effect sizes in these data sets. Although such a finding was not consistent with results obtained by Glass and Smith (1979), it was not particularly unexpected because fatally flawed studies that failed to manipulate independent variables separately were excluded from the data used in this meta-analysis. The contrasts between studies that relied on written or oral messages produced insignificant effects for both the data set that included the estimated effect size (z = .79) and the data set that excluded estimated effect sizes (z = .30). These results should not be surprising because early studies consistently used oral presentations and latter experiments relied on written messages. Indeed, the rank biserial correlation between study date and use of written messages as operationalizations was -.686 with the estimated effect size included and -.691 with the estimated effect size excluded. It is apparent that whereas early studies used oral operationalizations (as indicated by the inverse relationship) subsequent studies often relied on written messages. As the linear contrasts showed, however, the impact of these different research protocols was not reflected in any substantial effect on the magnitude of attitude change produced.

As a further test of the nature of effect sizes in the data set, disjoint cluster analysis of effect sizes was completed (Hedges & Olkin, 1983, based on work of Gibbons, Olkin, & Sobel, 1977). For this analysis, no estimated effect sizes or group studies were included. Separate passes were completed for corrected and uncorrected data sets. The square-mean root estimate of common sample size was 11.08 for both data sets. None of the differences between adjacently ranked clusters was significant.[5] Thus, it could not be concluded that the effect sizes fell into more than a single cluster.

Stability of Effect Sizes

Subsequent investigation determined the nature and distribution of effect sizes. Because measurement unreliability attenuates any effects, it was desired to correct observed effects for attenuation. Unfortunately, only a few studies actually reported measurement reliabilities for their data. Yet, the measurement protocols for attitude effects were surprisingly consistent across the studies. Thus, it was deemed acceptable to apply the average reliability for studies reporting such information to the studies that failed to report reliabilities.[6] Because the corrections assume at minimum that there are some available effect sizes reported, the estimated effect size from the Bostrom and Tucker (1969) study was omitted from this part of the analysis.

When corrected for attenuation and excluding the estimated minimum effect size data, the mean *r* was .268 for the unweighted sample and .252 for the weighted mean *r*. The dispersion of results is a useful way to isolate the uniformity of the effect sizes. Skewness computed with an unweighted mean was -.543 and was -.459 for the weighted mean data.

---

[5]Observed U values were as follows $U_1 = 5.2$, $U_2 = 5.005$, $U_3 = 4.46$, $U_4 = 4.412$, $U_5 = 4.255$, $U_6 = 4.239$, $U_7 = 3.68$, $U_8 = 3.513$, $U_9 = 3.483$, $U_{10} = 3.209$, $U_{11} = 3.043$, $U_{12} = 2.683$, $U_{13} = 2.445$.

[6]Although the correction for attenuation frequently is used in communication research (and here is contrasted with uncorrected coefficients), it is criticized on practical grounds in some circles. Bernstein (1988) argued, "The correction [for attenuation] is poor behavioral science even if it is acceptable mathematics. You probably have control over the predictor and might be able to add more items. . . . You may or may not have control over the criterion" (p. 409). In this meta-analysis, however, no claim was made about unreliability in the manipulation of evidence presumed to have a reliability of 1), and only correction for attitude measurement was involved. Thus, the correction should not prove misleading in this case.

Kurtosis was computed and found to reflect a platykurtic pattern (-2.99 for both weighted and unweighted measures), not surprising given the small number of data points.[7] For the effects corrected for attenuation, the situation was somewhat different with kurtosis for unweighted mean at -1.53 and for weighted mean at -.87. Skewness for weighted groups was -1.63 and for unweighted groups was r = -.543.

A further measure of the consistency of meta-analytic findings referenced the file drawer problem. In particular, if a small number of studies with findings that contradicted those of this meta-analysis could overturn the observed pattern, then the stability of these results might be in question. Cooper (1979) formulated a "fail-safe N" to isolate the number of unpublished studies failing to reject the null hypothesis that would have to exist for the overall probability level found in the meta-analysis to be reversed. For uncorrected data, the fail-safe number was 201.95 at alpha risk of .05. For data corrected for attenuation, the fail-safe number was 221.84 for alpha set at .05. Thus, one may be comfortable with the stability observed in this study. Nevertheless, two caveats should be raised. First, even though the original literature search was fairly exhaustive and not limited to published works, it also is true that studies that were seriously flawed were omitted from final analyses. Thus, by the admission made in this chapter, the file drawer of unpublished studies already contains two studies, reducing the fail-safe number may be considered a useful way to keep perspective on the antipublication bias of articles containing insignificant differences. In his review of the practices of authors and editorial board members of the *Journal of Personality and Social Psychology*, Greenwald (1975) found that authors finding significant differences were more than 8 times as likely to submit articles for publication than when they did not find significant differences. Thus, if the situation were equally balanced, with published work reflecting stronger than average Type I error rates (and assuming, for the sake of arguing conservatively, that all studies in the final data set were published—5 were not), then one would expect that there could be an additional 112 unpublished studies failing to find a significant evidence effect. Even so, after reviewing and classifying much unpublished work, the author has been unable to find such a large number of contrary research examples.

These questions of statistical significance, although illuminating, were not as central to the research question of this project as is the magnitude of effect. Orwin (1983) developed an alternative formula for use when contrasting standardized difference scores (which can be transduced from test statistics or *r*) against a standard. Drawing an analogy to the reasoning

---

[7]Though some sources use a formula in which the kurtosis of the standard normal curve is 3, the formula used here defines that value as O (Glass & Hopkins, 1954).

of Cohen (1977), one might consider a *d* of no more than .20 as a small effect. Then, one might ask how many studies would have to exist exhibiting a small enough effect size to drop the observed d below .2. When transformed to *d*, the average effect was .537 for uncorrected data and .559 for corrected data. The observed fail-safe numbers to reduce the effect size below an average *d* of .2 were 21.9 (uncorrected) and 23.31 (corrected). Thus, although such study numbers do not seem to exist as yet, they are not so great as to seem impossibilities in the future.

CONCLUSION

The results of this meta-analysis show that when group studies were removed from the set, an average effect sizes *r* of between .234 to .258 are revealed. Moreover, the mean effect size seemed to come from a homogeneous set of effect sizes. In addition, further analyses led to the conclusion that the mean effect reported here may be considered fairly stable because: (a) the distributions of effect sizes were compatible with a normal distribution that should underlie such data and (b) the fail-safe number of potential unpublished contradictory studies was reasonably substantial.

Other results suggested the possible potential for developing a list of mediating variables for the evidence-persuasion effect. First studies involving the use of evidence by communicators in group deliberations produced very different effects from those studying involving traditional speeches of advocacy. Although this meta-analysis provided no formal test, it may be that during group deliberations attention must be paid to information of a social nature as well as a content nature (the socioemotional and task dimensions). Thus, evidence may or may not make a difference depending on how much attention can be devoted to it. Bradley (1981) found, for instance, that an image of women as uninfluential sources of information was overcome in group deliberations if women used evidence—something that apparently was not stereotypically expected of women. On the other hand, in traditional messages of advocacy, evidence seems to be paid attention without consistent distraction. Such speculation may invite future research into the actual information processing of evidence in group versus formal speeches of advocacy.

The role of mediating variables also was implied by the significant linear contrast of effect sizes by the number of independent variables in each experiment. The negative *z* values for the contrasts indicated that effect sizes tended to decline as the number of independent variables in a research study increased. On one hand, the result may be treated as trivial because effect sizes are subject to ceiling effects and increasing the number of independent variables means dividing a total variance pool into additional parts as an artifact of the design. On the other hand, although some of the effect certainly may be explained by such a suggestion, it also should be noted that two other matters make an alternative view plausible. First, this meta-analysis examined main effects for evidence, which may or may not be subject to so volatile an amelioration of effect sizes as a function of increasing the number of effect tests in an experiment. Second, there was not evidence of any ceiling effect in the data set, suggesting that the explanation for the observed reduction in effects might lie elsewhere. Subsequent testing of these possibilities by use of causal modeling methods might prove useful in isolating the peculiar nature of a list of mediating variables. Based on this review, however, the list of such mediators should begin with the recognition of the apparent moderation of evidence main effect sizes when in the presence of the apparent moderation of evidence main effect sizes when in the presence of (listed in order of the studies producing lowest effect sizes to those dealing evincing largest effect sizes): group deliberations occurring when the evidence is introduced; use of highly ego-involving topics; use of one-sided messages; credibility level of sources; unclear message documentation; low strength of the argument the evidence is intended to support; low probative force of the evidence; low perceived importance of topic (or importance levels so high as to indicate high ego-involvement); low believability of evidence content; low credibility of evidence sources. Although others certainly could be listed from a general review of evidence research, the linear effect observed in this study was accompanied by these elements. Thus, inquiry might be dedicated to identifying roles they may play in evidence effects on attitude change. These influences also might be taken as limitations on interpreting effect sizes reported in this meta-analysis.

Interpretation of results should be tempered with the knowledge that observed effects tended to be modest, as is typical in much social science research. Cohen's (1977) oft-repeated guidance is to view any effect size as small if the r is approximately .10, medium if r is approximately .30, and large if r is about .5. Such advice suggests that the average effect size found here was not medium magnitude, although it was on the high side of "small effects." Using Cohen's guidelines, Wolf (1986) interpreted an effect size r of .28 as a "medium sized" effect. Thus, it could be possible to label the effect sizes found in this study (when corrected for attenuation, r of .268 for the unweighted sample and r of .252 for the weighted mean) as "approaching medium." Yet, such a labeling risks overstating the case. Thus, it may be claimed that the data show a high small effect (or perhaps a low medium effect). Although such results can seem disheartening, Rosenthal and Rubin (1982) suggested that one use the Binomial Effect Size Display (BESD) to evaluate the practical impact of effect sizes (see also Rosenthal, 1984a). By transforming *r* to a binomial effect size, one can display improvements that are suitable for both dichotomous and continuous data. The BESD computes the percentage of success by expressing improvements that are suitable for both dichotomous and continuous data. The BESD computes the percentage shift above the median contrasted with the proportion ordinarily below the median. The BESD values for this meta-analysis (uncorrected, including the estimated effect size using an unweighted mean) equal an improvement from 37.4% to 62.6%. With the weighted mean, the improvement is from 38.3% to 61.7%. The BESD values for the *r* values excluding the estimated effect size show an improvement form 37.1% to 62.9% for the unweighted mean, and 38% to 62% for the weighted mean. These improvements in attitude change effects all exceed a range of 23 percentage points. Thus, although modest by some standards, the improvement appears to make a meaningful contribution to persuasive effects.

SUMMARY

This meta-analysis showed an average effect size for testimonial assertion evidence effects on attitude change of an r ranging from .234 to .258. These results appeared to be consistent main effects, evincing an underlying normal distribution and a reasonably comfortable fail-safe number to assure stability. Although showing a high small effect (or perhaps a low medium effect), and subject to limitations from potential mediating sources, evidence use appeared to predict meaningful shifts in attitude.

REFERENCES

Anderson, D. C. (1958). *The effect of various uses of authoritative testimony in persuasive speaking*. Unpublished master's thesis, Ohio State University, Columbus.

Babich, R. M. (1972). Perceived information related to attitude change in topic, evidence and source variant messages. (Doctoral dissertation, University of Colorado, Boulder, 1971). *Dissertation Abstracts International, 43*, 516B–517B.

Bernstein, I. H. (with Garvin, C. P., & Teng, G. K.). (1988). *Applied multivariate analysis*. New York: Springer-Verlag.

Borgida, E., & Nisbett, R. E. (1977). The differential impact of abstract vs. concrete information on decisions. *Journal of Applied Social Psychology, 7*, 258–271.

Bostrom, R. N. (1983). *Persuasion*. Englewood Cliffs, NJ: Prentice-Hall.

Bostrom, R. N., & Tucker, R. K. (1969). Evidence, personality and attitude change. *Speech Monographs, 36*, 22–27.

Bradley, P. H. (1981). The folk-linguistics of women's speech: An empirical examination. *Communication Monographs, 48*, 73–90.

Cathcart, R. S. (1955). An experimental study of the relative effectiveness of four methods of presenting evidence. *Speech Monographs, 22*, 227–233.

Chen, W. K. C. (1935). *The influence of oral propaganda material upon students' attitudes*. New York: Archives of Psychology.

Cohen, J. (1977). *Statistical power analysis for the behavioral sciences* (rev. ed.). New York: Academic Press.

Cooper, H. M. (1979). Statistically combining independent studies: A meta-analysis of sex differences in conformity research. *Journal of Personality and Social Psychology, 37*, 131–146.

Cronin, M. W. (1973). An experimental study of the effects of authoritative testimony on small group problem-solving discussions. (Doctoral dissertation, Wayne State University, Detroit, 1972). *Dissertation Abstracts International, 33*, 6485A.

Fisher, J. L. (1972). *An experimental study of the relationship between ego-involvement and different types of evidence in communication*. Unpublished master's thesis, Louisiana State University, Baton Rouge, LA.

Fleshler, H., Ilardo, J., & Demoretcky, J. (1974). The influence of field dependence, speaker credibility set, and message documentation on evaluations of speaker and message credibility. *Southern Speech Communication Journal, 39*, 389–402.

Florence, B. T. (1975). An empirical test of the relationship of evidence to belief systems and attitude change. *Human Communication Research, 1*, 145–158.

Gibbons, J. D., Olkin, I., & Sobel, M. (1977). *Selecting and ordering populations: A new statistical methodology*. New York: Wiley.

Gilkinson, H., Paulson, S. F., & Sikkink, D. E. (1954). Effects of order and authority in an argumentative speech. *Quarterly Journal of Speech, 40*, 183–192.

Glass, G.V., & Hopkins, K.D. (1984). *Statistical methods in education and psychology* (2nd ed.). Englewood Cliffs, NJ: Prentice-Hall.

Glass, G., & Smith, M.L. (1979). Meta-analysis of research on the relationship of class size and achievement. *Educational Evaluation and Policy Analysis, 1*, 2–16.

Greenwald, A. G. (1975). Consequences of prejudice against the null hypothesis. *Psychological Bulletin, 82*, 1–20.

Hample, D. (1977). Testing a model of value argument and evidence. *Communication Monographs, 44*, 106–120.

Hedges, L. V., & Olkin, I. (1983). Clustering estimates of effect magnitude from independent studies. *Psychological Bulletin, 93*, 563–573.

Holtzman, P. D. (1966). Confirmation of ethos as a confounding element in communication research. *Speech Monographs, 33*, 464–466.

Kellermann, K. (1980). The concept of evidence: A critical review. *Journal of the American Forensic Association, 16*, 159–172.

Krusemark, R. (1974). *An experimental study of the effects of documentation and initial audience attitudinal position on responses to written persuasive communications*. Unpublished master's thesis, State University of New York, Buffalo, NY.

McCroskey, J. C. (1967a). Experimental studies of the effects of ethos and evidence in persuasive communication. (Doctoral dissertation, Pennsylvania State University, 1966). *Dissertation Abstracts International, 27*, 363A.

McCroskey, J. C. (1967b). The effects of evidence in persuasive communication. *Western Speech, 31*, 189–199.

McCroskey, J. C. (1967c). *Studies of the effects of evidence in persuasive communication*. East Lansing, MI: Michigan State University, Speech Communication Research Laboratory, SCRL 4–67.

McCroskey, J. C. (1969). A summary of experimental research on the effects of evidence in persuasive communication. *Quarterly Journal of Speech, 55*, 169–176.

McCroskey, J. C., & Dunham, R. E. (1966). Ethos: A confounding element in communication research. *Communication Monographs, 33*, 464–466.

McCroskey, J. C., Young, T. J., & Scott, M. D. (1972). The effects of message sidedness and evidence on inoculation against counterpersuasion in small group communication. *Speech Monographs, 39*, 205–212.

Mullen, B., & Miller, N. (1991). Meta-analysis. In C. M. Judd, E. R. Smith, & L. H. Kidder (Eds.), *Research methods in social relations* (6th ed., pp. 425–449). New York: Holt, Rinehart & Winston.

Orwin, R. G. (1983). A fail-safe N for effect size. *Journal of Educational Statistics, 8*, 157–159.

Reinard, J. C. (1988). The empirical study of the persuasive effects of evidence: The status after fifty years of research. *Human Communication Research, 15*, 3–59.

Reinard, J. C. (1984). The role of Toulmin's categories of message development in persuasive communication: Two experimental studies on attitude change. *Journal of the American Forensic Association, 20*, 206–223.

Reinard, J. C., Charles, R. L., & Crawford, J. E. (1974, April). *An experimental study of Toulmin's categories of argumentative development on attitudes*. Paper presented at the International Communication Association Convention, New Orleans, LA.

Reinard, J. C., & Reynolds, R. (1976, November). *An experimental study of the effects of Toulmin's pattern for argument development on attitude change: Another look*. Paper presented at the Western Speech Communication Association Convention, San Francisco, CA.

Reynolds, R. A., & Burgoon, M. (1983). Belief processing, reasoning and evidence. In R. N. Bostrom (Ed.), *Communication yearbook 7* (pp. 83–104). Beverly Hills, CA: Sage.

Rosenthal, R. (1984a). Assessing the statistical and social importance of the effects of psychotherapy. *Journal of Consulting and Clinical Psychology, 51*, 4–13.

Rosenthal, R. (1984b). *Meta-analytic procedures for social research*. Beverly Hills, CA: Sage.

Rosenthal, R., & Rubin, D. B. (1982). A simple, general purpose of display of the magnitude of experimental effect. *Journal of Educational Psychology, 74*, 166–169.

Smith, T. J. (1972). *The effects of truth and desirability evidence on judgments of the truth and desirability of a proposition*. Unpublished master's thesis, Michigan State University, East Lansing, MI.

Stiff, J. B. (1986). Cognitive processing of persuasive message cues: A meta-analytic review of the effects of supporting information on attitudes. *Communication Monographs, 53*, 75–89.

Toba, Y. (1975). A general theory of evidence as the conceptual foundation for auditing theory. *Accounting Review, 50*, 7–24.

Whitehead, J. L. (1971). Effects of authority-based assertions on attitude change and credibility. *Speech Monographs, 38*, 311–315.

Wolf, F. M. (1986). *Meta-analysis: Quantitative methods of research synthesis*. Newbury Park, CA: Sage.

5

Comparing the Persuasive Effectiveness One- and Two-Sided Message

Mike Allen
University of Wisconsin-Milwaukee

An enduring concern of those in public speaking is how a communicator should address potential counterarguments when advancing any thesis. Apart from any consideration of a particular strategy to address existing counterarguments, a more fundamental question exists for a communicator. Should a communicator consider potential counterarguments and include a refutation of them when formulating or organizing a speech? An examination of some of the available persuasion textbooks provides a divergent set of opinions about whether a communicator should use a one-sided message or two-sided message. A one-sided message consists of a message only presenting arguments in favor of a particular proposition. A two-sided message is a message that presents the arguments in favor of a proposition but also considers the opposing arguments. Every communicator engaged in creating a persuasive message must decide whether to consider opposing viewpoints. The end result is a communication that includes or excludes consideration of counter positions.

This review focuses initially on the lack of agreement among scholars providing advice to persuaders. This advice is contained in public speaking and persuasion textbooks that discuss message design strategies and their effectiveness. The review then discusses the descriptions and prescriptions stemming from some of the available theories in persuasion. The lack of consensus on the available evidence at both the practical and theoretical levels justifies the use of meta-analysis as a procedure to synthesize the experimental literature on the topic of message sidedness.

EXISTING ADVICE ON MESSAGE SIDEDNESS

Aristotle (1932, trans.) implicitly advocated the use of the two-sided message. His writing in *The Rhetoric* on this issue explains how to most effectively organize and structure the presentation of the pro and con information. However, later scholars, basing their recommendations on an accumulation of social scientific studies and theories, have advocated a variety of positions on this issue. Petty and Cacioppo (1981) concluded that an advertiser should use a one-sided message when the object is "well liked, widely consumed, has few competitors, and enjoys local customers" (p. 75). They recommended a two-sided message for advertisers when "the audience is well-informed about a product and its alternatives, the product is not widely preferred, or the audience is likely to be exposed to advertisements for competitive products" (p. 75). Petty and Cacioppo presented this position as consistent with their Elaboration Likelihood Model of persuasion. A full treatment of the theoretical issues involved in the ELM follows in the next section.

Reardon (1981) in her book, *Persuasion: Theory and Context,* concluded that the contextual information is important to making decisions about how to present information in a speech. Her suggestions involve incorporation of counterarguments and their refutation based on audience awareness of the counterarguments, level of intelligence, or hostility to the viewpoint advocated. The advice offered by Reardon is based on a consideration of situational features on a case-by-case basis by the communicator. The author does not conclude that there exists a general superiority of the one-sided or two-sided message strategy. Instead, there exist a series of conditions that the communicator should consider before adopting a particular message strategy.

In his book *The Art of Public Speaking* (Lucas, 1989), argued that to convince not only skeptical audiences, but audiences in general, the communicator should include refutations of counterarguments. This conclusion argues for use of a two-sided message in all situations. The justification for this position lies in a belief that the communicator's credibility is strengthened by the consideration of counterarguments. This advice for using a two-sided message in general is a contrast from both the earlier positions (Petty & Cacioppo, 1986; Reardon, 1981), which are based on features that may moderate or change the effectiveness of a particular strategy.

A review of the issue of advice offered in textbooks (Allen & Preiss, 1990) concludes that the advice given practitioners is inconsistent about message sidedness. This advice varies from author to author and textbook to textbook. The important feature to consider about this inconsistent set of advice is the fact that it stems from the same basic social scientific set of assumptions and data. All of the textbooks reviewed used the evidence from social scientific experiments as a basis for the generation of the claims. This points to disagreement over the interpretation of the same experimental evidence. The aforementioned examples of textbooks serve not as a random sample of available opinion but should be considered illustrative of the problems on this particular issue. The advice an advocate/student receives depends on which book or article they happen to read.

This constitutes a case of reasonable and intelligent scholars differing over the interpretation of a body of experimental evidence. These divergent interpretations lead the authors to prescriptive advice about the nature of messages consistent with their interpretation of the available data. This creates a problem for the practitioner seeking advice on message design. When a body of literature is analyzed and inconsistent conclusions advanced by scholars, the practitioner of communication cannot safely conclude the best course of action for planning a speech. Additionally, the ability to evaluate theoretical positions is undermined; how can a theory be assessed if any body of evidence remains inconsistent?

THEORETICAL EXPLORATIONS OF MESSAGE SIDEDNESS

The explanations for why different effects are obtained when comparing the persuasiveness of one- and two-sided messages takes a variety of forms. The two explanations receiving attention are the Elaboration Likelihood Model (ELM) and Inoculation theory. The ELM explains attitude change in terms of cognitive elaboration (Petty & Cacioppo, 1981, 1986). Inoculation theory bases an explanation on the previous cognitive experiences of the message receivers (McGuire, 1961a, 1961b; McGuire & Papageorgis, 1961, 1962).

The ELM argues that permanent attitude change as a result of persuasive communication is the result of cognitive elaborations made by the audience after receiving the message (Petty & Cacioppo, 1981, 1986). Elements of the situation work to inhibit or promote elaboration of message content. Message sidedness is not generally linked to the workings of the ELM as Petty and Cacioppo (1986) pointed out; however, the sidedness of a message, they concluded becomes a factor when "motivation and ability to think about the issue will determine the route to persuasion" (p. 215). The two-sided or one-sided messages, when seen as more believable or credible, create an increased desire to process the message by increasing the credibility of the source. This desire to process increases when certain situations occur, such as when a well-informed, hostile audience is exposed to a controversial message. The audience under these conditions is motivated to consider the message and to scrutinize the content. A two-sided message is better because the content appears well-informed and admits the reason for the hostility is rational but not acceptable because a superior set of reasoning exists that would promote a changed opinion. The two-sided or one-sided message permits under different conditions of motivation creates different effects on the attitudes of an audience.

Inoculation theory uses the metaphor of a disease to represent opinion and attitude change (McGuire, 1961a, 1961b). Inoculation is the introduction into the body of a weakened or inactive strain of a disease that permits the body to create antibodies that work on more active or effective forms of the disease. Similarly, a communicator presents the counterarguments of the opposition but refutes them to build up resistance in the audience so they will not sway from the desired opinion. Additionally, if an antibody exists in the audience, the speaker needs to overcome that initial resistance to be effective. This theory argues that a two-sided message is more effective in both the short and long run. Most of McGuire's work deals with sequential message exposures and is therefore not directly relevant to the issue of two-sided versus one-sided messages in a single exposure. However, the theoretical reasons for considering which form of message to use ultimately address the same issues of effectiveness and for the same reasons. This review recognizes that the work in inoculation theory does not include the primary research on this issue because the nature of the experimental design is different from prototypical single exposure designs.

METHODS

Literature Review[1]

A computer search of *Psychological Abstracts*, a manual search of *Psychological Abstracts*, the *Social Sciences Citation Index*, the *Index to Journals in Communication Studies Through 1985*, and examination all of the reference and bibliographies of located studies and reviews provided materials.[2] To be included in this meta-analysis a study had to compare the persuasiveness of a one-sided and a two-sided message.

Possible Moderating Variables

Each study was coded for a variety of possible features that may moderate the effect of message features. An examination of the experiments for information regarding the methodology provided the information necessary for the coding and evaluation of these features.

Type of Two-sided Message. The existing experimental literature offers two types of two-sided messages: *refutational* or *non-refutational*. Refutational two-sided messages are messages that mention counterarguments to the position advocated and then refute them. The intent is to introduce the contrary position and demonstrate why this position is inferior to the position advocated by the communicator. The nonrefutational message only mentioned the counterarguments without offering a refutation of them.[3]

Education of Level of Audience. Another potential moderator was the education level of the audience. Message receivers were either coded as high school or college students. Not all experiments could be coded because some experiments used participants not derived from school setting and no judgment was possible.

---

[1]More information is available in earlier reports of this data (Allen, 1993). One correction had to be made from the earlier report. The Jones and Brehm (1970) study originally had a sample size of 84. The correct sample size if 42. The error stems from the article that used an analysis of variance (F-test) to generate the results but then reports the results in the form of the t-test (by taking the square root of F). The degrees of freedom reflect the F test, but the actual sample is only one-half that.

[2]The author wishes to thank both Steve Booth-Butterfield and Sandi Smith for suggestions on possible sources of data. Without the help of both of these individuals, the report would have been far less complete.

[3]Information on the coding of each study, as well as other relevant information, is available from the author.

Favorability of the Audience. The favorability of the audience toward the conclusions advocated by the message source was coded. An audience could be favorable or unfavorable.

Statistical Analysis

The results of each study were converted to a common metric for averaging. For the purposes of this review, the correlation coefficient was used. The correlation coefficient was used because it is recommended in the case of binary variables due to the ease of interpretation of the results (Hunter & Schmidt, 1990; Rosenthal, 1984, 1987). Once an average is established, the average correlation is tested for homogeneity (Hunter & Schmidt, 1990). The test estimates the expected amount of variance due to sampling error and compares that estimate with the observed amount of variance in the sample of correlations. If 75% or more of the variance can be attributed to sampling error, the estimates are considered homogeneous. If less than 75% of the variance can be attributed to sampling error the estimates are considered heterogeneous and a moderator is probably present.

RESULTS

The results proceed to analyze the overall data and then each moderator separately. If the results for a particular moderator successfully account for the results, then two observations should be true: (a) Attempts to use other moderators should be unsuccessful, and (b) the successful moderator, when applied to the subgroups of other moderators, should create homogeneous results.

Overall Analysis

The initial results indicate that the two-sided message was slightly more persuasive than the one-sided message (r = .030, k = 70, N = 10,580). However, only 40% of the observed variance could be attributed to sampling error. The means the observed average correlation is not the best estimate of the average effect because a moderator variable(s) exists. Although the average effect indicates a very slight advantage for the two-sided message, this estimate should not be considered representative of the entire sample of studies or messages.

Type of Two-sided Message. Considering the moderating effect of the type of two-sided message (refutational or nonrefutational) generated results that were homogeneous. The two-sided message with no refutation of counterarguments demonstrates the one-sided message is superior (r = -.087, k = 26, N = 3159) with 92% of the observed variance attributable to sampling error. The two-sided message with refutation was superior to the one-sided message (r = .074, k = 43, N = 7317). A total of 76% of the observed variance could be attributed to sampling error. These results indicate that the originally heterogeneous overall result can be explained by the differing operationalizations of what constituted a two-sided message. The one-sided message is more persuasive than a two-sided message with no refutation. However, a two-sided message with refutation generates more favorable attitudes than a one-sided message. It should be noted that in no experiment did all three messages occur; therefore, a direct test within one experiment was not possible. Logically, the order of most effective messages should be two-sided with refutation, one-sided, and two-sided with no refutation. A follow up experiment testing an earlier version of this meta-analysis (Allen et al., 1990) confirms these findings and the results of that experiment are to within sampling error of the results. Additionally, a theoretical test of results (Hale, Mongeau, & Thomas, 1991) and a replication of this meta-analysis (O'Keefe, 1993) support the overall findings of this report.

If this moderator is the only moderator, than clustering the studies by other moderators should not produce homogeneous results. This should be true for any sample that contains multiple two-sided message types. The use of any other moderator should still produce results that are heterogeneous. However, after taking each subgroup and then dividing the studies by type of two-sided message should produce homogeneous results within each subgroup.

Education as a Moderator

There were two levels of education (high school and college). Two studies were conducted in high schools and 15 were conducted using college students. This analysis tests whether the status of the person's education moderates the results. It should be pointed out that studies did not use adult populations and report separate analyses for different levels of education. Therefore, education in this case is necessarily confounded with age and the test may be alternately interpreted as distinguishing between old and young. This "gap" in the literature should be a source of future research.

The analysis shows that the two studies using high school students both used two-sided messages with refutation. The average effect size was positive (*r* = .210, *k* = 2, *N* = 339), indicating the two-sided message with refutation was considered more persuasive. The observed correlation was homogeneous, the variance attributable to sampling error (100%).

The 31 studies using college students were initially analyzed combining across both types of two-sided messages. The average correlation favored two-sided messages (*r* = .007, *k* = 56, *N* = 7140). However, the average correlation was not homogeneous, only a relatively small percentage was attributable to sampling error (50%). This indicates the probable existence of some moderator variable.

The 31 studies were divided into smaller data sets based on the type of two-sided message. Six studies had used a two-sided message with no refutation and 10 studies used a two-sided message with refutation. The 5 studies using the nonrefutational message had an average effect size that favored the one-sided message (*r* = -.083, *k* = 24, *N* = 2929) and the observed average effect was homogenous (77% of variance attributable to sampling error). The 21 studies using a refutational two-sided message had a positive effect favoring the two-sided message (*r* = .078, *k* = 32, *N* = 4058) and the effect was homogenous (88% of the variance explainable as sampling error).

What should be pointed out is that the results indicate a consistent superiority for the two-sided refutational message. It is possible that a particular type of message works with persons of younger age or among adults of relatively divergent levels of education. The samples provided here do not contain sufficient information to undertake this analysis. The result is the possibility that educational or age differences may produce different results. However, the possibility of an additional alternative hypothesis should be treated as very speculative and without firm empirical or theoretical support. The possibility should justify continued research target toward that specific outcome.

Audience Favorability as a Moderator

Studies were examined that reported information on the initial favorability of the audience toward the conclusion advocated. There existed two codable initial positions of the audience (favorable or unfavorable). An overall analysis is presented of the studies, then each condition will be examined separately.

The overall analysis of seven relevant studies showed a small positive correlation (*r* = .029, *N* = 945) that was based on a heterogeneous sample (only 28% of the variance due to sampling error). This necessitated the use of the type of two-sided message being introduced as a possible moderating variable.

The nonrefutation two-sided message was used in three studies. The average correlation for those studies was negative ($r = -.107, N = 376$), however, the sample was heterogeneous (only 31% of the variance due to sampling error). The refutational two-sided message was used in four studies and the average correlation was positive ($r = .118, N = 569$) and based on a homogeneous sample of effects (100% of the variance attributable to sampling error).

The results are consistent in direction with the previous findings. The average correlation was positive for the two-sided message with refutation and negative for the two-sided nonrefutational message. However, unlike previous moderators, there was a heterogeneous average after considering the type of two-sided message. This suggests the possibility of another moderator operating. However, with only three studies examining this phenomena the ability to identify the additional moderator does not exist with any confidence.

The need to identify the moderator may or may not exist. One position says that the feature of interest is the main effect and moderators are of little interest. "The fact that message replications interact with treatments may invite a search for moderators (or 'blocking' variables), but whether that search succeeds or fails, the main effect (generalized across replications) will still be of primary interest" (Jackson, O'Keefe, Jacobs, & Brashers, 1989, p. 377). One concern driving this position is the nature of the search for moderator variables: "If one partitions the studies into subsets with large and small (or positive and negative) effect sizes, the ability to find a 'moderator' is limited only by one's tolerance for the incoherent, the implausible, and the bizarre" (p. 382). This position makes the existence of heterogeneity in the particular sample irrelevant because the main effect is consistent with the previous findings.

An alternative position argues that the main effect is only interpretable and therefore useful within the context of an understanding of what constitutes the moderator or interaction. In the presence of disordinal interactions, the main effect can be zero while the interaction term accounts for a significant portion of the variance (see Hunter, Hamilton, & Allen, 1989, for a discussion of disordinal interactions and messages). The current chapter urges caution in interpreting the main effect for hostile audiences without additional research to interpret this effect.

CONCLUSIONS

The results generally support the conclusion that the apparent inconsistency of earlier literature reviews stemmed from divergent operationalizations of what constitutes a two-sided message. When the difference between a two-sided message with and without refutation is incorporated into the analysis, the heterogeneous results become homogeneous. The reclassification of messages does not require any additional moderator variables and is sufficient to explain the effect.

The results are inconsistent with the ELM's expectations about the effects of sidedness of messages. The ELM does not predict the findings based on some feature of the message. However, if the type of two-sided message creates some difference in the processing of message information for receivers, the findings could reinterpreted as consistent with the model. This is particularly important because some of the moderator tests are inconclusive based on small sample sizes. It may be that for some combination of audience features a more sophisticated processing explanation is required consistent with the ELM (Petty & Cacioppo, 1986).

Inoculation approaches argue for the effect observed in this meta-analysis. The introduction of a weakened form of counterargument is sufficient to increase the attitude change of the message receivers. The causal model advanced by Hale et al. (1991) suggests that the message design stimulates more favorable thoughts and therefore more attitude change.

The implications of the results for application to practical advice giving should be obvious. In all previously examined conditions the results indicate that a communicator should use a two-sided message with a recognition and refutation of the available counterarguments. This message type produces the most favorable attitude response from the message receivers—this effects the reaction of the receivers toward the message sender. Research should consider and explore the effect that such message design has on communicator credibility. The follow-up experiment conducted to test the findings of this meta-analysis (Allen et. al., 1990) contained a measure of source credibility. The findings of this experiment suggest that evaluations of source credibility are consistent with the pattern of attitude change. This suggests that type of message not only changes attitudes but also the receiver's evaluation of the source as well. No causal explanation is forwarded; however, the possibility of a causal exploration deserves continued consideration.

The results should come as no surprise to most students of classical rhetoric or teachers of public speaking. The idea that a person would merely mention a counter position without refutation should be discouraged. The operationalization of the two-sided message without including refutation points to a possibly inadequate understanding of the function and effectiveness of messages.

This difference in operationalization and the resulting problems point to the need for a theory of messages and message effects. Without such theories, past and future experiments may contain problems that may not be as easily or readily identifiable as in the message-sidedness literature. Much concern has been made about the issue of research to generalize on the basis of a limited pool of messages. The effect has been referred to as the "messages-as-fixed-effect fallacy." The results of this investigation demonstrate that no generalized message by treatment interaction was observed (which would have been indicated by a positive moderator test). This indicates that either the concern about this problem may be unwarranted in this area or that so little is known about messages that the ability to generate the variability necessary does not exist in this set of experiments.

The real test of these results will be how they contribute to an overall theory of messages. The previous ideas about messages tended to indicate an indeterminacy of language and provided a series of contextual features that prevent clear generalizations. The evidence accumulated and analyzed here indicates the possibility that simple generalizations may be possible. Such generalizations, however, without a clear and comprehensive theory of message effects will be limited. The conclusions should serve to help practitioners and assist in curriculum development. However, the larger picture needs to be addressed for these results to be placed within the context of theoretical and future experimental issues.

REFERENCES

Allen, M. (1991). Comparing the persuasiveness of one-sided and two-sided messages using meta-analysis. *Western Journal of Speech Communication, 55*, 390–404.

Allen, M. (1993). Determining the persuasiveness of message sidedness: A prudent note about utilizing research summaries. *Western Journal of Communication, 57*, 98–103.

Allen, M., Hale, J., Mongeau, P., Berkowitz-Stafford, S., Stafford, S., Shanahan, W., Agee, P., Dillon, K., Jackson, R., & Ray, C. (1990). Testing a model of message sidedness: Three replications. *Communication Monographs, 57*, 275–291.

Allen, M., & Preiss, R. (1990). Using meta-analyses to evaluate curriculum: An examination of selected college textbooks. *Communication Education, 39*, 103–116.

Aristotle (1932). *The rhetoric of Aristotle* (L. Cooper, trans.). New York: Appleton-Century-Crofts.

Hale, J., Mongeau, P., & Thomas, R. (1991). Cognitive processing of one- and two-sided persuasive messages. *Western Journal of Communication, 55*, 380–389.

Hunter, J., Hamilton, M., & Allen, M. (1989). The design and analysis of language experiments in communication. *Communication Monographs, 56*, 341–363.

Hunter, J., & Schmidt, F. (1990). *Methods of meta-analysis*. Newbury Park, CA: Sage.

Jackson, S., O'Keefe, D., Jacobs, S., & Brashers, D. (1989). Messages as replications: Toward a message-centered strategy. *Communication Monographs, 56*, 364–384.

Jones, R., & Brehm, J. (1970). Persuasiveness of one- and two-sided communications as a function of awareness there are two sides. *Journal of Experimental Social Psychology, 6*, 47–56.

Lucas, S. (1989). *The art of public speaking* (3rd ed.). New York: Random House.

McGuire, W. (1961a). Persistence of the resistance to persuasion induced by various types of prior belief defenses. *Journal of Abnormal and Social Psychology, 64*, 241–248.

McGuire, W. (1961b). Resistance to persuasion conferred by active and passive prior refutation of the same and alternative counterarguments. *Journal of Abnormal and Social Psychology, 63*, 326–332.

McGuire, W., & Papageorgis, D. (1961). The relative efficacy of various types of prior belief-defense in producing immunity against persuasion. *Journal of Abnormal and Social Psychology, 62*, 327–337.

McGuire, W., & Papageorgis, D. (1962). Effectiveness of forewarning in developing resistance to persuasion. *Public Opinion Quarterly, 26*, 24–34.

O'Keefe, D. (1993). The persuasive effects of message sidedness variations: A cautionary note concerning Allen's (1991) meta-analysis. *Western Journal of Communication, 57*, 87–97.

Petty, R., & Cacioppo, J. (1981). *Attitudes and persuasion: Classic and contemporary approaches*. Dubuque, IA: Brown.

Petty, R., & Cacioppo, J. (1986). *Communication persuasion: Central and peripheral routes to attitude change*. New York Springer-Verlag.

Reardon, K. (1981). *Persuasion*. Beverly Hills,CA.: Sage.

Rosenthal, R. (1984). *Meta-analytic procedures for social research*. Beverly Hills, CA: Sage.

Rosenthal, R. (1987). *Judgment studies: Design, analysis, and meta-analysis*. New York: Cambridge University Press.

6

The Effect of Language Intensity on Receiver Evaluations of Message, Source, and Topic

Mark A. Hamilton
University of Connecticut

John E. Hunter
Michigan State University

When is persuasion facilitated by more intense language, and when is it facilitated by less intense language? Information processing theory and Reinforcement Expectancy Theory offer different answers to this question. Before comparing the predictions of these two theories, we examine the definition of message intensity as it has evolved from the early 1960s to the present. The second section of the chapter provides an information processing theory account of message intensity effects. We start with a causal process model that explains the effect of message intensity on receiver evaluations of message and source, and also present the mathematical prediction model of attitude change from information-processing theory. We describe how message intensity can influence each of the components in this model. The third section provides a Reinforcement Expectancy Theory account of message intensity effects. We introduce the mathematical prediction model for attitude toward source and topic derived from traditional reinforcement theory and then consider receiver expectations of source as possible moderators of the effect of message intensity on attitude change.

The meta-analysis that follows examined the effect of language intensity on eight variables: perceived language intensity, extremity of source position, perceived dynamism of the source's presentation, perceived message clarity, perceived source competence, perceived source trustworthiness, perceived source liking, and attitude change toward topic. The findings indicate that information-processing theory provides a better explanation of language intensity effects than Reinforcement-Expectancy Theory.

DEFINITIONS OF LANGUAGE INTENSITY

Intensity is a stylistic feature of language that is conveyed through the properties of emotionality and specificity (Hamilton, Hunter, & Burgoon, 1990). Emotional intensity is the degree of affect reflected in the source's language, ranging from mild to intense. To illustrate the polar ends of the emotional intensity continuum, compare the mildly worded sentence "She angered him" to the intensely worded sentence "She enraged him." Use of markers like "enraged" or "terrified" indicate that the source is emotionally charged about an issue.

Linguistic specificity is the extent to which a marker denotes a narrow or broad semantic category. Precise lexical items have narrow semantic breadth. Specificity narrows the semantic category to which the referent belongs. Greater lexical precision should allow receivers to better recognize the attitude object or related concept to which the source refers. To the extent that the attitude object of the message is clear, receivers will associate their affective responses to the object. That is, specificity amplifies the impact of emotional intensity on receivers. For example, the sentence "The King had many wives" is less precise than "The King had eight wives."

The extent to which variations in the emotionality of language and linguistic specificity can have an impact on receivers depends on two message features—the *density* of the markers in the text and the *power* of those markers.

Marker Density

At various points in the text it is possible to insert words that differ in intensity. Each of these points represents a lexical marker of intensity. *Marker density* is the ratio of lexical markers to the total number of words in a message (Bradac, Hopper, & Weimann, 1989). In the context of intensity studies, we refer to this ratio as the density of intensity markers. The greater the density of intensity markers in a message, the greater the opportunity for a difference between high- and low-intensity markers to influence receiver evaluations of message, source, and topic.

Marker Power

The intensity of a word varies quantitatively. High- and low-intensity markers can differ by a large amount or by a small amount. If a very high-intensity word is used as the high-intensity marker and a very low-intensity word is used as the low-intensity marker, then the power of that marker position in the message is very high. If the high- and low-intensity markers differ by only a little, then the power of that marker position is very low. If all the markers in the high- and low-intensity versions of the message have high marker power, then the two messages will show a distinct difference in intensity. If all the markers have weak power, then the two messages will show a subtle difference in intensity.

In most studies, the high- and low-intensity versions of the message start with exactly the same template message. Because all the marker positions are the same, the two messages have the same marker density. However, differences in researcher creativity and message content can produce messages that differ considerably in marker power. Thus, even with similar density, the intensity difference between the two message versions can still vary quite a bit. The strength of the intensity manipulation will vary across studies. Some of that variation will be due to marker density and some to marker power. Marker density can be estimated if authors publish their messages—marker power is much harder to estimate.

Extremity of Source Position

In contrast to defining the term *intensity* as a stylistic message feature, some researchers have defined it as extremity of source position. For example, Bowers (1963) defined *intensity* as the extent to which a message differs from advocating a neutral position. Language intensity can, in fact, increase the perceived extremity of position advocated by the source (Hamilton & Stewart, 1993), but the two concepts are distinguishable. Not all researchers are aware of the distinction between the two concepts. Some may have thought they were manipulating a stylistic message feature when they were actually varying the extremity of the source's position.

The difference between the position advocated by the source and the premessage attitude of receivers is message discrepancy (see Chapter 1, this volume). By manipulating "intensity" as source position, researchers were actually manipulating message discrepancy. Nearly all message manipulations in the intensity literature confound stylistic intensity and message discrepancy. They differ, however, in the extent of the confound.[1] There are easy scaling methods for measuring source position, and some studies have measured both the perceived stylistic intensity of the message and the perceived discrepancy of the message. Distinguishing between these two consequent variables is important. We show that receiver perceptions of stylistic intensity have a positive effect on source evaluation, whereas perceived extremity of source position generally has a negative effect on evaluations of source.

Manipulations of Message Intensity

The confounding of the stylistic intensity and extremity of source position concepts in the language intensity literature can be demonstrated most easily by considering the operational method for constructing "high-intensity" and "low-intensity" versions of a message. Start with a message such as a speech advocating some given policy. Then go through the speech looking for points at which different words could be used. For each of the identified points in the text, select a low-intensity word and a high-intensity word. The position of these words in the text can then be called a "marker" of intensity. The question is this: What makes one choice a "high-intensity" marker and the other choice a "low-intensity" marker? Researchers have answered this question in two different ways.

Extremity of Source Position.

Some authors define intensity as substantive differences in the positions taken by the source. Consider the statement "There have been cases where stigmatized people have become so despondent that they committed suicide." In ordinary English, the marker "some" would be low in intensity,

---

[1]Some studies very effectively control discrepancy while manipulating linguistic style. For example, the messages used in Hamilton, Hunter, Stewart, and Zhao (1991) had an impact on perceived language intensity (the measure of linguistic style), but no effect on perceived source position (the measure of discrepancy). Other studies actively seek to manipulate message discrepancy. For example, in Burgoon, Jones, and Steward (1975, Experiment1) the intensity manipulation check was receivers' ratings of the position taken by the speaker.

whereas the marker "many" would be high in intensity. These markers differ in substance as well as style. The word "many" implies a much higher frequency of suicide than the word "some." Thus the use of the word "many" creates a message that takes a somewhat different position than the speech using the marker "some." If all markers were of this form, the high- and low-intensity messages would, taken as a whole, be quite different in substantive content. Most importantly, the messages would differ in the position advocated. In that sense, the high- and low-intensity messages would no longer be making the same point.

Stylistic Intensity.

Other authors define *intensity* as stylistic differences in the message. Consider the statement "Because of the unintended consequences, the adoption of this policy would be ______." In ordinary English, the marker "ill-considered" would be low in intensity, whereas the marker "stupid" would be high in intensity. In terms of logical content, both markers say the same thing. In terms of style, one marker is much more intense than the other. If all markers were stylistic, the speeches would differ in tone, but the logical content would be the same. In that sense, the high- and low intensity message would be making the same point.

Perceived Intensity

We define the term *perceived intensity* as the intensity of the message as it is decoded by the individual receiver. Typically, persuasion researchers choose the topic and arguments in a message so that all receivers in their target audience will have similar reactions. However, their assumption of uniform receiver perceptions is often due to researcher ignorance of the audience rather than a reflection of true uniformity. As we show here the size of the correlation between manipulated intensity and perceived intensity is rather modest. Thus, even with the best of intentions and even with message pretesting, current researchers achieve only a very limited control over individual differences in the perceived intensity of the message.

Measuring Perceived Intensity.

Researchers measure intensity by asking receivers to make judgments after listening to or reading the message. How accurate are receiver reports of intensity? Their reports contain two sources of measurement error: systematic error and random error of measurement. By using multiple items on a perceived intensity scale and applying reliability theory, we can assess the extent of random measurement error. Many current studies achieve a very high level of reliability in the perceived intensity scale. Furthermore, we can use reliability estimates to correct statistical outcome measures for the attenuating effects of random measurement error.

Systematic error is difficult to determine for the perceived intensity variable (as for most variables). How high is the construct validity of current perceived intensity measures? We do not now know the answer to that question. The current approach to assessing the construct validity of the perceived intensity measure is the classic indirect approach. We use our measures to estimate correlations with other theoretical constructs such as source credibility and attitude change. If the measure acts as it is predicted to act by a theory that is believed to be true, then we know the construct validity is high. If the measure acts differently from the theoretical predictions, we often do not know whether the theory is wrong or the measure has low construct validity. Path models based on information processing theory have been tested using current perceived intensity scales (Hamilton, in press). The models achieve good fit to the data, suggesting that the construct validity of perceived intensity scales is rather high—although we cannot say just how high.

The Correlation between Manipulated and Perceived Intensity.

The lexicon of experimental designs describes the perceived intensity ratings of the high- and low-intensity messages as the *manipulation check.* That is, the designed difference in message intensity determined by the differential choice of intensity markers can be considered to be manipulated intensity. The perceived intensity scale can be regarded as the manipulation check variable that assesses the extent to which the design manipulation actually alters the desired dependent variable.

It is important to remember that *manipulated intensity* is conceived as a binary variable with values "high" and "low." These values are the same across studies that use very different template messages about very different topics. This uniformity of values across messages is a statistical fiction. The actual message intensity is quantitative, not binary. As we show, some language intensity manipulations are stronger than others. Thus, even though the same binary description of the intensity manipulation is applied in each study, the actual strength of the intensity manipulation differs from one study to the next.

One way to measure the difference in the strength of the intensity manipulation is to consider the correlation between manipulated and perceived intensity. To the extent that an experiment achieves a strong intensity manipulation, there should be a larger correlation between manipulated intensity and perceived intensity. However, a low correlation can be produced by two very different causes: a weak intensity manipulation or randomness in message decoding.

Message Decoding. The linguistically insensitive receiver may overlook markers. This is especially important if the markers that are overlooked are the key high-intensity markers. Conversely, the linguistically hypersensitive receiver may read more emotional meaning into a marker than is there in the sense of strict linguistic content. Receivers may also have idiosyncratic associations with particular words. To the extent that the high- and low-intensity messages are differentiated by a large number of markers, the idiosyncratic differences in marker intensity should average out and have little effect on the manipulated message intensity. However, if the message versions depend only on a small number of critical markers, the random effects may be large. To the extent that there are systematic differences in sensitivity to emotional markers, the use of multiple markers would not eliminate the impact of this individual differences variable. Rather, this variation would reduce the size of the observed correlation between manipulated intensity and perceived intensity.

INFORMATION-PROCESSING THEORY

Information processing theory (Hamilton, in press; Hamilton, Hunter, & Boster, 1993; Hunter, Danes, & Cohen, 1984; McGuire, 1968a, 1969, 1989) was used to develop a causal process model of the effect of message intensity on receiver evaluations of message, source, and topic. The theory was also used to predict the effect of message intensity on attitude change. We consider the causal model of language intensity effects first, then the attitude change prediction model.

Previous causal modeling work reanalyzed the data from individual studies (Hamilton, in press) and meta-analyzed findings (Hamilton & Thompson, 1994) to generate the causal model shown in Figure 6.1. The causal model indicates that intensity has both positive and negative effects on perceived source credibility. The positive effect of manipulated intensity on perceived source competence is mediated by three variables—perceived language intensity, the perceived dynamism of the source's presentation, and perceived message clarity. The negative effect of intensity on competence was mediated by the perceived extremity of the position advocated by the source. The positive effect of intensity on perceived source trustworthi-

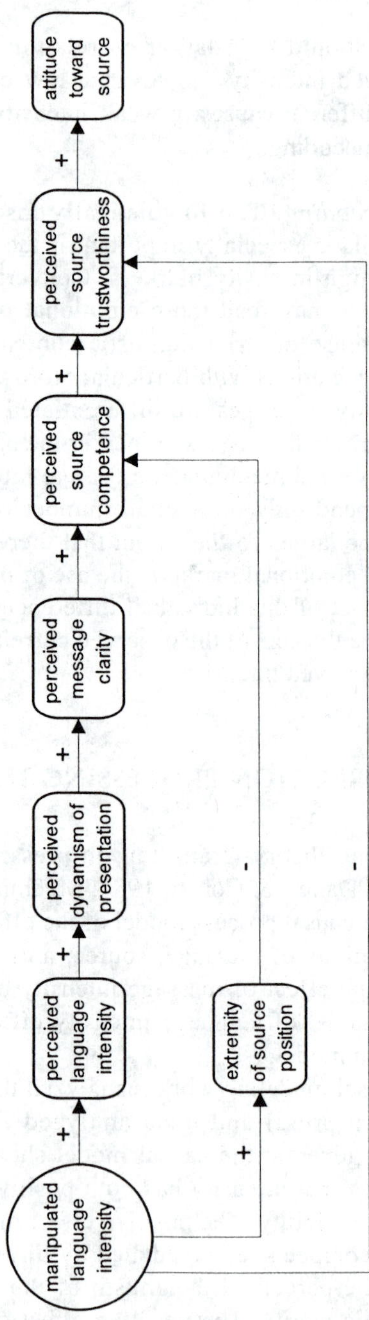

Figure 6.1. Predicted model of the effect of language intensity on attitude toward source

ness was mediated by perceived intensity, perceived dynamism, perceived message clarity, and perceived source competence. The negative effect of intensity on trustworthiness was not mediated by extremity of source position. The positive effect of intensity on perceived source liking (attitude toward the source) was mediated by perceived intensity, perceived dynamism, message clarity, source competence, and source trustworthiness.

The variables in the source attitude model shown in Figure 6.1 correspond to the stages of the traditional information processing model. Message exposure is the presentation of the intensity manipulations contained in the persuasive message. In the attention stage, receivers generate internal representations of the message in working memory based on the lexical items that convey intensity. The more the internal representation excites the receiver, the greater the perceived intensity of the message. Excitement depends on the emotional intensity and specificity of the lexical items contained in the message, magnified by the density of the markers. A more exciting presentation should lead receivers to evaluate the source's presentation as more dynamic and allocate more attention to the message Greater attention to the message, in turn, should improve receiver comprehension of message arguments, and better comprehension should increase the perceived clarity of the message. Thus, as dynamism increases, so will receivers' processing of message content, increasing the perceived clarity of the message (McGuire, 1969, p. 207). A clear message should, in turn, increase perceived source competence.

During the information comparison stage, receivers compare the new information contained in message arguments to the old information residing in memory; they also assess the expertise of the source. The goal during this processing phase may be to satisfy the receiver's need for information seeking on the topic, or to assess the justification for the source's position on the topic. If the receiver needs to defer to the source, premessage source competence should increase the subjective probability of message arguments as they are processed. The more compelling the arguments contained in the message, the higher the postmessage source competence. However, the greater the discrepancy between the position advocated by the source and the initial position of receivers, the more receivers will derogate a source's expertise. More competent sources should be perceived as more believable or trustworthy. In the informatic integration phase, receivers integrate old knowledge about source and topic with new knowledge gleaned from the message. As described by Anderson (1971, 1981, 1982), changes in belief structure produce attitude change.

Predicting Attitude Change From Language Intensity

We used the attitude change prediction model (see Chapter 1, Equation 1, this volume) to explain the effect of language intensity on receiver attitude toward topic. Language intensity can have an impact on each of the four components of the prediction model—message strength, source evaluation, message discrepancy, and counterarguing. The effect of language intensity on message strength was described earlier,[2] as was the effect of intensity on perceived source evaluation (Figure 6.1).

Counterarguing as a Moderator.

Language intensity increases message discrepancy by making the position advocated by the source seem more extreme. If we assume a strong message, a credible source, and minimal counterarguing, intensity should increase attitude change by increasing discrepancy. To the extent that receivers respond negatively to the extremity of position taken by the source, the increase in discrepancy that results from greater language intensity will inhibit attitude change by increasing counterargument. Alone, the increase in counterargument triggered by intensity may be minimal, but when magnified by ego-involvement with an issue, counterargument may be extensive. Thus, receiver ego-involvement with the attitude object should moderate intensity induced counterarguing .

If language intensity increases message discrepancy, then intensity in an attitude-discrepant message should enhance attitude change when attitude change is an increasing monotonic function of discrepancy, and inhibit attitude change when attitude change is a nonmonotonic function of discrepancy. Attitude change will be a nonmonotonic function of discrepancy when counterarguing is extensive, and this is most likely when receivers are ego-

---

[2]The strength of a message will depend on its verbal content, and if the message is presented orally, on the delivery of that content. Some messages are presented orally, but many are not. We were interested in studying message strength across contexts, so we focused primarily on verbal content. Propositional content (the nature of the arguments presented in the message) and lexical items (the particular words used to indicate thoughts and emotions) contribute to message strength. Lexical items that increase message strength are referred to as intense language. A broader conceptualization of message strength that would include the use of opinionated or obscene language was not attempted in this chapter. The meta-analysis of language intensity effects presented here shows a different pattern of results that the meta-analyses of opinionated language effects (Hamilton & Costa, 1988) and obscene language effects (Hamilton, 1989; in press).

involved with the topic (Hamilton & Thompson, 1994). Thus, when counterarguing is slight to moderate, intensity will enhance attitude change. When counterarguing is extensive, intensity will inhibit attitude change.

It is interesting to note that several previous reviews of the literature on language intensity effects (Bradac, Bowers, & Courtright, 1979; Burgoon, 1989,1990; Burgoon et al., 1975) have proposed that language intensity is inversely related to attitude change in discrepant messages. In the studies cited as evidence for this proposition, the topics used for the persuasive messages were highly ego-involving for receivers, so they should have elicited profuse counterarguing. Burgoon et al. (1975) used high-ego-involvement topics for the student receivers in their three studies: restricted access to college (Experiment 1), and mandatory on-campus living (Experiments 2 and 3). The receivers in these studies should have perceived the discrepant message as threatening. The more intense the language, the more severe that threat. Once past the inflection point on the discrepancy curve, further increases in discrepancy (due to intensity) for these ego-involved receivers should have produced diminishing attitude change. For low to moderate ego-involved receivers, however, greater discrepancy leads to greater attitude change, so intensity should enhance attitude change for attitude discrepant messages delivered to low or moderate ego-involved receivers.

Exogenous Stress and Counterarguing. Information-processing theory predicts a curvilinear relationship between message-irrelevant cognitive stress and attitude change. In Chapter 1 of this volume, Hamilton and Hunter discussed the role of anxiety in the multiplicative version of the McGuire (1968b) two-factor model. McGuire argued that message-irrelevant anxiety would decrease attention and comprehension of message content, but increase acceptance of the message conclusion by disrupting counterarguing. At low anxiety, comprehension would be greatest, but yielding would be least; at high anxiety, comprehension would be least, but yielding would be greatest. At moderate anxiety, an optimal combination of reception and yielding factors would produce the maximum amount of attitude change.

Hovland, Janis, and Kelly (1953) argued that emotional messages such as fear appeals are more effective among relaxed receivers than among anxious receivers. Recent work on fear appeal effects by Hale and Mongeau (1991) supports the Hovland et al., prediction. Averaging across studies, Hale and Mongeau found that the correlation between fear and attitude change is slightly positive among low-anxiety receivers and slightly negative among high-anxiety receivers.

Suppose that the emotional content of a high fear appeal or high-intensity message increases receiver stress. Within the two-factor model, if language intensity increases stress from a low to moderate level, then it should enhance attitude change; if intensity increases stress from a moderate to high level, then it should inhibit attitude change. The proposition that anxiety or stress moderates the impact of language intensity on attitude change has been offered by others (Bradac, Bowers, & Courtright, 1979; Burgoon et al., 1975; Carmichael & Cronkhite, 1965), although the theoretical basis of their prediction was unclear. We tested the proposition that for relaxed receivers, intensity should be positively correlated with attitude change; for stressed receivers, intensity should be negatively correlated with attitude change.

Summary of Information Processing Predictions.

The attitude change prediction model (see Equation 1, Chapter 1, this volume) claims that message strength, source evaluation, message discrepancy, and counterarguing will interact multiplicatively on attitude change. That is, there should be little if any persuasive effect of intensity on attitudes when the message is weak, discrepancy is near zero, or when the source is evaluated poorly (perceived as incompetent, biased, or dislikable). The moderating role of counterargument is more complex. Source position, ego-involvement, and accumulated information should determine the effect of message discrepancy on attitude change (see Equation 2, Chapter 1, this volume). Receivers who are reactive to the position taken by the source, ego-involved, and have a large amount of accumulated information can be characterized as prone to counterargue. For the credible source delivering a strong, discrepant message, intensity will enhance persuasion when counterarguing is low, but inhibit persuasion when counterarguing is high. Finally, language intensity should enhance persuasion for relaxed receivers, but inhibit persuasion for stressed receivers.

REINFORCEMENT EXPECTANCY THEORY

Based on their qualitative review of the intensity literature, Bradac, Bowers, and Courtright (1979) drew conclusions about the effect of intense language on receiver attitudes toward source and topic. Their conclusions were presented as a formal theory and causal model by Bradac, Bowers, and Courtright (1980). The assumptions of reinforcement theory (Insko, 1965; Insko & Cialdini, 1969; Staats & Staats, 1957) were implicit in the causal model and axioms that Bradac et al. (1980) presented. In the model, language intensity influences attitudes through a two-step process: Language intensity affects source evaluation, and source evaluation affects attitude change. The axiomatic theory of Bradac et al. (1980) and Burgoon (1989) subsumed a number of propositions presented as part of language expectancy theory in Burgoon and Chase (1973), and Burgoon et al. (1975). This axiomatized reinforcement theory has more recently been referred to as Reinforcement Expectancy Theory (Klingle & Burgoon, 1995).

Intensity and Source Evaluation

In traditional reinforcement theory, attitude toward source depends on the position the source advocates in the message (*m*) and the receiver's premessage attitude toward topic (*a*). Source change is a multiplicative function of source position and premessage attitude (Hunter et al., 1984). Stated simply, reinforcement theory predicts that if the position of the source is congruent with that of the receiver, then the receiver will find the experience rewarding and the source will be evaluated more positively. If the position of the source is discrepant with that of the receiver, then the receiver will find the experience punishing and the source will be evaluated more negatively. Bradac et al. (1980) implicitly assumed this source change equation with language intensity acting as an amplifying moderator variable. They claim that intensity will enhance perceived source credibility (competence and trustworthiness) and similarity in attitude congruent messages, and inhibit source similarity (and source credibility we presume) in attitude discrepant messages. Mathematically, this means that source change will be the product of source position (*m*), premessage attitude (*a*) and language intensity (*i*), such that

$$\Delta s = \alpha m \cdot a \cdot i \qquad (1)$$

where Δ is the premessage to postmessage change in the receiver's attitude toward the source, *m* is the position advocated by the source, *a* is the receiver's initial attitude, *i* is language intensity, and α is the message impact parameter.

Intensity and Attitude Change

In traditional reinforcement theory, attitude change toward topic should be in the direction advocated by the source, weighted by premessage source evaluation when relevant (Hunter, et al., 1984). Intensity should act as a magnifier of message effects, producing more agreement with the message. In contrast to traditional reinforcement theory, Bradac et al.'s (1980, p. 221) causal model of language effects claims that attitude change will depend on postmessage rather than premessage source evaluations. Hamilton and Thompson (1994) have shown that postmessage evaluations of source are, in fact, a better predictor of attitude change than premessage evaluations of source.

Message discrepancy is irrelevant to attitude change toward topic in traditional reinforcement theory. Thus, discrepancy would not moderate the effect of intensity on attitude change. However, if attitude change were a function of postmessage source evaluation, then message discrepancy could have an impact on attitude change mediated through source evaluation (see Equation 1). This would explain the Bradac et al. proposition that language intensity enhances attitude change if the message is attitude congruent, but inhibits attitude change if the message is attitude discrepant (Bradac, Bowers, & Courtright, 1979, 1980; Burgoon, 1989; Burgoon & Chase, 1973; Burgoon, et al, 1975, p. 242). Attitude change would be predicted as follows:

$$\Delta a = \alpha m \cdot s \cdot i \qquad (2)$$

where α is a message impact parameter, m is the position advocated by the source, s is the relevant source evaluation variable (competence, trustworthiness, or liking), and i is language intensity. Language intensity in Equation 2 operates like the message strength variable in information processing theory. In fact, the three lexical features discussed by Bradac et al. (1980) (intensity, immediacy, diversity) might be interpreted as forms of message strength.

Competing Predictions.

There is a key difference between the reinforcement model described by Equation 2 and the information-processing model described in Chapter 1 of this volume (Equations 1 and 2). Information processing theory explicitly accounts for the receiver's premessage attitude toward topic, *a*. Reinforcement Expectancy Theory, on the other hand, incorporates premessage attitude toward topic indirectly, through postmessage source evaluation.

Both information processing theory and Reinforcement Expectancy Theory predict that greater intensity in low-discrepancy (attitude-congruent) messages can enhance attitude change, although Reinforcement Expectancy Theory implies a larger positive effect than information-processing theory. The theories differ dramatically in their predictions of intensity effects at high discrepancy. Information processing theory predicts a positive correlation between intensity and attitude change for low-ego-involved receivers, and a negative correlation between intensity and attitude change for high-ego-involved receivers. Reinforcement Expectancy Theory predicts a negative correlation between intensity and attitude change regardless of ego-involvement.

Language Expectancy Propositions

As we noted in our discussion of counterarguing, language intensity influences perceived message discrepancy by affecting receiver perceptions of the source's position. High-intensity language should make a message appear more discrepant; low-intensity language should make a message appear less discrepant. Consider the role of receiver expectations within reinforcement theory.

If a receiver has an expectation about the position the source will take, then a message that is less discrepant than expected will be viewed more positively than a message that meets expectations. This would be a positive violation of expectations, because the message will be more pleasant for receivers than was expected. The theory predicts that positive violations of expectations enhance attitude change (Burgoon, 1989; Burgoon et al., 1975). If a receiver has an expectation about the position the source will take, then a message that is more discrepant than expected will be viewed more negatively than a message that meets expectations. This would be a negative violation of expectations because the message will be less pleasant for receivers than was expected. The theory predicts that negative violations of expectations inhibit attitude change.

If a receiver does not have any expectations or the message is as discrepant as expected, then there will be no violation of expectations, so receiver expectations will not influence attitude change. Instead, attitude change will be as predicted by traditional reinforcement theory (see Equation 2).

Burgoon et al. (1975) extended their basic reinforcement model to include two types of expectancy effects. They believed that receivers have expectations of a source's language use that are tied to source gender and premessage source credibility. Burgoon et al. hypothesized that source gender and premessage credibility moderate the effect of language intensity on attitude change. Expectancy theory (Burgoon, 1989; Burgoon et al., 1975) predicts that greater intensity will enhance attitude change for high credibility sources and inhibit attitude change for low credibility sources. The theory also predicts that greater intensity will enhance attitude change for male sources and inhibit attitude change for female sources.

METHOD

The procedures used in the meta-analysis followed those recommended by Hunter and Schmidt (1989). The correlation was used to express the strength of relation between intensity variables and receiver evaluations of message, source, and topic. All parameters were weighted by study sample size. We calculated the standard deviation of the correlation based on the observed variance in the set of correlations uncorrected for sampling error, the standard deviation of the correlation based on the estimated population variance corrected for sampling error, and a chi-square test for significant variation within the set of studies. The chi-square (χ^2) test is a powerful means of testing the hypothesis that variance within a set of correlations is due to sampling error.

An exhaustive literature review was conducted to locate studies of language intensity effects. References from obtained studies, indices of dissertation abstracts, and electronic information searches were used to identify relevant articles, conference papers, dissertations, and theses. For the sake of consistency across studies, the uncorrected correlations were used in the meta-analyses. Few authors in the intensity literature reported the reliability of their attitude measures, yet unreliable dependent measures probably did not substantially attenuate the correlation between intensity and receiver attitudes in the studies reviewed.[3]

The effect of manipulated intensity on the perceived dynamism of the source's presentation, perceived message clarity, perceived source competence (or expertise), perceived source trustworthiness (or character), and perceived source liking (attitude toward source) was examined. The effect of perceived intensity on the same dependent variables was also calculated, although the number of studies was substantially smaller than for manipulated intensity.

Table 6.1 identifies the studies used to determine the correlation between manipulated intensity and attitude change in the various moderator conditions. In the process of calculating correlations between manipulated language intensity and attitude change, we uncovered two types of studies.

---

[3]Hamilton and Thompson (1994) included 10 items in their attitude scale. Kochevar (1967) and McEwen and Greenberg (1970) both used 4 attitude items. Carmichael and Cronkhite (1965) used 16 semantic differential items to measure attitudes. The lowest reliability for a single attitude measure item in a similar experiment, Hamilton et al. (1990), was .71. Using this worst-case estimate of single-item reliabilities, and applying that value to the Spearman-Brown formula, it is possible to calculate the approximate reliability of a 4- and 16-item attitude scale. To achieve a scale reliability of .90 or higher, the average single item reliabilities would have to be above .70 for a 4-item scale and above .38 for a 15-item scale. These calculations suggest that even the four-item attitude scales used by Kochevar (1967) and McEwen and Greenberg (1970) had reliabilities of .90 or higher. The Carmichael and Cronkhite (1965) attitude scale most certainly achieved high reliability.

Table 6.1. Studies Used for Estimating the Effect of Manipulated Intensity on Receiver Attitudes by Condition.

	Message discrepancy	Ego-involvement	Premessage credibility	Source gender	Irrelevant stress
Lomas (1940)	both	low			
Bowers (1963) college	congruent		high		
Bowers(1963) peace corps	congruent		high		
Bowers (1963) fashion	congruent		high	female	
Bowers (1963) education	discrepant	high	high		
Carmichael & Cronkhite (1965)					both
Kochevar (1967)	congruent				
Baseheart (1969)	congruent		high		
McEwen & Greenberg (1970)	discrepant	low	high		
Cagle (1972, fashion)	congruent		high	female	
Cagle (1972, education)	discrepant	high	high		
Marks (1972)	congruent				
Burgoon et al. (1975, E1)	discrepant	high		both	
Burgoon et al. (1975, E2)	discrepant	high			both
Burgoon et al (1975, E3)	discrepant	high	both		
Williams & Goss (1975)	discrepant	high			
Bradac et al. (1979)	congruent			female	
Hamilton et al. (1990)	both	low	both	both	both
Hamilton et al. (1991, E1)	both	low	both	both	
Hamilton et al. (1992, E1)	both	low	high		
Hamilton & Stewart (1993)	congruent		high	both	
Hamilton & Thompson (1994) parochial schools	both	low	both		
Hamilton & Thompson (1994) segregation	both	low	both		

Some contained moderator variables that allowed us to calculate separate effects per moderator condition. Others fixed the moderator variable at a specific level. For instance, receivers could be placed in either attitude-congruent or attitude-discrepant conditions in some experiments. In other experiments, insufficient information was available for classifying receivers by discrepancy condition, so all receivers were classified according to pretest data that estimated how discrepant the population in general was from the source's position. Similarly, receivers may have been presented with either a high- or low-credibility source in an experiment. This allowed the calculation of separate effects for the high- and low-credibility source for that study. Other experiments may have fixed the source's credibility at a high, moderate, or low level based on pretest results. Still other experiments may not have manipulated credibility at all.

We used intensity marker density as a measure of message strength. Intensity effects should be greater for the high-density message than for the low-density message. In the studies on which our meta-analysis was based, separate analyses based on positive and negative postmessage source evaluations (for example, competent vs. incompetent source) were not generally available, so premessage evaluations of source had to be used instead. Finally, messages were considered *attitude congruent* if they were low in discrepancy, or *attitude discrepant* if they were high in discrepancy.

RESULTS

We began by examining the effect of intensity marker density on receiver perceptions of language intensity and extremity of source position. The results of this analysis would be used in the causal process model and the attitude prediction model. Marker density should moderate the size of the effect of manipulated intensity on perceived intensity, extremity of position, and subsequent variables in the causal chain described in Figure 6.1. Marker density should also moderate message strength, the multiplier of message discrepancy (see Equation 1, Chapter 1, this volume).

The second section of the meta-analysis tested the links in the source attitude model shown in Figure 6.1. We determined the effect of manipulated and perceived intensity on receivers' perceptions of dynamism, message clarity, source competence, source trustworthiness, and source liking. We then revised the causal model proposed in Figure 6.1 to reflect our meta-analytic results.

In the third section of the meta-analysis, we tested the predictions of information processing theory—that message strength (density), source evaluation (premessage credibility), message discrepancy (attitude congruent messages or attitude discrepant messages), and counterargument (ego-involvement, cognitive stress) would moderate the impact of manipulated intensity on receiver attitudes. We also tested the Reinforcement Expectancy Theory proposition related to source gender.

Intensity Manipulations

The effect of intensity marker density on receivers' message perceptions was examined first. Marker density was determined by counting the number of intensity markers per total words in the persuasive message. The ratio, or percentage of intensity markers per total words, was calculated for each message. Table 6.2 displays marker density for studies in the meta-analysis. The average density was .18, or approximately one intensity marker per five words in the message.

Perceived Intensity.

The correlation between manipulated intensity (high versus low) and perceived intensity was calculated where possible (see Table 6.2). Across studies, the average correlation between manipulated and perceived intensity was moderate (r = .36) but heterogeneous. The size of the correlation between manipulated and perceived intensity was correlated with marker density, $r(7) = .82$. We regressed the correlation between manipulated and perceived intensity on marker density. Once the effect of density was partialled out, 44% of the variance in the residuals was due to sampling error ($SD_\rho = 07$, $\chi^2 = 15.94$, $df = 6$, $p > .01$).

Extremity of Source Position.

The correlation between manipulated intensity (high versus low) and perceived extremity of source position (also known as assertion intensity) was calculated where possible (see Table 6.2). Across studies, the average correlation between manipulated intensity and extremity of position was moderate (r = .37) but heterogeneous across studies. The size of the correlation between manipulated and extremity of position was correlated with marker density, $r(5) = .73$. We regressed the correlation between manipulated intensity and extremity of position on marker density. Once the effect of density was partialled out, 57% of the variance in the residuals was due to sampling error ($SD_\rho = .07$, $\chi^2 = 8.88$, $df = 4$, $p > .05$).

Table 6.2. Marker Density and Strength of the Intensity Manipulations.

	N	Marker Density	Perceived Intensity	Extremity of source position
Bowers (1963)	360	.08		
Carmichael & Cronkhite (1965)	36	.08		
Kochevar (1967)	55	.09		.35
Baseheart (1969)	95	.14	.49	
McEwen & Greenberg (1970)	111	.09	.29	
Cagle (1972)	80	.08		
Marks (1972)	192	.09		
Goss & Williams (1973)	99	.14		
Burgoon et al. (1975, E1)	108	.12		.13
Burgoon et al. (1975, E2)	14	.12		.15
Burgoon et al. (1975, E3)	99	.12		
Williams & Goss (1975)	108	.14	.29	
Bradac et al. (1979)	183	.12		
Hamilton et al. (1990)	287	.24	.39	
Hamilton et al. (1991, E1)	496	.18	.29	
Hamilton et al. (1992, E1)	282	.19	.12	
Hamilton & Stewart. (1993)	386	.53	.62	.49
Hamilton & Thompson (1994)	107	.06		.46
Weighted average *r*		.18	.36	.37
Total *N* across studies (*TN*)		3229	1765	799
Number of studies (*k*)		18	7	5
Observed *SD*		.12	.16	.16
Estimated population *SD*			.16	.14
90% best estimate			.55	.56
90% worst estimate			.19	.16
Variance due to sampling error			20%	11%
χ^2 homogeneity test		--	62.92*	26.03*

Note. *$p < .001$.

Marker density was a substantial moderator of the effect of manipulated intensity on perceived intensity and extremity of source position. However, marker power and idiosyncratic decoding responses could account for as much as 56% of the residual variance in perceived intensity and 43% of the residual variance in extremity of position.

Test of the Causal Process Model

Estimates of the effect of intensity on the perceived dynamism of the source's presentation can be found in Table 6.3. The effect of manipulated

Table 6.3. Correlation of Intensity with Perceived Source Dynamism and Perceived Message Clarity.

Intensity Variable	N	Dynamism		Clarity	
		Manipulated	Perceived	Manipulated	Perceived
Kochevar (1967)	55	.21		.18	
Baseheart (1969)	95	.61		.18	
McEwen & Greenberg (1970)	111	.27	.73	.25	.78
Marks (1972)	192	.09			
Hamilton et al. (1990)	287			.07	.39
Hamilton et al. (1991, E1)	496			.09	.27
Hamilton et al. (1992, E1)	282	.00	.49		
Hamilton & Stewart (1993)	386	.41	.71		
Hamilton & Thompson (1994) parochial	107	.41			
Hamilton & Thompson (1994) segregation	107	.38			
Weighted average r		.27	.63	.13	.37
Total N across studies		1335	777	1152	894
Number of studies		8	3	5	3
Observed *SD*		.19	.11	.06	.16
Estimated population *SD*		.18	.1	0	.16
90% best estimate		.5	.76		.57
90% worst estimate		.04	.5		.17
Variance due to sampling error		14%	11%	100%	9%
χ^2 homogeneity test		56.53*	25.26*		31.85*

Note. *$p < .001$

intensity on the perceived dynamism was moderate (r = .27), but heterogeneous across studies. According to the model shown in Figure 6.1, the size of the correlation between manipulated intensity and dynamism should be a product of the manipulated-perceived intensity correlation and the perceived intensity-dynamism correlation. In fact, we found that the larger the correlation between manipulated and perceived intensity, the larger the correlation between manipulated intensity and dynamism: $r(6) = .88$. We regressed the manipulated intensity-dynamism correlation on the manipulated-perceived intensity correlation. Once the effect of the manipulated-perceived intensity correlation had been partialled out, sampling error explained 45% of the variance in the residuals of this regression: $SD_\rho = .08$, $\chi^2(3) = 8.93$, $p = .03$. Although the size of the correlation between manipulated and perceived intensity was a substantial moderator of the effect of manipulated intensity on dynamism, 55% of the residual variance may have been due to other factors, such as the correlation between perceived intensity and dynamism.

Next, we examined the effect of perceived intensity on perceived dynamism. The size of the correlation between perceived intensity and dynamism appeared to be a function of the size of the correlation between manipulated intensity and perceived intensity. There was a strong relationship between the two sets of correlations: $r(3) = .85$. We regressed the perceived intensity-dynamism correlation on the manipulated-perceived intensity correlation. Sampling error explained 100% of the variance in the residuals of this regression. If the correlation between perceived intensity and dynamism is a function of the strength of the intensity manipulation (size of the correlation between manipulated and perceived intensity), then this would increase variance in the correlation between manipulated intensity and dynamism.

Perceived Message Clarity.

Estimates of the effect of intensity on perceived message clarity can be found in Table 6.3. Manipulated intensity slightly increased perceived message clarity (r = .13), an effect that was homogeneous across studies. The effect of perceived intensity on clarity was less uniform. The perceived intensity-clarity correlation was regressed on the manipulated-perceived intensity correlation. Sampling error explained 56% of the variance in the residuals: $SD_\rho = .05$ $\chi^2(2) = 5.37$, $p > .05$. Although the size of the correlation between manipulated and perceived intensity was a substantial moderator of the effect of perceived intensity on clarity, 44% of the residual variance may have been due to other factors, such as the mediating effects of attention and comprehension.

The Effect of Language Intensity on Evaluations of Source.

We began by testing the proposition that message discrepancy moderates the effect of manipulated intensity on perceived competence as proposed by Bradac et al. (1979). If this proposition were true, it would have implications for the testing of the proposed antagonistic effects model shown in Figure 6.1. In eight studies, receivers were classified into attitude congruent or attitude discrepant conditions, then the correlation between manipulated intensity and perceived competence was calculated for the congruent and discrepant conditions. In only one of the eight studies, Goss and Williams (1973), did the data approximate the pattern predicted by Bradac et al. The pattern in the Goss and Williams study was most likely due to sampling error.[4] Thus, the proposition that message discrepancy moderates the effect of manipulated intensity on perceived source competence and trustworthiness failed.

Next, we looked at the main effect of language intensity on competence, trustworthiness and liking for studies manipulating language intensity (and not vocal intensity). Estimated effects from these studies can be found in Table 6.4. Manipulated language intensity had no impact on competence ($r = 0$), with homogeneous effects across studies. However, perceived intensity did enhance competence ($r = .33$), with homogeneous effects across studies.

Manipulated intensity slightly reduced trustworthiness, ($r = -.04$), with homogeneous effects across studies. The effect of perceived intensity on trustworthiness was heterogeneous across studies. If competence is antecedent to trustworthiness, as shown in Figure 6.1, then the size of the effect of perceived intensity on trustworthiness might depend on the size of the effect of perceived intensity on competence. In fact, the two sets of correlations (perceived intensity with competence, and perceived intensity with trustworthiness) were highly correlated: $r(5) = .78$. We regressed the perceived intensity-trustworthiness correlation on the perceived intensity-competence correlation. Sampling error explained 53% of the variance in the residuals: $SD_\rho = .05$ $\chi^2(4) = 9.42, p > .05$.

Manipulated language intensity slightly reduced receivers' liking of the source ($r = -.07$), with sampling error explaining 100% of the variance across studies. The effect of perceived intensity on liking ($r = .02$) was heterogeneous across studies. If trustworthiness is antecedent to liking, as

[4]Only by using a one-tailed significance test on the Goss and Williams data could the correlation for the congruent condition be argued to be marginally more positive than the correlation for the discrepant condition ($z = 1.71, p = .044$). If any correction is made to adjust the alpha level downward for the number of tests conducted, then this study no longer shows a significant difference.

Table 6.4. Correlation of Intensity With Evaluations of Source.

	N	Competence		Trustworthiness		Liking	
Intensity Variable		Manipulated	Perceived	Manipulated	Perceived	Manipulated	Perceived
Kochevar (1967)	55	.17		-.14			
Baseheart (1969)	95	.11		-.17			
McEwen & Greenberg (1970)	111	-.11	.37	-.04	0.28		
Cagle (1972) fashion	40	.15		-.02			
Cagle (1972) education	40	-.03		.09			
Marks (1972)	192	-.06		-.06			
Williams & Goss (1975)	108	-.11		-.28			
Burgoon et al. (1975, E1)	142	.02		.11			
Burgoon et al. (1975, E3)	99	-.31		-.03		-.09	
Bradac et al. (1979)	183	.08		-.08		-.05	
Hamilton et al. (1990)	287	-.06	.29	-.06	.12	-.13	-.07
Hamilton et al. (l991, E1)	496	.04	.34	.02	.11	-.07	-.15
Hamilton et al. (1992, E1)	282	.05	.37	.05	.4	-.01	.41
Hamilton & Stewart (1993)	386	-.01	.29	-.07	.07		
Weighted average *r*		0	.33	-.04	.17	-.07	.02
Total *N* across studies		2516	1562	2516	1562	1347	1065
Number of studies		14	5	14	5	5	3
Observed *SD*		.09	.03	.08	.12	.04	.24
Estimated population *SD*		.05	0	.04	.11	0	.23
90% best estimate		.06		.01	.3		.32
90% worst estimate		-.07		-.08	.03		-.28
Variance due to sampling error		69%	100%	82%	21%	100%	5%
χ^2 homogeneity test		20.17		17.07	23.89*		59.43*

Note. *p < .001

shown in Figure 6.1, then the size of the effect of perceived intensity on liking might depend on the size of the effect of perceived intensity on trustworthiness. In fact, the two sets of correlations covaried almost perfectly: $r(3) = .99$. We regressed the perceived intensity-liking correlation on the perceived intensity-trustworthiness correlation. Sampling error explained 100% of the variance in the residuals.

The Effect of Vocal Intensity on Evaluations of Source.

We tested the hypothesis that the presence of vocal intensity would moderate the effect of manipulated intensity on perceived source competence, trustworthiness, and liking, such that vocal intensity plus language intensity would lead to more negative source evaluation than language intensity alone. In the Hamilton and Thompson (1994) study, the message manipulation varied both vocal and verbal intensity. In all other studies, only verbal intensity was varied.

Manipulated language intensity plus vocal intensity reduced competence: $r = -.16$ ($N = 107$, $k = 2$), with little variance across studies ($r \pm .04$). The effect of language intensity alone on competence ($r = 0$) was less negative than the effect of the language and vocal intensity manipulation on competence. Manipulated language intensity plus vocal intensity reduced trustworthiness: $r = -.44$ ($N = 107$, $k = 2$), with little variance across studies ($r \pm .01$). The effect of language intensity alone on trustworthiness ($r = -.04$) was less negative than the effect of language and vocal intensity on trustworthiness. Manipulated language intensity plus vocal intensity substantially reduced liking: $r = -.38$ ($N = 107$, $k = 2$) with little variance across studies ($r \pm .02$). The effect of language intensity alone on liking ($r = -.07$) was less negative than the effect of language and vocal intensity on liking. Thus, for perceived competence, trustworthiness, and liking, the addition of vocal intensity to the intensity manipulation resulted in additional source derogation.

Summary and Integration of the Causal Model.

Based on the results of our meta-analyses, we estimated the correlations among the following variables: manipulated intensity, perceived intensity, extremity of source position, perceived dynamism, perceived message clarity, perceived source competence, perceived trustworthiness, and perceived liking.[5] We used values from Hamilton (in press) to estimate the correlations

---

[5]Based on the findings of our meta-analysis, we excluded the two Hamilton and Thompson (1994) studies manipulating vocal intensity when estimating the effect of manipulated intensity on perceived competence, trustworthiness, and liking. Although the Hamilton (1989) study examined obscenity effects, the correlations among the source evaluation variables in that study were homogeneous with the correlations from the intensity studies.

between dynamism, clarity, competence, trustworthiness, and liking. Four data sets (TN = 825) were used to estimate the correlations between dynamism and competence, competence and trustworthiness, and dynamism and trustworthiness: Hamilton (1989), Hamilton and Stewart (1993), Hamilton and Thompson (1994), and the combined Kochevar-McEwen-Greenberg data (Kochevar, 1967; McEwen & Greenberg, 1970). The three correlations were homogeneous across studies: dynamism and competence (r = .36, SD_ρ = .03), competence and trustworthiness (r = .67, SD_ρ = .04), and dynamism and trustworthiness (r = .19, SD_ρ = .07).

A number of correlations were based on but one or two studies. The correlations involving liking were based on the Hamilton and Thompson (1994) data, and the Hamilton (1989) data: dynamism and liking (r = .12, SD_ρ = 0), competence and liking (r = .67, SD_ρ = 0), and trustworthiness and liking (r = .78, SD_ρ = .06). The correlations involving extremity of source position were taken from Hamilton and Stewart (1993): source position and dynamism (r = .19), source position and competence (r = -.19), and source position and trustworthiness (r = -.19). The correlations involving message clarity were based on the combined Kochevar-McEwen-Greenberg data: clarity and dynamism (r = .63), clarity and competence (r = .47), and clarity and trustworthiness (r = .36). Unfortunately, two of the correlations involving message clarity were not available: clarity with source position, and clarity with liking.

Next, we estimated the size of the paths for the model shown in Figure 6.1. The resulting model is shown in Figure 6.2. The only discrepancy between the proposed model of Figure 6.1 and the obtained model in Figure 6.2 was that manipulated intensity did not have a direct, negative effect on perceived source trustworthiness.

Predicting Attitude Toward Topic

If information processing theory is correct, then message discrepancy, premessage source credibility, and marker density should moderate the effect of language intensity on receiver attitude toward topic. When the message is attitude-congruent, the source has low credibility, or marker density is low, intensity should have little if any effect on attitude change. When the message is attitude-discrepant, premessage source credibility is high, or marker density is high, intensity should have an effect on attitude change; the direction of that effect will depend on receiver counterarguing—intensity will enhance persuasion for low-ego-involved receivers, but inhibit persuasion for high-ego-involved receivers. A strong, discrepant message from a credible source would constitute a threat to receivers involved with their premes-

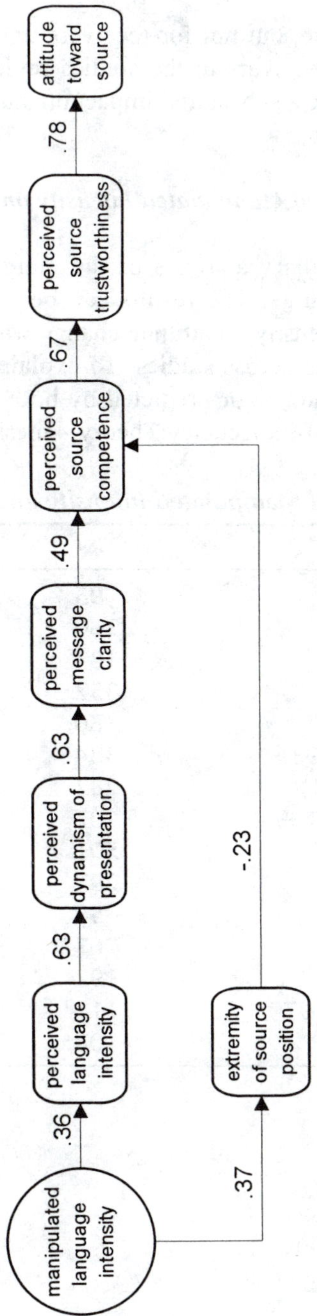

Figure 6.2. Obtained model of the effect of language intensity on attitude toward source

sage position on the topic, but not for receivers uninvolved with their pre-message position. The receivers in the studies reviewed were students, so any issue that would have a substantial impact on student lifestyles had been coded as highly involving.

The Main Effect of Manipulated Intensity on Attitude Change.

We conducted a preliminary analysis of the main effect of manipulated intensity on attitude change. The results can be found in Table 6.5. The effect of manipulated intensity on attitude change was approximately zero ($r = .02$), but heterogeneous across studies. To explain this heterogeneity, we turned first to the key moderator predicted by both information processing theory and Reinforcement Expectancy Theory—message discrepancy.

Table 6.5. Correlation of Manipulated Intensity and Attitude Change.

Study	*N*	*r*
Baseheart (1969	95	.07
Bowers (1963)	360	-.08
Bradac et al. (1979)	183	.04
Burgoon et al. (1975)	352	-.07
Cagle (1972)	80	-.01
Hamilton & Steward (1993)	384	.18
Hamilton et al. (1992, E1)	282	.02
Hamilton & Thompson (1994)	107	.05
Hamilton et al. (1991, E1)	501	.09
Hamilton et al. (1990)	287	.02
Kochevar (1967)	55	.04
Lomas (1940)	767	-.05
Marks (1972)	192	.2
McEwen & Greenberg (1970)	111	.09
Williams & Goss (1975)	108	-.35
Weighted Average *r*		.02
Total *N* across studies		3864
Observed *SD*		.11
Estimated population *SD*		.09
90% best credibility value		.13
90% worst credibility value		-.1
Variance due to sampling error		34%
χ^2 Homogeneity test		44.36*

Note. $^{*}p < .001$

Message Discrepancy.

For attitude-congruent messages, manipulated intensity had no impact on attitude change (r = .00, TN = 1831, k = 11), with the variance across studies explained by sampling error (SD_ρ = .04, χ^2 = 14.17, p > .05). For attitude-discrepant messages, the effect of manipulated intensity on attitude change was not so homogeneous. When receivers had high involvement with the topic, intensity inhibited persuasion (r = -.19, TN = 680, k = 6), but the variance could not be accounted for by sampling error alone (SD_ρ = .09, χ^2 = 11.83, p < .05). When receivers had low involvement with the topic, intensity enhanced attitude change, (r = .11, TN = 1820, k = 11), but the variance could not be accounted for by sampling error alone (SD_ρ = .07, χ^2 = 18.85, p < .05)

Premessage Source Credibility as a Moderator Variable.

Source credibility might explain much of the variance in the two discrepant message conditions. First, we considered discrepant messages delivered to high-involvement receivers. Only one of these studies allowed classification of receivers into low- and high-credibility source conditions—Burgoon et al. (1975, Experiment 3). In the low-credibility condition of that study, intensity had no impact on attitude change (r = .01, n = 48). The high-credibility condition from Burgoon et al. (Experiment 3) was combined with the remaining studies in the *discrepant message*-from-*credible source*-to-*involved receivers* condition. For those studies, manipulated intensity had a negative effect on receiver attitudes (r = -.20, TN = 632, k = 6), with the variance explained by sampling error (SD_ρ = .08, χ^2 = 10.22, p >.05).

Next, we considered discrepant messages delivered to low-involvement receivers. For the *low-credibility* source, intensity had no impact on receiver attitudes (r = .03, TN = 303, k = 4) with the variance accounted for by sampling error (SD_ρ = .03, χ^2 = 4.24, p > .05). For the *high-credibility* source, intensity had a positive effect on receiver attitudes (r = .15, TN = 949, k = 6), with sampling error explaining 100% of the variance across studies. The effects observed for the low credibility source delivering a discrepant message did not differ for the high- (.01) or low- (.03) involvement receivers, and neither was different from a correlation of zero. The effects for the high-credibility source delivering a discrepant message were strikingly different for the high- (.15) and low- (-.20) involvement receivers.

To summarize, at low message discrepancy or low credibility, manipulated intensity has no impact on receiver attitude toward topic, regardless of receiver involvement. For the credible source delivering a discrepant message, the effect of manipulated intensity on attitudes depends on receiver involvement—intensity inhibits persuasion for high-involvement receivers, and enhances persuasion for low-involvement receivers. The moderating effects of message discrepancy, source credibility, and involvement are shown in Figure 6.3. Thus, there were two conditions that showed an intensity effect—a credible source delivering a discrepant message to involved receivers (the inhibition condition), and a credible source delivering a discrepant message to uninvolved receivers (the enhancement condition).

Message Strength as a Moderator Variable.

The information processing model predicts that the size of the effects in the inhibition and enhancement conditions depended on message strength (intensity marker density). We examined the inhibition condition first. Unfortunately, there were no intensity studies in which a credible source delivered a discrepant, *high-density* message to involved receivers. All such studies used low-density messages. Next, we examined the enhancement condition. There were six studies in which a credible source delivered a discrepant message to uninvolved receivers. The effect size across the six studies was homogeneous, so there was little moderating effect of density. Categorizing the studies into high- and low-density subsets and then comparing their average correlations showed that indeed there was no difference between the two groups.

Message-Irrelevant Cognitive Stress as a Moderator.

In view of the fact that receiver involvement with topic moderated the impact of manipulated intensity on attitude change for high-discrepancy messages, it was necessary to control for topic involvement when testing the cognitive stress moderator proposition. Only those studies that manipulated message-irrelevant stress on a particular topic, allowing a direct comparison of relaxed and stressed receivers, were used in the analysis. This permitted the most generous test of the stress as moderator proposition. Among relaxed receivers, manipulated intensity enhanced attitude change ($r = .11$, $TN = 218$, $k = 3$) with 100% of the variance explained by sampling error. Among stressed receivers, manipulated intensity inhibited attitude change ($r = -.19$, $TN = 213$, $k = 3$), with approximately zero variance across studies ($SD_\rho = .01$, $\chi^2 = 5.13$, $p > .05$). The findings for the relaxed and stressed receiver correlations were in the direction proposed by information processing theory.

Source Gender as Moderator.

As with the test of the receiver stress moderator proposition, it was necessary to control for topic when testing the gender moderator proposition.

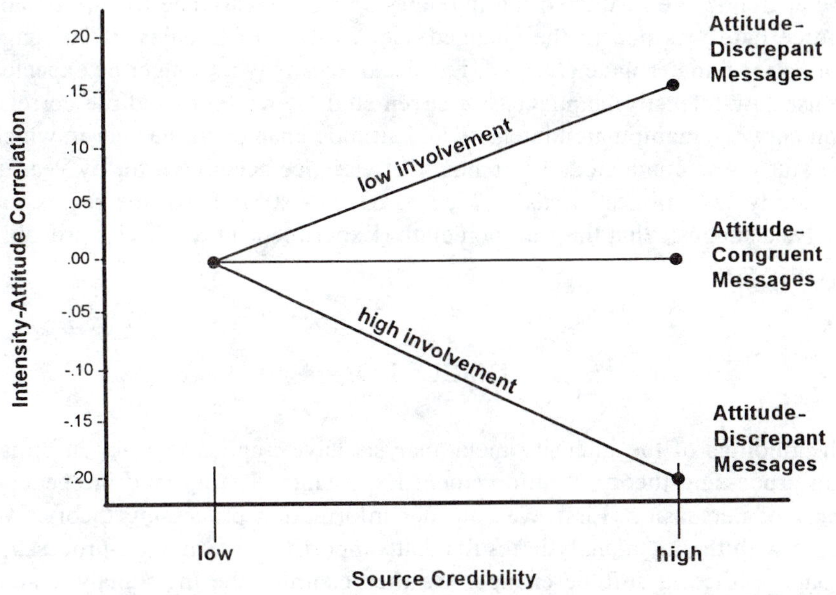

Figure 6.3. Effect of manipulated intensity on receiver attitudes by condition

Only those studies that manipulated source gender on a particular topic, allowing a direct comparison of male and female sources, were used in the analysis. This permitted a generous test of the expectancy theory proposition. For male sources, manipulated intensity increased receiver attitude change ($r = .14$, $TN = 670$, $k = 4$) with 100% of the variance across studies explained by sampling error. For female sources, the effect of manipulated intensity on attitude change ($r = .03$, $TN = 651$, $k = 4$) showed marginal heterogeneity across studies (SD_ρ = 09, $\chi^2 = 9.51$, $p = .02$). The study by Burgoon et al. (1975, Experiment 1) was identified as an outlier. This study was excluded and the reduced set of studies examined for homogeneity. For the male sources, the effect of intensity on attitude change was again homogeneous ($r = .14$, $TN = 602$, $k = 3$) with 100% of the variance explained by sampling error. For the female sources, the effect of intensity on attitude change was also homogeneous ($r = .07$, $TN = 575$, $k = 3$, $SD_\rho = .03$, $\chi^2 = 3.53$, $p > .05$). The correlations for the male and female sources were within sampling error of one another.

Changed Norms Hypothesis. Was the Burgoon et al. (1975, Experiment 1) finding an outlier produced by Type I error as the preceding analysis suggests, or was it an important anchor point revealing a weak social trend? We evaluated the hypothesis that the variance for the female source data was due to the changed socialization of females. If language norms for females have changed, female sources may no longer be expected to use low-intensity language. For seven studies, we regressed the correlation between manipulated intensity and attitude change on the year in which the study was conducted. The amount of variance accounted for by year of the study was modest ($beta = .27$, $t = .63$, $p > .05$). Thus, the regression analysis suggests that the Burgoon et al. (Experiment 1) result was probably a Type I error.

DISCUSSION

The findings of the intensity meta-analysis have implications for information processing theory, Reinforcement Expectancy Theory, and the general study of persuasion. First, we consider information processing theory. We begin with the meta-analytic results that support the information-processing model predicting attitude change. We then examine the meta-analytic support for the causal process model from information processing theory. The results of the meta-analyses are consistent with findings from primary studies that show very strong support for the theory.

Second, we consider Reinforcement Expectancy Theory. The meta-analytic results did not support the language expectancy propositions, nor the underlying basic reinforcement model. Analysis of the evidence from primary studies shows the same lack of support for the theory as the findings from the meta-analysis. Finally, we consider alternatives to standard meta-analytic procedures and show that they yield incorrect conclusions.

Information Processing Theory

Attitude Change Prediction Model.

Language intensity influenced attitude change only for discrepant messages delivered by credible sources. Messages from low-credibility sources had no effect on attitude change. The moderating effect of credibility would likely have been even larger had postmessage credibility data been available for use as a moderator variable in place of premessage credibility.

Message Discrepancy. Information processing theory predicts that there will be more attitude change in response to high-discrepancy messages than low-discrepancy messages. Message discrepancy should moderate the effect of intensity on attitude change because intensity is primarily a multiplier of change. Low-discrepancy messages induce little change and hence provide little opportunity for an intensity effect to appear. This prediction was borne out by the meta-analysis for high- and low-discrepancy messages. For low-discrepancy (attitude-congruent) messages, the average intensity effect was zero.

In many studies, language intensity increases message discrepancy by increasing the perceived extremity of position taken by the source. Attitude change should be an increasing monotonic function of discrepancy for receivers low to moderate in counterargument. Receiver ego-involvement should increase counterargument (see Equation 2, Chapter 1, this volume). For receivers prone to counterargue, attitude change should be a nonmonotonic function of discrepancy, such that maximum attitude change occurs at moderate discrepancy. As a result, when a credible source delivers a discrepant message, intensity enhances attitude change if receivers are low in ego-involvement with topic, and inhibits attitude change if receivers are high in ego-involvement with topic, as shown in Figure 6.3. Marker density did not magnify the pattern of effects shown in Figure 6.3, although the lack of studies in one of the conditions rendered the test inconclusive.

Cognitive Stress. It was also predicted that the high-stress conditions would be radically different than other attitude change conditions. This prediction was also borne out: The intensity effect was negative for the high-stress conditions ($r = -.19$). The finding that intensity reduces attitude change in the high irrelevant stress conditions is consistent with the predictions of the McGuire (1968a, 1968b) two-factor model based on information processing theory (see Chapter 1, this volume). According to the two-factor model, cognitive stress inhibits comprehension and counterarguing. Thus, relaxed receivers are likely to comprehend message content, but will also be prone to counterargue the message; stressed receivers are less likely to comprehend message content, but are less likely to counterargue the message. These two factors combine to predict maximal attitude change at moderate cognitive stress.

Among relaxed receivers, intensity should increase stress from a low to moderate level, enhancing persuasion. Among moderately stressed receivers, intensity should increase stress from a moderate to high level, inhibiting persuasion. In the meta-analysis, intensity increased attitude change in the low-stress conditions that did not preclude persuasion; that is, when a discrepant message was delivered by a credible source to uninvolved receivers. In the high-stress conditions, intensity decreased attitude change.

In summary, the message discrepancy, source credibility, ego-involvement, and stress moderators predicted by information processing theory explained the variability in the results of the meta-analysis that were not due to sampling error. In the primary studies that have tested the information processing prediction model (Hamilton et al., 1990; Hamilton & Stewart, 1993; Hamilton & Thompson, 1994), attitude change has been shown to be a multiplicative function of message discrepancy, postmessage source evaluation, message strength, and counterarguing. The Multiple Correlation values for the attitude change equations in these studies average above .60.

The Causal Process Model.

The proposed process model shown in Figures 6.1 and 6.2 was derived from information processing theory. The density of intensity markers in the message moderated the effect of manipulated language intensity manipulations on perceived intensity and extremity of source position. The findings suggest that except when intensity marker density is unnaturally high, much of the variance in perceived intensity and extremity of source position depends on marker power and the differential decoding ability of receivers.

The model shown in Figure 6.2 depicts a sequence in which perceived intensity triggers a positively linked chain beginning with perceived dynamism and ending with liking of source. The increased excitement from emotionally intense language increases the perceived dynamism of the presentation. Dynamism enhances perceived message clarity. This effect is thought to occur because dynamism increases receiver attention to the message, attention to the message increases comprehension, and comprehension results in greater clarity (Hamilton, in press; McGuire, 1969). Message clarity, in turn, increases perceived source competence. The more competent the source's performance, the greater the believability or trustworthiness of the source. Finally, as information is integrated into existing knowledge structures, trustworthiness improves perceived liking of the source (attitude toward source).

The model shown in Figure 6.2 depicts one negative effect of intensity on receiver evaluations of source. The negative effect of intensity on postmessage source competence, mediated by the perceived extremity of source position, was small. The path model based on the meta-analysis did not show a negative effect of intensity on trustworthiness as predicted in Figure 6.1. The effect of perceived intensity on trustworthiness and liking was shown to vary either directly or indirectly with the effect of perceived intensity on competence. That is, variation in the effect of perceived intensity on competence amplified variation in the effect of perceived intensity on trustworthiness and liking.

Reinforcement Expectancy Theory

Reinforcement Expectancy Theory predicts that intensity will enhance perceived source credibility for the attitude-congruent message and inhibit credibility for attitude-discrepant messages. Perceived credibility, in turn, should influence attitude change. Thus, intensity should enhance the attitude change for attitude-congruent messages and inhibit change for attitude-discrepant messages. The results of the meta-analysis disconfirmed the theory in two respects. First, message discrepancy did not moderate the effect of intensity on perceived credibility as predicted by Reinforcement Expectancy Theory. There have been two direct tests of the proposition that discrepancy moderates the effect of intensity on perceived source credibility (Hamilton et al., 1990; Hamilton & Thompson, 1994). In both studies, message discrepancy did not moderate the effect of intensity on perceived competence or perceived trustworthiness. Thus, the Reinforcement Expectancy Theory prediction failed at both the meta-analytic level and at the level of the individual study.

Second, Reinforcement Expectancy Theory could not account for the finding that intensity facilitated persuasion for the high-credibility source delivering a discrepant message to low-involvement receivers. The two language expectation propositions fared just as poorly as the reinforcement predictions in the meta-analysis. Neither premessage credibility nor source gender moderated the effect of intensity on attitude change as predicted by Reinforcement Expectancy Theory.

Premessage Credibility as a Moderator.

Expectancy theory (Burgoon, 1989; Burgoon et al., 1975) predicts that greater intensity will enhance attitude change for high-credibility sources and inhibit attitude change for low-credibility sources. Most persuasion theories, including information processing theory, predict that intensity should enhance attitude change for the high-credibility source, but have little effect for the low-credibility source. Expectancy theory is unique, however, in its prediction that intensity will inhibit attitude change for the low-credibility source. Advocates of expectancy theory cite Burgoon et al. (Experiment 3) as a key study supporting their proposition.

The Burgoon et al. (1975, Experiment 3) Study. On the attitude change measure in this study, premessage credibility did not moderate the effect of intensity on attitude change. Greater intensity had no effect on attitude change for the low credibility source (r = .01, n = 48), and slightly decreased attitude change for the high-credibility source (r = -.13, n = 51).

The two correlations are within sampling error of one another and fit the pattern predicted by Figure 6.3. The *latitude of acceptance* measure in the Burgoon et al. study *did* match the pattern predicted by expectancy theory. Should the standard attitude change results be ignored in favor of the rarely used latitude of acceptance results?

Two studies from Burgoon et al. (1975), Experiments 2 and 3, used the same high- and low-intensity messages regarding mandatory on-campus housing for students. The effect of manipulated intensity on attitude change for the low cognitive stress condition in Experiment 2 ($r = -.06$, $n = 56$) is exactly replicated by the correlation between manipulated intensity and attitude change in Experiment 3 ($r = -.06$, $N = 99$). In addition to being exactly replicated by Experiment 2, the attitude change results from Experiment 3 were consistent with the findings on the postmessage credibility measures in that study, whereas the results from the latitude of acceptance measure were not consistent with the credibility results. Thus, we could find no grounds on which to reject the results obtained on the standard attitude measure in favor of those obtained on the rarely used latitude of acceptance measure. In summary, the proposition that premessage credibility moderates the effect of intensity on attitude change was not supported by the results of Burgoon et al. (1975, Experiment 3) or at the level of meta-analysis.

Source Gender as a Moderator.

Expectancy theory proposes that source gender moderates the effect of language intensity on attitude change, such that intensity enhances persuasion for the male source, and inhibits persuasion for the female source (Burgoon, 1989; Burgoon et al., 1975). This prediction is predicated on the assumption that males use more intense language than females. If such a norm exists, then receivers may expect the male source to use more intense language and the female source to use less intense language.

Advocates of expectancy theory might construe the results of two studies as evidence for the proposition that intensity inhibits attitude change for female sources: Bowers (1963) and Burgoon et al. (1975, Experiment 1). Calculation of effect size shows that language intensity appeared to inhibit persuasion for the female source in the Burgoon et al. study ($r = -.23$, $n = 77$), but the negative intensity effect for the female source in the Bowers study was much smaller ($r = -.11$, $n = 180$). A 95% confidence interval around both correlations includes zero.

After reviewing the results across more recent tests of the gender moderator proposition, Hamilton and Stewart (1993) concluded that the Burgoon et al. finding does not replicate. They noted that Cagle (1972) was unable to replicate the Bowers (1963) finding using the same source and topic at the same university a decade later: $r(40) = .24$. The difference between the correlations in the Bowers and Cagle studies was at the margin of that expected by sampling error. Hamilton and Stewart (1993) also cited studies by Bradac, Courtright, and Bowers (1979) and Hamilton et al (1990) that found no relationship between intensity and attitude toward topic for female sources. In fact, the Hamilton and Stewart (1993) data show that intensity actually enhanced persuasion for the female source: $r(170) = .17$.

Hamilton and Stewart (1993) suggested that the unreplicability of Burgoon et al. (1975, Experiment 1) may be due to the fact that language norms have changed for female sources, such that intensity may have inhibited persuasion 20 years ago, but not any more. The Burgoon et al. finding would be the negative anchor point at the temporally distant end of this social trend. We tested for the presence of this weak social trend in intensity effects for female sources in the meta-analysis. Date of the study accounted for little of the variance across studies. More to the point, the inhibiting effect of intensity on persuasion is greater in the Burgoon et al. study (-.23), conducted in 1974, than it is for the Bowers study (-.11), conducted in 1962. Moreover, the line-of-best-fit predicts a positive correlation between intensity and attitude change for the female source beyond 1974, the year in which the Burgoon et al. (1975, Experiment 1) study was conducted. Even if the proposition were true at some earlier time, it holds no practical value for the present-day female source. The meta-analytic results indicate that the Burgoon et al. (1975, Experiment 1) result was a Type I error.

Implications for Persuasion Theory.

The results of our meta-analysis demonstrate the advantages of quantitative summaries of a research domain over narrative reviews. Previous attempts to synthesize the intensity literature based on qualitative summaries have resulted in erroneous conclusions. A number of widely held beliefs about intensity effects were dispelled by the meta-analysis: Greater intensity does not inhibit attitude change for low-credibility or female sources; message discrepancy does not moderate the impact of manipulated intensity on perceived source competence; manipulated intensity does not bolster attitude change in attitude-congruent messages, or always inhibit attitude change in attitude-discrepant messages.

The meta-analysis shows that intensity effects are explained by information processing theory but not Reinforcement Expectancy Theory. The results of individual studies also show much stronger support for information processing theory than for Reinforcement Expectancy Theory. Regardless of the level of analysis, information processing theory provides the better account of the effect of language intensity on receivers evaluations of message, source, and topic.

REFERENCES

Anderson, N. H. (1971). Integration theory and attitude change. *Psychological Review, 78*, 171-206.

Anderson, N. H. (1981). *Foundations of information integration theory.* New York: Academic Press.

Anderson, N. H. (1982). *Methods of information integration theory.* New York: Academic Press.

Baseheart, J. R. (1969). *The effects of transformation complexity and language intensity on receiver comprehension and attitude change.* Unpublished doctoral dissertation, Michigan State University, East Lansing, MI.

Bowers, J. (1963). Language intensity, social introversion and attitude change. *Speech Monographs, 30*, 345-352.

Bradac, J., Bowers, J.A., & Courtright, J. (1979). Three language variables in communication research: Intensity, immediacy and diversity. *Human Communication Research, 5*, 257-269.

Bradac, J., Bowers, J., & Courtright, J. (1980). Lexical variations in intensity, immediacy and diversity: An axiomatic theory and causal model. In R.N. St. Clair & H. Giles (Eds.), *The social and psychological contexts of language* (pp. 193-223). Hillsdale, NJ: Erlbaum.

Bradac, J., Courtright, J., & Bowers, J. (1979). Effects of intensity, immediacy and diversity on receiver attitudes toward a belief-discrepant message and its source. In H. Giles, W. P. Robinson, & P. M. Smith (Eds.), *Language: Social psychological perspectives* (pp. 217-221). Oxford: Pergamon.

Bradac, J., Hopper, R., & Weimann, J. (1989). Message effects: Retrospect and prospect. In J. Bradac (Ed.), *Message effects in communication science* (pp. 294-317). Newbury Park, CA: Sage.

Burgoon, M. (1989). Messages and persuasive effects. In J. J. Bradac (Ed.), *Message effects in communication science* (pp. 129-164). Newbury Park, CA: Sage.

Burgoon, M., & Chase, L. (1973). The effects of differential linguistic patterns in attempting to induce resistance to persuasion. *Speech Monographs, 40*, 1-7.

Burgoon, M., Jones, S., & Stewart, D. (1975). Toward a message-centered theory of persuasion: Three empirical investigations of language intensity. *Human Communication Research, 1*, 240-256.

Cagle, J. A. (1972). *Clozentropy, language intensity and attitude change.* Unpublished doctoral dissertation University of Iowa, Iowa City, IA.

Carmichael, C., & Cronkhite, G. (1965). Frustration and language intensity. *Speech Monographs, 32*, 107-111.

Goss, B., & Williams, M. L. (1973). The effects of equivocation on perceived source credibility. *Central States Speech Journal, 24*, 162-167.

Hale, J.L., & Mongeau, P.A. (1991, May). *Testing a causal model of the persuasive impact of fear appeals.* Paper presented to the International Communication Association annual convention, Chicago, IL.

Hamilton, M. (1989). Reactions to obscene language. *Communication Research Reports, 6*, 67-69.

Hamilton, M..A. (in press). The phase interfaced omnistructure underlying the processing of persuasive messages. In F. Boster & G. Barnett (Eds.), *Progress in communication science*. Norwood, NJ: Ablex.

Hamilton, M., & Costa, C. (1988, November). *The effect of opinionation in language*. Paper presented at the Speech Communication Association Convention, New Orleans, LA.

Hamilton, M.A., Hunter, J.E., & Boster, F.J. (1993). The elaboration likelihood model as a theory of attitude formation: A mathematical analysis. *Communication Theory, 3*, 50-65.

Hamilton, M., Hunter, J., & Burgoon, M. (1990). An empirical investigation of an axiomatic model of the effect of language intensity on attitude change. *Journal of Language and Social Psychology, 9*, 235-255.

Hamilton, M., Hunter, J., Stewart, B., & Zhao, H. (1991, May). *Message centered persuasion theory: Three more empirical investigations*. Paper presented at the International Communication Association annual conference, Chicago, IL.

Hamilton, M. A., & Thompson, W. L. (1994). Testing an information processing model of message intensity effects. *World Communication, 23*, 1-14.

Hamilton, M.A., & Stewart, B. (1993). Extending an information processing model of language intensity effects. *Communication Quarterly, 41*, 231-246.

Hamilton, M. A., Thompson, W. L., Daly, T., & Kukunoor, K. (1992, May). *Language intensity and attitude change on significant social issues: An information processing model*. Paper presented at the International Communication Association annual convention, Chicago, IL.

Hovland, C., Janis, I., & Kelly, H. (1953). *Communication and persuasion*. New Haven, CT: Yale University Press.

Hunter, J., Danes, J., & Cohen, S. (1984). *Mathematical models of attitude change* (Vol. 1). New York: Academic Press.

Hunter, J., & Hamilton, M. (1991). PATH [A computer program to perform least-squares path analysis]. (Program available from second author at the University of Connecticut, Storrs, CT)

Hunter, J. E., & Schmidt, F. L. (1990). *Methods of meta-analysis: Correcting error and bias in research findings*. Newbury Park, CA: Sage.

Insko, C.A. (1965). Verbal reinforcement of attitude. *Journal of Personality and Social Psychology, 2*, 261-623.

Insko, C.A., & Cialdini, R.B. (1969). A test of three interpretations of attitudinal reinforcement. *Journal of Personality and Social Psychology, 12*, 333-341.

Klingle, R. S., & Burgoon, M. (1995). Patient compliance and satisfaction with physician influence attempts: A reinforcement expectancy approach to compliance-gaining over time. *Communication Research, 22*, 148-187.

Kochevar, J. (1967). *The effects of message intensity on evaluations of the source, message and the topic*. Unpublished master's thesis, Michigan State University, East Lansing, MI.

Lomas, C.W. (1940). *An experimental study of the effect of provocative language on audience reaction to political speeches.* Unpublished doctoral dissertation, Northwestern University, Evanston, IL.

Marks, R. R. (1972). *The effects of language intensity*. Unpublished doctoral dissertation, Ohio University, Athens, OH.

McEwen, W., & Greenberg, B. (1970). The effects of message intensity on receiver evaluations of source, message and topic. *Journal of Communication, 20*, 340-350.

McGuire, W. J. (1968a). Personality and attitude change: An information-processing theory. In A. Greenwald, T. Brock, & T. Ostrom (Eds.), *Psychological foundations of attitude* (pp. 171-196). New York: Academic Press.

McGuire, W. J. (1968b). Personality and social influence. In E. Borgatta & W. Lambert (Eds.), *Handbook of social psychology* (2nd ed., pp. 136-314). Reading MA: Addison-Wesley.

McGuire, W. (1969). The nature of attitudes and attitude change. In G. Lindzey & E. Aronson (Eds.), *The handbook of social psychology* (2nd ed., Vol. 3, pp. 136-314). Reading, MA: Addison-Wesley.

McGuire, W. (1989). Theoretical foundations of campaigns. In R. Rice & C. Atkin (Eds.), *Public communication campaigns* (pp. 43-65). Newbury Park, CA: Sage.

Williams, M. L., & Goss, B. (1975). Equivocation: Character insurance. *Human Communication Research, 1*, 265-270.

7

Forewarning and Persuasion

William L. Benoit
University of Missouri-Columbia

Communication scholars generally accept the assumption that one's expectations constitute an important influence on communication generally, and on persuasion specifically. This study investigates the effect of a particular type of expectation—expecting to read, hear, or watch a persuasive message—on attitude change. This is an important question for at least three reasons: (a) to increase the effectiveness of persuasive messages, (b) to have reasonable expectations about the effectiveness of persuasive messages, and (c) to enhance our ability to critically evaluate the persuasive messages we receive.

First, if the persuasive message is presented to a group, it may be possible to control their expectations. If the audience receives a short introduction of the speaker and/or the speech, we may be able to affect the nature of that introduction. Further, a persuasive message can be designed in ways that stress or downplay our persuasive intent. If it turns out that forewarning reduces the effectiveness of persuasive messages, we may wish to avoid calling attention to our persuasive intent. This is not to suggest that persuaders should try to mislead their audiences; however, simply omitting a statement of persuasive intent to permit the audience to receive a persuasive message in a more open frame of mind does not seem to be an especially unethical act. Thus, an understanding of the effects of forewarning on persuasion may help persuaders to create favorable audience expectations (or at least avoid creating unfavorable ones).

Second, again as a persuader, there exist situations in which persuaders can not effect the audience's expectations concerning the persuasive message. However, knowing how audience expectations affect reception of messages may allow persuaders to compensate for the possibility of damaging effects of audience expectations. Persuaders may counteract undesirable expectations, or take advantage of favorable ones. At the very least, we can avoid unreasonable expectations about a persuasive message's probable effectiveness.

Finally, as listeners, readers, and viewers of persuasive messages, and as students of communication, an understanding of how our expectations might influence our reactions to persuasive messages can help us to become more informed consumers. It may not be possible to completely set aside or "control" our expectations, but at least we shouldn't be forced to react blindly to them.

So, for these three reasons, this meta-analysis investigates how forewarning influences the effectiveness of persuasive messages. Research on forewarning and persuasion has tended to focus on two questions: (a) does type of forewarning affect persuasion, and (b) does presence or absence of a delay between the warning and the persuasive message affect persuasiveness?

TYPE OF FOREWARNING

Allyn and Festinger (1961) are generally acknowledged to have conducted the first research into the effects of forewarning on the effectiveness of a persuasive message. In their study, one group of high school students were told that they would hear a speech by a person with a "very strong opinion that teenagers are a menace on the roads and should be strictly controlled by effective new laws" (p. 36). This type of warning has come to be known as forewarning of "topic and position," because the warning informs auditors about the topic (teenaged drivers) and the position the persuader can be expected to adopt (teenaged drivers should be controlled). Notice that the warning was given to the audience before the persuasive message itself.

In contrast, a study by McGuire and Papageorgis (1962) told the forewarned auditors that they were studying "some correlates of persuasion' and that they could expect to "read some passages which attacked their beliefs on certain health issues" (p. 29). The second type of warning is generally called forewarning of "persuasive intent," because the warned subjects expect to be exposed to a persuasive message (which will attack their beliefs), but they do not know the exact topic or position of the persuader. Here again, the warning is separate from, and prior to, the persuasive message.

Why might type of forewarning make a difference in persuasive effects? It could be argued, for example, that only if auditors knew in advance what a persuasive message was going to advocate ("topic or position") could they prepare defenses against it. If true, only this type of forewarning would reduce a message's persuasiveness. On the other hand, it is possible that any sort of forewarning (even a vague "intent to persuade") could make an audience skeptical or critical of the subsequent persuasive message and reduce its persuasiveness. This would mean that any sort of warning would reduce attitude change from a persuasive message.

Although both types of warnings have been studied, the results appear mixed. Some research has found warnings to inhibit persuasion (e.g., Kiesler & Kiesler, 1964, with warning of persuasive intent; Petty & Cacioppo, 1977, with warning of topic/position).

DELAY

Another important controversy emerges over whether or not a delay between the forewarning and the attacking message is necessary for the warning to inhibit persuasion. Neither Allyn and Festinger (1961) nor McGuire and Papageorgis (1962) reported a delay between warning and message. However, later research (e.g., Fukada, 1986; Petty & Cacioppo, 1977) did include such a delay.

Why do some theorists believe that a delay is necessary for a forewarning to inhibit attitude change? It is possible that forewarning reduces the effectiveness of a persuasive message by permitting the audience to think about the topic and prepare some "attitude defenses" against the persuasive message. If they are correct in this assumption, then forewarning should inhibit persuasion only when there is a delay between the warning and the persuasive message, a delay that gives the auditors time to develop attitude defenses. On the other hand, it is also possible that delay between warning and persuasive message is not necessary for the warning to inhibit persuasion. Once warned to expect that a message will attempt to persuade auditors to change their minds, the auditors may be "on their guard"—skeptical and doubtful of whatever the attacking persuasive message said. If true, this would mean that warnings reduce persuasion regardless of whether there is a delay between warning and message.

As with type of forewarning, the results of studies that test the effects of forewarning with and without delays seem mixed. Freedman and Sears (1965) reported that forewarning with a delay reduced persuasion, but Apsler and Sears (1968) did not find that a warning with a delay interfered with a persuasive message. Thus, this area of research is ripe for meta-analysis.

The fundamental question to be answered in this meta-analysis is how much of an effect, if any, forewarning exerts on the effectiveness of a persuasive message. Secondarily, if forewarning does affect persuasion this meta-analysis will determine whether a moderator variable, such as type of warning (topic/position or persuasive intent) or presence of a delay (between warning and message), influences the effects of forewarning.

METHOD

In the sections that follow, the procedures employed to conduct this meta-analysis are described. First, the procedure used to locate studies of forewarning is specified. Next, the criteria used to select the specific studies included in this analysis is discussed. Third, method for coding the selected studies is explained. Finally, the procedures for analyzing the results of the individual studies are described.

Obtaining the Initial Pool of Studies

A number of studies investigating the effects of forewarning or anticipation on persuasion can be found in the literature, beginning with the first study in this area by Allyn and Festinger (1961). Studies collected from psychology and communication journals were supplemented in three ways. First, literature reviews on forewarning and persuasion (Cialdini & Petty, 1981; Papageorgis, 1968) were examined to determine whether additional articles are mentioned in them. Second, the references of each study located were examined to discover other relevant articles. Finally, a list of key studies was developed to consult the *Social Sciences Citation Index* (once the researcher has identified some key older articles in the area of interest, this index reveals which more recently published works reference those key articles). This generated a list of about 30 articles, each of which was considered for possible inclusion in the meta-analysis reported here.

Selection of Studies for Meta-Analysis

The second task was to determine which of these studies formed a coherent group of articles for meta-analysis. Six criteria were used to determine which studies would be analyzed for this essay. Each criterion is discussed briefly, and studies excluded are listed for interested readers (some studies were excluded for more than one reason, although for simplicity only one is mentioned here).

First, because this investigation is a meta-analysis, only essays that report experimental studies are included. Literature reviews (e.g., Cialdini & Petty, 1981; Papageorgis, 1968) were excluded from this analysis. These essays would be useful, however, for readers who wish to read further on forewarning and persuasion (of course, each of the studies included in the bibliography contain literature reviews of varying lengths).

A number of experimental studies examine the effects of various expectations on attitude change. However, many of these experiments are not directly relevant. Because this essay is concerned with the effects of expecting to receive a persuasive communication on the persuasiveness of that message, a second criterion for selecting is that an experiment must have exposed subjects to messages and measured the persuasiveness of those messages. A number of studies concerned with anticipatory attitude change measure audience attitudes after the warning, and indeed include no persuasive message at all (e.g., Cialdini, Levy, Herman, & Evenbeck, 1973; Cialdini, Levy, Herman, Kozlowski, & Petty, 1976; Cooper & Jones, 1970; Dinner, Lewkowski, & Cooper, 1972; Gaes & Tedeschi, 1978; Hass, 1975; Hass & Mann, 1976; Sears, Freedman, & O'Connor, 1964). Although this research may tell us something about cognitive processing, the fact that subjects were never exposed to a persuasive message (even though those in the warned condition were promised one) means that this work has little if any relevance to the study of warnings on the effects of persuasive messages. Accordingly, these experiments were not included in this study.

A third criterion for selecting studies for this meta-analysis is that studies forewarn auditors of the persuasive message to be included. For example, Sears (1967) was interested in the effects of expecting to discuss the topic after reading a persuasive message. The warning in this study was not to expect a persuasive message, but to expect to discuss the topic. Therefore, it was not included in this meta-analysis.

Fourth, a study must include both a warned and an unwarned condition. In Deaux's (1968) experiment, all subjects were told to expect to hear a disagreeing speech. This provides no basis of comparison to determine whether warned subjects reacted differently from unwarned subjects to the persuasive message. Similarly, Hass and Grady (1975) reported that for comparisons among various forewarning conditions (three types of forewarning, as well as the presence or absence of delay between forewarning and message). Neither of these studies were included in the analysis because they lacked an unwarned group.

Furthermore, to be included in this meta-analysis, a study must provide sufficient information to conduct the analysis. Several studies were excluded for this reason (Hass & Linder, 1972; Infante, 1973; McGuire & Millman, 1965; Watts & Holt, 1979), although attempts were made to obtain this information. Two studies were excluded because (except for a brief summary), they were not reported in English (Fukada, 1983; Ueno, 1981).

Finally, an experiment must use attitude change (or opinion change, belief change, change in behavioral intent) as the dependent variable to be included in this meta-analysis. Brock (1967) studied counterargument production (the number of unfavorable ideas that auditors thought about during reception of the persuasive message) rather than attitude change or persuasion. Accordingly, this study was not included in the analysis performed here.

Application of the selection criteria to the studies initially collected for this investigation yielded 12 studies for meta-analysis. Studies selected for analysis were Allyn and Festinger (1961), Apsler and Sears (1968), Dean, Austin, and Watts (1971) Experiments 1 and 2, Freedman and Sears (1965), Fukada (1986), Hollander (1974), Kiesler and Kiesler (1964), McGuire and Papageorgis (1962), Petty and Cacioppo (1977) Experiment 1 and 2, and Petty and Cacioppo (1979). This pool should be adequate for determining the effect of forewarning on attitude change from persuasive messages.

Coding the Studies

Each study was coded for two potential moderator variables. One such factor was type of forewarning. As discussed earlier, some studies warned subjects only of a general persuasive intent, whereas others warned subjects of the topic and position of the persuasive message. Second, each study was coded for presence of absence of delay. Some studies gave auditors some time to think (generally 5–10 minutes) between the warning and the persuasive message, whereas others presented the message immediately after the warning.

The first step in the data analysis was to convert results of these studies to a common statistic. The correlation coefficient was selected because it is relatively easy to interpret. Four studies reported no significant difference between forewarned and unwarned subjects (Allyn & Festinger, 1961;[1] Apsler & Sears, 1968; Dean et al.,1971; Hollander, 1974) but failed to report A or F score. A figure of 1.00 was assumed for the nonsignificant F tests, and a figure of one-half the smallest significant T (with the appropriate degrees of freedom) was assumed for the t-tests. Conversion formulas provided in Hunter and Schmidt (1990) were used for this analysis. Then the ratio of the mean observed variance in these studies to the error variance was calculated. A value of .75 or above indicated that moderator variables are not present (Hunter & Schmidt, 1990). Table 7.1 lists the individual studies analyzed in this meta-analysis.

RESULTS OF THE META-ANALYSIS

The mean correlation for the studies selected for meta-analysis was .18 (k = 12, n = 1359, average n = 113). This means that there is a relatively small but noteworthy effect of forewarning on persuasion. Specifically, when warned to expect a persuasive speech, auditors were less persuaded by it than when they were not warned. Thus, forewarning does provide a modest reduction in the effectiveness of persuasive messages. Table 7.2 provides information on the sample of studies employed in this meta-analysis.

Second, the ratio of error variance to observed variance was .75. This indicates that no moderator variables influence the operation of forewarning in persuasion. In other words, it is likely that neither type of forewarning for presence of delay (not other potential moderator variables) affects the persuasion-inhibiting effects of forewarning. Not surprisingly, inspection of the mean correlations for each of the four subgroups of studies

---

[1]Although Allyn and Festinger (1961) concluded that audience expectations inhibited persuasion, after much thought, this study was treated as if it found no significant difference in this meta-analysis. They reported that there was no difference in mean attitude change between groups. However, they also indicate that a chi-square reveals that more individuals reported change in the warned than the unwarned group. Because mean attitude change, rather than number of people reporting change, has become the standard procedure for assessing the effects of forewarning in subsequent research, that nonsignificant result was taken as the best indication of the results of this study. Whether it is the "best" indicator may be arguable, but it seems undeniable that it is the most appropriate finding to integrate with subsequent research in this meta-analysis.

Table 7.1. Individual Studies Used in Meta-Analysis.

Study	Warn Type	Delay	Diff.	*N*	*r*
Allyn & Festinger (1961)	T/P	no	no	96	.10*
Apsler & Sears (1968)	T/P	yes	no	76	.11*
Dean et al. (1971)I	T/P	no	yes	80	.22
Dean et al. (1971)II	T/P	no	no	71	.12*
Freedman & Sears (1965)	T/P	yes	yes	232	.14
Fukada (1986)	PI	yes	yes	60	.27
Hollander (1974)	T/P	no	no	119	.09*
Kiesler & Kiesler (1964)	PI	no	yes	96	.29
McGuire & Pagageorgis (1962)	PI	no	yes	287	.12
Petty & Cacioppo (1977) 1	T/P	yes	yes	76	.33
Petty & Cacioppo (1977) 2	T/P	yes	yes	56	.29
Petty & Cacioppo (1979)	PI	no	yes	110	.25

T/P = warning of topic/position
PI = warning of persuasive intent
*r estimated as discussed in text (nonsignificant difference).

Table 7.2. Description of Studies Used in Meta-Analysis.

Number of studies	12
Total number of subjects	1359
Mean number of subjects	113
Range of subjects	56–287

(studies using persuasive intent forewarning, studies using topic/position forewarning, studies with delay between warning and messages, and studies without a delay), reported in Table 7.3, reveals no substantial differences.

DISCUSSION

Forewarning an audience to expect a persuasive message tends to make that message less persuasive. This effect, although modest, is likely to occur regardless of type of warning (persuasive intent or topic/position) and regardless of presence of delay. Although most persuasion textbooks that

Table 7.3. Mean Correlation of Studies in Meta-Analysis.

All studies	.18
Studies using persuasive intent	.19
Studies using topic/position	.17
Studies with delay	.20
Studies without delay	.16

discuss forewarning correctly indicate that it can inhibit persuasion, some also report that delay is important for forewarning (especially forewarning of topic/position) to have an effect on persuasion (see, e.g., Petty & Cacioppo, 1986a; Smith, 1982). This meta-analysis does not support the need for a delay between warning and message for warning to inhibit that message's persuasiveness. This section discusses the implications of these findings for students of communication and persuasion, implications for persuasion theory, a possible explanation for the observed effects of forewarning, and potential future research on forewarning.

Implications of the Findings

Because forewarning of either persuasive intent or topic and position can inhibit persuasion, persuaders may wish to take steps to prevent audience expectations from undermining their persuasive efforts. I do not recommend deceiving the audience about the purpose of a persuasive message. Leading an audience to expect that you would agree with them when you are actually trying to change their mind (or leading them to believe that you will adopt a more acceptable position in your message than you actually take in it) could severely undermine your credibility when the audience discovers the truth, as your speech unfolds. In addition to this practical concern, ethical considerations should keep persuaders from deceiving your audience. However, there is no reason that persuaders must explicitly call attention to their persuasive intent or their position on the topic, either at the beginning of their message or as they are being introduced to the audience.

Of course, at times it will be unavoidable that an audience realizes a message is intended to be persuasive (the audience may be aware of general persuasive intent or of the topic and position taken in the message). In these cases, the persuader may wish to attempt to compensate for the inhibiting effects of forewarning. The persuader could stress a lack of bias, emphasize that the audience's best interests were considered (and not just the persuader's own selfish interests), explain that both sides of the issue were carefully considered before a position was taken, or simply ask the audience to keep an open mind. At the very least, persuaders should moderate their expectations for success, keeping in mind that their persuasive task is more difficult when the audience is forewarned. It is worth noting, of course, that although forewarning is likely to reduce the persuasiveness of a message, it does not guarantee that it will be a total failure.

Also, as targets of persuasion (and students of communication) we should keep in mind the effects of expectations on persuasion (and communication generally). This meta-analysis suggests that people are likely to react differently to a persuasive message when they are forewarned of its persuasiveness than they are unaware of its persuasiveness. Whether this inhibiting effect is considered desirable for undesirable, students of communication and persuasion should be aware that expectations can alter reactions to messages in systematic ways.

Implications for Persuasion Theory

Furthermore, these results, although fairly modest, have some implications for theory in persuasion. First, our assumptions concerning the fundamental nature of attitude change have been shifting from the "hypodermic needle" view, which assumes that persuasive messages are injected in to the audience and then (if designed effectively) change the audience's attitudes. More recently, theorists and researchers are recognizing the importance of the audience in persuasion. Auditors decide which messages to attend, audiences construe or interpret messages, and are capable of making active choices concerning acceptance or rejection of messages (of course, receivers do not spend the same amount of time and effort thinking about every persuasive message they encounter; the point is that they do not simply react passively to all messages). The fact that auditors react differently to messages when they anticipate that the message will be persuasive underscores the importance of the audience in persuasion. Persuasion theory must take into account audience expectations along with message factors and other variables.

Few theories specifically address the role of forewarning in persuasion. One notable exception is the Elaboration Likelihood Model (see Cialdini & Petty, 1981; Petty & Cacioppo, 1981, 1986a, 1986b). The ELM argues that forewarning of persuasive intent reduces the effectiveness of a subsequent persuasive message, but a delay is necessary for forewarning of topic/position to be effective (especially on highly involving topics). The results obtained in this meta-analysis, however, indicate that a delay is not a necessary in either type of forewarning.

A Possible Explanation for Forewarning Effects

Why would forewarning reduce persuasion? It appears that forewarning reduces persuasion by encouraging auditors to adopt a less receptive state of mind. McGuire and Papageorgis (1962) suggested that forewarning subjects of an impending persuasive message motivates auditors to prepare defenses against that message. Similarly, Petty and Cacioppo (1977) argued that "the warnings motivated persons to consider more fully their own positions, generating cognitive defenses for the impending attack" (p. 654). In line with this explanation, some theorists argue that a delay between the warning and the persuasive message is necessary to provide time for receivers to construct their defenses to provide time for receivers to construct their defenses (Freedman & Sears, 1965), especially with topic and position warnings. However, this meta-analysis does not find that a delay is necessary for forewarning to erode a message's persuasiveness. Does this finding invalidate this explanation of how forewarning may inhibit persuasion?

To answer this question, it might be useful to consider the effects of credibility on attitude change. Except in certain circumstances (e.g., if the topic is very important or involving to auditors, or if the speech agrees with the audience, trying to reinforce rather than change their attitudes), attributing a message to a highly credible (expert) source can increase that message's persuasiveness. However, a message's persuasiveness is enhanced most by credibility is when the source is identified as *before* the audience receives the message (see Allen & Associates, 1990; Husek, 1965; Mills & Harvey, 1972).

An explanation for this effect is that being informed that a source is an expert puts the audience not a more receptive state of mind, that it reduces auditor's motivation to carefully scrutinize—generate counterarguments, or unfavorable cognitive responses to—the persuasive message. On the other hand, being told that a message was from a credible source after the message has already been processed does not help persuasiveness as much, presumably because it is too late for knowledge that the source is an expert to put the audience in a more favorable state of mind for processing the message (for a fuller discussion, see Benoit, 1991; O'Keefe, 1987).

Thus, learning that a source is expert before that source's message is processed may tend to put the audience in a more receptive state of mind, enhancing the persuasiveness of that message. One the other hand, knowledge that a message will attempt to change an audience's attitudes (warning of either persuasive intent or topic and position) may tend to put the audience in an unreceptive or more critical state of mind. Thus, either type warning, with or without delay, could interfere with the success of a persuasive message by provoking the audience to produce unfavorable cognitive responses to that message—more unfavorable thoughts than would have been produced without the warning.

Consistent with this explanation, Kiesler and Kiesler (1964) reported that a message is less persuasive when a statement identifying its persuasive intent is given to the audience before the message (a warning), but no less persuasive when the same statement is presented to them after the message. Hence, it is not the information in the warning that reduces persuasion, but the fact that the information in the warning is learned before the message. Presumably, when auditors are informed of a message's persuasive intent before receiving that message they tend to adopt a less receptive state of mind toward the persuasive message. It appears, then, that a critical state of mind during message processing, not a delay between warning and message, reduces the effectiveness of persuasion.

Further Research

Finally, I want to suggest that more research on forewarning and persuasion is needed. First, measurement of auditors' cognitive responses (favorable and unfavorable thoughts in response to the persuasive message) would test the explanation offered here: that warning tends to place auditors in a less receptive state of mind. Although cognitive responses have been measured, some of the work does not directly answer the question of whether warned auditors produce a greater number of unfavorable thoughts during reception of a persuasive message than unwarned auditors (e.g., Brock, 1967, did not include an unwarned group; Petty & Cacioppo, 1977, measured cognitive responses during the delay between warning and message). Only Petty and Cacioppo (1979) attempted to measure thoughts that auditors had during message reception. They found that warnings did increase unfavorable and decrease favorable thoughts, but only on involving or important topics. Additional research along these lines would provide more confidence in this explanation of forewarning effects in persuasion.

Individual studies have suggested that other possible moderating variables might exist, but not enough experiments have been conducted on them to justify separate meta-analysis. For example, Hollander (1974) suggested that gender might influence the effects of forewarning. Apsler and Sears (1968), as well as the study just mentioned by Petty and Cacioppo (1979), argued that involvement in (or relevance, or importance of) the topic of the persuasive message might affect the impact of warning on persuasion. At this point we have enough research to show that warning influences the effects of a persuasive message, but we do not have enough information about important ways in which this effect might be limited.

CONCLUSION

Twelve experiments on the effects of forewarning on persuasive messages were subjected to meta-analysis. Forewarning was found to exert a modest effect (a mean r of .18), reducing the effectiveness of persuasive messages. Comparing the observed variance to the error variance indicates that it is unlikely that this effect is influenced by a moderator variable (e.g., type of forewarning or presence of delay between the warning and the persuasive message).

REFERENCES

Allen, M., & Associates (Nov. 1990). *An examination of timing of communicator identification and level of source credibility and attitudes*. Paper presented at the Speech Communication Association, Chicago, IL.

Allyn, J., & Festinger, L. (1961). The effectiveness of unanticipated persuasive communications. *Journal of Personality and Social Psychology, 62*, 35–40.

Apsler, R., & Sears, D. O. (1968). Warning, personal involvement, and attitude change. *Journal of Personality and Social Psychology, 9*, 162–166.

Benoit, W. L. (1991). A cognitive response analysis of source credibility. In B. Dervin & M. J. Voigt (Eds.), *Progress in communication sciences* (Vol. 10, pp. 1–19). Norwood, NJ: Ablex.

Brock, R. C. (1967). Communication discrepancy and intent to persuade as determinants of counterargument production. *Journal of Experimental Social Psychology, 3*, 296–309.

Cialdini, R. B., Levy, A., Herman, C. P., & Evenbeck, S. (1973). Attitudinal politics: The strategy of moderation. *Journal of Personality and Social Psychology, 25*, 100–108.

Cialdini, R. B., Levy, A., Herman, C. P., Kozlowski, L. T., & Petty, R. E. (1976). Elastic shifts of opinion: Determinants of direction and durability. *Journal of Personality and Social Psychology, 34*, 663–672.

Cialdini, R. B., & Petty, R. E. (1981). Anticipatory opinion shifts. In R. E. Petty, R. M. Ostrom, & T. C. Brock (Eds.), *Cognitive responses in persuasion* (pp. 217-235). Hillsdale, NJ: Erlbaum.

Cooper, J., & Jones, R. A. (1970). Self-esteem and consistency as determinants of anticipatory opinion change. *Journal of Personality and Social Psychology, 14*, 407–412.

Dean, R. B., Austin, J. A., & Watts, W. A. (1971). Forewarning effects in persuasion: Field and classroom experiments. *Journal of Personality and Social Psychology, 18*, 210–221.

Deaux, K. K. (1968). Variations in warning, information preference, and anticipatory attitude change. *Journal of Personality and Social Psychology, 9*, 157–161.

Dinner, S. H., Lewkowicz, B. E., & Cooper, J. (1972). Anticipatory attitude change as a function of self-esteem and issue familiarity. *Journal of Personality and Social Psychology, 24*, 407–412.

Freedman, J. L., & Sears, D. O. (1965). Warning, distraction, and resistance to influence. *Journal of Social Personality and Social Psychology, 1*, 262–266.

Fukada, H. (1983). [Forewarning effects in fear-arousing communication.] *Japanese Journal of Psychology, 54*, 459–469. (Japanese, English summary)

Fukada, H. (1986). Psychological processes mediating persuasion-inhibiting effect of forewarning in fear arousing communication. *Psychological Reports, 58*, 87–90.

Gaes, G. G., & Tedeschi, J. T., (1978). An evaluation of self-esteem and impression management theories of anticipatory belief change. *Journal of Experimental and Social Psychology, 14*, 579–587.

Hass, R. G. (1975). Persuasion or moderation? Two experiments on anticipatory belief change. *Journal of Personality and Social Psychology, 31*, 1155–1162.

Hass, R. G., & Grady, K. (1975). Temporal delay, type of forewarning, and resistance to influence. *Journal of Experimental and Social Psychology, 11*, 459–469.

Hass, R. G., & Linder, D. E. (1972). Counterargument availability and the effects of message structure on persuasion. *Journal of Personality and Social Psychology, 23*, 219–233.

Hass, R. G., & Mann, R. W. (1976). Anticipatory belief change: Persuasion or impression management? *Journal of Personality and Social Psychology, 34*, 105–111.

Hollander, S. W. (1974). Effects of forewarning factors on pre- and post-communication attitude change. *Journal of Social Psychology, 30*, 272–278.

Hunter, J. E., & Schmidt, F. L., (1990). *Methods of meta-analysis: Correcting error and bias in research findings*. Newbury Park, CA: Sage.

Husek, T. R. (1965). Persuasive impacts of early, late, or no mention of the negative source. *Journal of Personality and Social Psychology, 2*, 125–128.

Infante, D. A. (1973). Forewarnings in persuasion: Effects of opinionated language and forewarner and speaker authoritativeness. *Western Speech, 37*, 185–195.

Kiesler, C. A., & Kiesler, S. B. (1964). Role of forewarning in persuasive communications. *Journal of Abnormal and Social Psychology, 68*, 547–579.

McGuire, W. J., & Millman, S. (1965). Anticipatory belief lowering following forewarning of a persuasive attack. *Journal of Personality and Social Psychology, 2*, 471–479.

McGuire, W., & Papageorgis, D. (1962). Effectiveness of forewarning in developing resistance to persuasion. *Public Opinion Quarterly, 26*, 24–34.

Mills, J., & Harvey, J. (1972). Opinion change as a function of when information about the communicator is received and whether he is attractive or expert. *Journal of Personality and Social Psychology, 21*, 52–55.

Papageorgis, D. (1968). Warning and persuasion. *Psychological Bulletin, 70*, 271–282.

Petty, R. E., & Cacioppo, J. T. (1977). Forewarning, cognitive responding, and resistance to persuasion. *Journal of Personality and Social Psychology, 35*, 645–655.

Petty, R. E., & Cacioppo, J. T. (1979). Effects of forewarning of persuasive intent and involvement on cognitive responses and persuasion. *Personality and Social Psychology Bulletin, 5*, 173–176.

Petty, R. E., & Cacioppo, J. T. (1981). *Attitudes and persuasion: Classic and contemporary approaches.* Dubuque, IA: Brown.

Petty, R. E., & Cacioppo, (1986a). *Communication and persuasion: Central and peripheral routes to attitude change.* London: Springer-Verlag.

Petty, R. E., & Cacioppo, J. T. (1986b). The elaboration likelihood model of persuasion. In L. Berkowitz (Ed.), *Advances in experimental social psychology* (Vol. 19, pp. 123–205). New York: Academic Press.

O'Keefe, D. J. (1987). The persuasive effects of delaying identification of high- and low-credibility: A meta-analytic review. *Central States Speech Journal, 38*, 63–72.

Sears, D. O. (1967). Social anxiety, opinion structure, and opinion change. *Journal of Personality and Social Psychology, 7*, 142–151.

Sears, D. O., Freedman, J. L., & O'Connor, E. F. (1964). The effects of anticipated debate and commitment on the polarization of audience opinion. *Public Opinion Quarterly, 28*, 615–627.

Smith, M. J. (1982). *Persuasion and human action: A review and critique of social influence theories*. Belmont, CA: Wadsworth.

Ueno, T. (1981). [The effects of forewarning on resistance to persuasion.] *Japanese Journal of Psychology, 52*, 173–177. (Japanese, English summary)

Watts, W. A., & Holt, L. E. (1979). Persistence of opinion change induced under conditions of forewarning and distraction. *Journal of Personality and Social Psychology, 37*, 778–789.

Ueno, T. (1981). [The effects of forewarning on resistance to persuasion.] *Japanese Journal of Psychology, 52*, 173–177. (Japanese, English summary)

Watts, W. A., & Holt, L. E. (1979). Persistence of opinion change induced under conditions of forewarning and distraction. *Journal of Personality and Social Psychology, 37*, 778–789.

8

The Effects of Distraction During Persuasion

David B. Buller
John R. Hall
The University of Arizona

Over 25 years ago, McGuire (1969) argued that attention was fundamental to suasory success. However, for the most part, attention to persuasive messages has been taken as axiomatic by theorists, whereas researchers typically employ methodologies that heighten the salience of persuasive stimuli. In practice, attention to persuasive messages is far from guaranteed; it is unstable, fickle, and capricious. Persuasive messages compete for receivers' consideration with other messages, environmental cues, and internal responses. As a result, some messages receive detailed examination, whereas others remain ignored or only partially processed. Attentional sets affect the depth and nature of cognitive processing, determining message influence. Thus, before applying conclusions from persuasion research to actual discourse, it is crucial to explore how receivers become engaged by persuasive messages and to identify the objects on which receivers focus during persuasive attempts.

One related issue that captured the interest of scholars 35 years ago is the effect of distracting stimuli during persuasive communication. Since 1961, when Allyn and Festinger demonstrated a positive effect of distraction on attitude change, nearly 40 studies have tested competing explanations of distraction's effects, with conflicting and, at times, confusing results. Some have suggested that distraction enhances persuasion by reducing subvocal counterargument with persuasive assertions. Others assert that distraction reduces persuasion by hindering receiver comprehension of reasonable arguments. A meta-analysis (Buller, 1986) demonstrated strongest support for the comprehension-based explanation and revealed that the conceptualization of distraction requires expansion. The analysis suggested that some distraction carries supplemental meaning by highlighting source characteristics and that this "communication-relevant" distraction may involve a different form of message processing and response to persuasive appeals than "communication-irrelevant" distraction that reduces comprehension. Moreover, communication-relevant distraction may be relatively common and have potentially greater impact on day-to-day persuasion than communication-irrelevant distraction.

In this chapter, we first review the meta-analysis of distraction, focusing on early explanations consisting of counterarguing and message comprehension hypotheses. We then consider a new approach to distraction that distinguishes between distractors that are communication-relevant because they provide additional meaning or cause receivers to interpret specific facets of appeals and those that are irrelevant to the communication exchange. In so doing, we discuss probable differences in message-processing sequences, considering how the two types of distractors may produce different outcomes. Speculations about message variables that may function as communication-relevant distractors are offered.

THEORETICAL BACKGROUND OF META-ANALYSIS

Of the theoretical explanations for distraction's effects during persuasive communication, counterargument disruption and message-comprehension reduction are most prominent and stimulated considerable debate. The former explanation predicts enhanced persuasion whereas the latter suggests declines in persuasion due to distraction.

Counterargument Disruption

Festinger and Maccoby (1964), in one of the first studies on distraction, proposed that distraction enhances persuasion by interrupting receivers' subvocal counterarguing, which is positively related to resistance to persuasion. Subsequently, several studies tested this explanation (see M. Burgoon, Cohen, Miller, & Montgomery, 1978; Freedman & Sears, 1965; Insko, Turnbull, & Yandell, 1974; Keating & Brock, 1974; Kiesler & Mathog, 1968; Vohs & Garrett, 1968; Watts & Holt, 1979; Zimbardo, Snyder, Thomas, Gold, & Gurwitz, 1970).

However, problems in this research undermines support for the hypothesis. First, several studies failed to measure counterarguing, relying instead on reduced attitude change as post hoc evidence of counterargument disruption. Second, studies measuring counterarguing use measures with questionable validity. There remains disagreement about whether counterarguing measures operationalize counterargumentation appropriately and accurately reflect cognitions during message reception or are biased reconstructions of cognitions following attitude change (Miller & Baron, 1973; Osterhouse & Brock, 1970; Romer, 1979). Third, few studies actually estimated the relationship between counterarguing and attitude change. The two studies examining counterarguing found a positive relationship to attitude change in one but no relationship in the other. Nonetheless, Baron, Baron, and Miller (1973) concluded that the hypothesis has been supported across a variety of topics, speakers, and situations.

Message-Comprehension Explanation

In reviewing the conflicting results of early studies on distraction, McGuire (1966, 1969) speculated that distraction was more likely to reduce persuasion than to enhance it. He argued that distractors interfere with message comprehension. This reduction in argument understanding should decrease persuasion.

Studies by Silverman and Regula (1968), Vohs and Garrett (1968), Haaland and Venkatesen (1968), M. Burgoon, Fraedrich, and Bachman (1979), and Romer (1979) provided data supporting McGuire's message-comprehension explanation. One limitation has arisen in this explanation: A large decline in message comprehension is required to reduce attitude change. In fact, three studies reported increased attitude change despite decreased message comprehension (Insko, Turnbull et al., 1974; Rule & Rehill, 1970; Zimbardo et al., 1970).

Revisions to the Explanations

In response to the conflicting findings, revisions have been offered to both explanations. Petty expanded the counterarguing hypothesis, positing that distraction interrupts information processing in general, of which counterarguing is only one part (Harkins & Petty, 1981; Petty & Cacioppo, 1986; Petty, Wells, & Brock, 1976). Petty et al. proposed, and provided some support for their argument, that distraction reduces the most dominant or plentiful thoughts during persuasive messages. When counterarguments are dominant, distraction enhances persuasion by reducing resistance; however, when supportive, favorable thoughts are dominant, distraction harms persuasion by reducing agreement. Likewise, Harkins and Petty reported that distraction had the most negative effect on attitude change under the condition of greatest information processing, although this effect might be cited as support for the message comprehension explanation. Insko, Turnbull et al. (1974) and Lammers and Becker (1980) provided some evidence that distraction reduced favorable thoughts.

The message-comprehension explanation has undergone revision linking it with the counterarguing hypothesis. Noting the relatively small relationship between comprehension and attitude change, Vohs and Garrett (1968) proposed that low to moderate levels of distraction interrupted counterarguing and improved persuasion, whereas high levels of distraction interfered with message comprehension and harmed persuasion. The data on this revised explanation is uncompelling. Only one study (Romer, 1979) supported this nonmonotonic relationship and two others provided only suggestive trends (Haslett, 1976; Rosenblatt, 1966). However, many researchers seem to believe implicitly that extremely high levels of distraction, by necessity, reduce comprehension and attitude change (Buller, 1986).

META-ANALYSIS

Methodological Overview

The meta-analysis was performed on a set of 31 studies reporting 41 experimental manipulations of distraction that satisfied two criteria: (a) the relationship between distraction and attitude change represented the central focus of the study and (b) distraction was experimentally manipulated during presentation of a persuasive message. In addition, studies on violations of linguistic and nonverbal expectations were included because they invoked distraction explanations and Janis, Kaye, and Kirschner's (1965) study on eating during persuasion was incorporated because several distraction researchers had cited distraction to account for their findings.

Standardized effect-size estimates (*r*) were calculated from each study, following procedures developed by Glass, McGaw, and Smith (1981) and converted to correlations. Summary statistics were calculated using Hunter, Schmidt, and Jackson's (1982) methods (see Buller, 1986, for a complete discussion of methods).

Counterargument Disruption Hypothesis

The meta-analysis provides little support for the counterargument disruption hypothesis, even though distraction generally reduced counterarguing and was inversely related to attitude change ($r = -.50$). The overall average correlation between distraction and counterarguing contained nontrivial variation, as did the overall correlation between distraction and attitude change, prompting a search for moderators. However, the analysis of favorable thoughts showed that distraction did not interrupt these cognitions ($r = .00$).

The subset analysis revealed that distraction consistently lowered counterarguing. Distractions that involved speaking, listening to a human voice, watching a visual stimulus, being instructed to focus primarily on the distracting task, and a manual task accompanying a moderately strong message (as opposed to a strong message) reduced counterarguing ($r = -.15$ to $-.28$). However, distraction was only weakly related to counterarguing when the distraction involved being instructed to focus primarily on the source and when manual distraction accompanied a strong message or a message of unknown strength ($r = .00$ to $-.06$). Further, more attitude change occurred in only three of the cases where distraction disrupted counterargumentation; that is, listening to a human voice, watching a visual stimulus, or engaging in manual distraction with a moderately strong message ($r = .12$ to $.21$). Although these three subsets had relatively strong relationships between distraction and counterarguing, the distraction involving speaking had almost no relationship with attitude change ($r = .03$), in spite of a stronger relationship with counterarguing. In addition, the remaining subsets produced negative correlations between distraction and attitude change ($r = -.07$ to $-.25$).

Taken together, the meta-analysis showed that reduced counterarguing was not consistently associated with increased attitude change. Further, it was not abundantly clear why counterargument disruption would be the prevailing process in the three situations where consistent findings emerged. In fairness, the questionable validity of the counterargument measures casts some doubt on whether we can confidently rule out counterargument disruption as the causal mechanism in distraction's effect. However, the majority of stable estimates of the relationship between distraction and attitude change were negative.

Message Comprehension Explanation. The message comprehension explanation fared much better in the meta-analysis. As noted, the majority of stable estimates of the relationships between distraction and attitude change showed that distraction generally inhibits persuasion (r = -.05 to -.25). Further, in all but one analysis where distraction reduced message comprehension, it also reduced attitude change (r = -.10 to -.51).

Support for the message comprehension explanation also was weakened by methodological shortcomings. In this case, the lack of comprehension measures, rather than questions about their validity, created problems. Still, almost all of the studies that did measure message comprehension supported the message comprehension explanation.

COMMUNICATION-RELEVANT AND -IRRELEVANT DISTRACTION

Beyond supporting the message comprehension thesis at the expense of the counterarguing hypothesis, meta-analysis suggested that the various operationalizations probe at least two different conceptual definitions of distraction. In particular, distraction produced by tasks or cues that encourage receivers to focus on source personality or credibility appears to differ from distraction that shifts the receivers' focus away from the communication. Buller (1986) suggested that receivers considered the former type of distraction relevant to the communication exchange and depended on judgments about the source when responding to messages. These "communication-relevant" distractors, as he called them, provided supplemental meaning that was integrated into receivers' message processing. When the distraction focused attention on positive characteristics (e.g., high credibility), persuasion was enhanced, whereas when attention was focused on negative attributes, persuasion was diminished. By contrast, "communication-irrelevant" distractors (e.g., bells, train noises, and cartoons) seemed to interfere with information reception. In this case, persuasive outcomes were affected to the extent that the redirection of attention reduced receivers' abilities to understand reasonable persuasive appeals. When understanding was lowered, persuasion decreased.

Meta-Analysis on Communication-Relevant Distraction

Theoretical Background. Evidence of communication-relevant distraction came from two sets of studies in which the distracting task increased receivers' focus on the personality of the source. In the first set of studies, participants were explicitly instructed to focus on the personality of the source (as opposed to focusing on the message content) (Allyn & Festinger, 1961; Freedman & Sears, 1965; Miller & Levy, 1967). The second set of studies appeared to engender the same type of focus on the source using violations of linguistic and nonverbal expectations (J. Burgoon, Stacks, & Burch, 1982; M. Burgoon et al., 1978; Stacks & J. Burgoon, 1981; Woodall & J. Burgoon, 1981). The latter set provided the best evidence of communication-relevant distraction, whereas the former set provided insight into cognitive processing of communication-relevant cues.

Results. Studies on personality focus and violations of conversational expectations were combined into a single subset analysis. As expected, credibility moderated the impact of this form of distraction on attitude change. When receiving a message from a highly credible source, personality-focus distraction and violations of expectations enhanced persuasion (r = .15). These same distractions reduced persuasion when the source was low in credibility (r = -.10). Furthermore, these communication-relevant distractions were unrelated to counterarguing (r =.00) or message comprehension (r = -.02), underscoring the primacy of source evaluation in attitude change.

Theoretical Implications. The distinction between communication-relevant and communication-irrelevant distraction has two notable implications. First, most of the theoretical and empirical work to date, including that related to the counterarguing hypothesis, has focused on communication-irrelevant distraction. Distraction is conceived of as an interference to message processing rather than an event that provides additional meaning or alters the decoded message. In the meta-analysis, only studies involving personality-focus tasks and violations of linguistic and nonverbal expectations investigated communication-relevant distractions. Other message variables may function as similar distractors, although they have not been associated with the distraction concept. For example, Wiener and Mehrabian (1968) implied that linguistic variation (verbal immediacy) may encourage persuasion by accentuating or attenuating the speaker/proposition link. In this sense, linguistic variation might represent a distraction from the true state of affairs—incongruity of message content with receivers' preexisting attitudes or beliefs. By refocusing the receiver's attention on source characteristics, credibility or attraction provides sufficient supplemental information to motivate attitude change.

The second implication of the distinction between communication-relevant and -irrelevant distraction is that there may be two alternative sequences of processing "distracting" cues at work. Although both types of distraction appear to produce changes in attention, communication-irrelevant distractors merely divert the receiver's attention away from the persuasive appeal with *unpredictable* results. They can produce a sustained disruption and lower comprehension, reducing persuasion or represent a temporary, albeit annoying, diversion with little effect on persuasion. Conversely, communication-relevant distractors appear to stimulate sustained attention on specific, *predictable* aspects of the persuasive appeal. Thus, the information-processing sequence for a communication-irrelevant distraction likely involves attention shift, evaluation of relevance of distraction, message comprehension effects, and resolution, whereas the sequence for a communication-relevant distraction involves attention shift, encouraging sustained comprehension, evaluation of relevance, message comprehension, interpretation of distractor and/or nonmessage aspects of communication, and resolution.

In summary, the distinction between the two forms of distraction is based on differences in the attention process and may involve different sequences of information processing that produce different persuasive outcomes. Combining them under a single, generic label does nothing to resolve the inconsistent findings in the literature. Moreover, confusing the two concepts limits the applicability of distraction's effects because it focuses undue attention on communication-irrelevant distraction, while largely ignoring the probably more common communication-relevant distractions. To identify the differences we presume exist between the two types of distractors, we offer an informal model of the role of *communication-relevant* distraction in persuasive communication.

A MODEL OF DISTRACTION

Communication can be viewed as the intentional use of commonly understood codes to affect human cognitions (J. Burgoon, Buller, & Woodall, 1996), whereas *persuasion* can be viewed as the process of employing these commonly understood codes to intentionally affect certain types of human cognitions: receivers' beliefs and evaluations of attitudinal objects. The proposed model of distraction includes four steps: (a) attention, (b) comprehension, (c) evaluation and attribution, and (d) resolution. It is unlikely that these steps follow linearly and is quite likely that some steps occur nonrecursively. For instance, message complexity may increase the difficulty of comprehension, but this same complexity may enhance the receiver's willingness to attend to the stimulus. Receivers must attend to, comprehend, and assign significance to persuasive appeals and subsequently resolve cognitive inconsistencies before persuasive messages can be said to cause attitude *change*.

Attention

Within this model, we presume that stimuli can be either communication relevant or communication irrelevant. Take as an example a mass-media campaign encouraging college students to avoid sun exposure, thereby reducing the risk of certain types of skin cancer. In this instance, communication-relevant stimuli can be considered under two labels: (a) message attributes and (b) source attributes. Within this framework, communication-relevant message attributes might include (a) propositional content embedded within the appeal (e.g., What is the source asking the receiver to believe or feel?) and (b) the style of message delivery (e.g., How are the propositions presented? How creative or complex are the script writing, production and post-production values? What are the medium characteristics such as picture resolution of the camera and videotape as well as signal-to-noise ratio of the audio signal?). Communication-relevant source variables, as used here, include: (a) the sponsor of the appeal, and (b) the speaker in the appeal. Communication-irrelevant stimuli might include: (a) the quality of television set at the receiver's end, (b) competing stimuli in the environment during airing of the message, and (c) emotional and physiological states of the receiver.

Each of these stimuli, for various reasons, can capture attention. For instance, propositional content might induce attention: "If you sunbathe, you run a greater risk of skin cancer than persons who do not." Admittedly, the message is not creative, but the message is clear and, if the receiver focuses on the topic, the message may persuade. Alternatively, a statement from someone else in the environment may divert the receivers' attention away from the message and, given the message's brevity, one might miss it entirely and not be persuaded. Obviously, the receiver's focus of attention is important to determining the appeal's success; however, the term *attention* has been employed ambiguously in the literature.

First, some stimuli attract attention because their collative features such as novelty, complexity, and relevance spontaneously elicit interest (Berlyne, 1960). These properties effect an involuntary surge of arousal, an orienting response, reflex, or reaction (Kahneman, 1973). In this context, attention implies a "grabbing" of one's attention. A second form of attention involves voluntary sustained concentration. Used in this sense, attention implies an interpretive process, aimed at understanding or explaining stimuli—in this case, the message. Concentration can be elicited by an orienting response that begs interpretation (violation of linguistic expectations) or an induced need to understand (forewarning that an issue is of central importance; Kahneman, 1973; Neisser, 1976; Schneider & Shiffrin, 1977; Shiffrin & Schneider, 1977; Treisman, 1960). Focusing attention on communication-relevant stimuli has relatively predictable results on persuasive communication because reactions are based on specific aspects of the communication exchange.

By comparison, communication-irrelevant distraction, which diverts the receiver's attention away from the exchange, has less predictable results. If the stimuli "grabbing" attention are sufficiently interesting or intrusive and focus is diverted for some time, message comprehension is reduced. However, if the stimuli are not interesting or intrusive, the diversion may be temporary, and message comprehension may be disrupted minimally. How long an individual's attention remains diverted depends upon the characteristics of the stimuli, medium of transmission (e.g., audio stimuli may be automatically alerting while visual cues are not; Posner, Nissen, & Klein, 1976), and internal states of the individual such as interest in topic and utility of message.

Comprehension

Assuming that our hypothetical viewer attends to our mediated message (because of speaker attributes, interest in topic, or clever video production), the viewer will be compelled to extract some meaning. First, the viewer must recognize the source's syntactic and semantic units before agreeing or disagreeing with attitudinal positions offered. Obviously, if the receiver does not understand what belief or attitude the speaker is requesting the receiver to adopt, it is unreasonable to suggest that the message *causes* attitude change.

However, the verbal argument represents only one part of the message that our viewer will likely extract. Any persuasive attempt embeds not only propositions but relational or sociopragmatic information. In other words, receivers consistently judge not only linguistic propositions, but also the mode of presentation used to convey those propositions, given the nature of the assertions, the context, and the speaker's "reward value" (i.e., the source's authority, dominance, status, and expertise, representing an overall evaluation in terms of polarity, magnitude, and centrality; J. Burgoon, 1978; J. Burgoon & Hale, 1988). The term *mode of presentation* can be considered the sum of choices made regarding the use of grammatical constructions, lexical items, illocutionary force, nonverbal cues, and production decisions employed by a source to change the receiver's beliefs or attitudes—in short, the "style" in which the propositional content is delivered. Typical questions that bear on "mode of presentation" include "Is the public service announcement slick?", "Does the presentation make sense?", "Are the production values professional?", and "Does the spokesperson seem patronizing?" The viewer will consider both the propositional content and the relational/socio-pragmatic information contained in the message to arrive at an evaluation of the persuasive attempt.

Evaluation and Attribution

Once comprehension occurs, the derived message must be valenced. The polarity of valencing is assumed to be determined by the congruity or incongruity of the receiver expectations regarding propositional content (congruity with held beliefs, opinions, attitudes, and values) and the appropriateness of the mode of presentation, given the credibility and attraction of the source.

The mode of presentation may represent an important determinant of receiver attributions. Certainly, not everyone in our society enjoys equal rights in expressing particular propositions or illocutions. In the persuasive situation, there is an implicit or explicit request for action and there are, presumedly, receiver expectations about how those requests should be framed given the context, nature of request, and relationship between the speaker and receiver. One cannot determine the meaning of a message and its effects on receivers by solely examining linguistic meaning. In our mediated campaign, the receiver might reasonably ask, "Do I agree with the source's assertions?", "Is it appropriate that the producer of this message used slick graphics and special effects to manipulate my emotions?", "Is it appropriate for the source to use fear appeals including graphic visuals depicting skin cancer?", or "Does the source have the right to command me to stop sunbathing?" Obviously, cognitive inconsistencies may arise during evaluation. It is quite possible that a valued source will make undesirable assertions or a disliked source present valued assertions. Following balance, congruity, and tension-reduction theories (Bostrom, 1981; Festinger, 1957; Festinger & Maccoby, 1964; Insko & Adewole, 1979; Insko, Murashima, & Saiyadain, 1966; Insko, Songer, & McGarvey, 1974), it is assumed that receivers are motivated to resolve these inconsistencies.

Resolutions

Once a message is derived based on message comprehension and source attributions, the receiver must decide whether or not to modify preexisting beliefs and attitudes. Resolving cognitive inconsistencies requires effort. The receiver's willingness to invest effort is probably dependent on stimulus characteristics (novelty, plausibility, and importance) and receiver self-efficacy. According to McGuire's (1969) *cognitive miser* principle, Zipf's (1949) work on word frequency, Festinger's (1957) dissonance theory, and

Langer's work on mindless information processing (Langer, 1978, 1985; Langer & Imber, 1980; Langer & Piper, 1987), it is assumed that people tend to choose the path of least effort, all else being equal. Thus, there is a presumed preference and predisposition to process information "intuitively," given an opportunity (Brainerd & Reyna, 1990). This predisposition might be used strategically to mitigate the perceived discrepancy between assertions and already held attitudes by shifting focus (i.e., distracting) to (in the case of positive source characteristics) or away from (in the case of negative source characteristics) speaker characteristics.

STRATEGIC DISTRACTION

We have presented a simplistic, speculative model of cognitive processing; however, our concern is "distraction," which implies a stimulus-invoked *shift* in attention during a communication event. It seems reasonable to suggest that competing stimuli can trigger attentional shifts in the receiver's entering cognitive focus and that these competing stimuli, as discussed earlier, may be of two types. Stated more formally, communication-relevant distraction is best viewed as the redirection of a receiver's entering cognitive focus by stimuli that are intrinsic to the communication process (e.g., message, medium, or speaker attributes). Communication-irrelevant distraction is viewed as any shift in receiver's entering focus caused by stimuli that are extrinsic to the communication process. Within this model, it is assumed that communication-irrelevant stimuli distract because they "grab" the receiver's attention. This somatic response does not guarantee the receiver's continued focus. However, if the diversion persists, comprehension declines and persuasion becomes less likely. Conversely, it is assumed that communication-relevant stimuli encourage sustained concentration, thereby supplementing the meaning of propositional content. In particular, these distractions are likely to increase the impact of source attributes, enhancing the success of credible or rewarding sources and decreasing the success of less credible ones.

So how might communication-relevant distractors be used strategically to enhance persuasion? Based on the empirical evidence provided by the meta-analysis, it seems appropriate to suggest three simple prescriptions during counterattitudinal advocacy:

1. When delivering a counterattitudinal message, remove or reduce communication-irrelevant distractors to promote message comprehension, especially when the message contains highly persuasive arguments.

By our model, it is to the source's advantage that source attributes be integrated into message processing when the source is highly rewarding (e.g., dominant, credible, attractive); communication-relevant distractions represent one means of ensuring this. The distraction should benefit almost any type of persuasive message; however, it will be most valuable with arguments that are less persuasive in their own right.

2. If a counterattitudinal message is offered by a high reward source, use communication-relevant distractors that draw attention to source characteristics and away from the message.

By contrast, one should avoid directing attention to undesirable source attributes. With a low-reward source, distractors that attract attention to the message, away from source characteristics, are advantageous. However, once again, the message strength may make a difference. It is unlikely that weak arguments will fair much better than undesirable source characteristics:

3. If the message is offered by a low-reward source, use communication-relevant distractors that draw attention to the message and away from source characteristics.

Forms of Communication-Relevant Distraction

To follow the last two prescriptions requires understanding what communication-relevant distractors divert attention to source and message characteristics. The meta-analysis only focused on a few communication-relevant distractions; however, several potential communication-relevant distractions are at the disposal of communicators.

Diverting Attention to Source Characteristics. In the meta-analysis, violations of language intensity and nonverbal expectations were the distractions that diverted attention to source characteristics. These may be among the most easily manipulated and successful forms of communication-relevant distractors. Language intensity refers to the "degree to which a persuasive message deviates from neutrality. [It] can be manipulated within sentences by the use of future tense verbs, adverbial qualifications, and sex and death metaphors" (M. Burgoon, 1989, p. 151). Beyond these, opinionated language (message containing the claim and the source's attitude toward those who agree or disagree with that claim), fear appeals, and obscenity are forms of language intensity (M. Burgoon, 1989) that also may divert attention to source characteristics when violating linguistic norms (Bradac, Bowers, & Courtright, 1979). For example, Miller and Lobe (1967) and Miller and Basehart (1969) reported that highly credible sources were more persuasive when using opinionated language than less credible sources. Similarly, Hewgill and Miller (1965) showed that highly credible speakers were more effective when using high levels of fear but less credible speakers were more effective when they evoked only a low level of fear.

Other verbal forms may serve as communication-relevant distractions and increase attention to source characteristics. Gruner (1985) found that a moderate amount of humor, providing that it was situationally appropriate, can enhance perceptions of the source. Another form of communication-relevant distraction may be message organization. Although organization can facilitate comprehension and disorganization generally reduces comprehension and source credibility (Bettinghaus & Cody, 1987; McCroskey & Mehrley, 1969), a moderate amount of disorganization may call attention to source attributes. Provided the disorganization is not sufficient to jeopardize the credibility of highly credible speaker, it may encourage receivers to concentrate on favorable source attributes.

On the nonverbal side, violations of proxemic expectations were included in the meta-analysis and successful by increased attention to source characteristics. J. Burgoon et al. (1996) identified several additional nonverbal behaviors that may operate as communication-relevant distractions highlighting source attributions. In particular, faster speaking tempo, disfluencies, greater vocal variety, and louder speech are more successful when displayed by high- rather than low-reward sources. Eye contact also may divert attention to source characteristics. Kleinke (1980) found that eye contact increased compliance when receivers felt that the source could legitimately make a request but reduced compliance when receivers felt the source could not legitimately make the request.

Distraction to Message. Although the meta-analysis did not directly examine communication-relevant distractions that draw attention to the message, the experiments in which receivers were set to focus either on the message or on the source suggest that such distractions would be successful. Two behaviors that may potentially distract a receiver to focus more on the message are rhetorical questions and forewarning. Rhetorical questions may mark (i.e., draw attention to) important arguments (Zillman, 1972) or they may motivate people to think about the arguments if they are not doing so already (Petty, Cacioppo, & Heesacker, 1981). There is, however, some risk in using rhetorical questions as they may interfere with comprehension and reduce persuasive impact (Munch & Swasy, 1988; Petty & Cacioppo, 1986; Petty et al., 1981). Forewarning has been shown to increase counterargumentation when receiving a persuasive message. This suggests that it motivates people to pay more attention to the message than when not forewarned. However, the fact that counterarguments increase when subjects are forewarned suggests that such communication-relevant distraction is best used with strong arguments.

To conclude the discussion and further illustrate the utility of the foregoing prescriptions, we apply them to our public health example on skin cancer messages. In the case of the high-reward source, we would intentionally highlight the source of the appeal in our mediated public service announcements (PSA). For example, we can employ linguistic variation that emphasizes the source's ownership of the persuasive propositions, perhaps by using intense language (in the form of opinionated language or fear appeals) and by varying nonverbal style, because the receiver is likely to entertain counterattitudinal assertions by a valued source. Thus, we might enhance our PSA by adding the sound of a frying hamburger underneath a visual of a young college student tanning in a lounge chair with the narration, "If you fry, you could die."

Augment this sequence with a dissolve to a popular young rock musician and it would be surprising if the young viewer did not attend. Although the receiver's interest may not be realized until near the end of the PSA, sufficient attention may be elicited to ensure conscious entertainment of the proposition during the next viewing. Thus, distracting the viewer to concentrate on source rather than counterattitudinal assertions may provide a cognitive "foot in the door." Conversely, with a low-reward speaker, one might want to deemphasize (or at the very least not highlight) source ownership of the assertions. Instead, one might best accentuate reasonable arguments by employing rhetorical questions. Alternatively, we could manipulate medium characteristics: We could quicken the pace of visual cuts, employ a variety of digital video effects, and use multitrack audio editing techniques to draw attention to the presentation rather than the presenter.

We began this discussion by reviewing the distraction literature and revealing a confusion that has occurred between communication-relevant and -irrelevant distractors. Obviously, meta-analysis may be viewed not only as a useful statistical tool for calculating average effect sizes across studies, but as an investigative probe for uncovering ambiguities across research programs and stimulating provocative theorizing that deserves further study.

REFERENCES

Allyn, J., & Festinger, L. (1961). The effectiveness of unanticipated persuasive communication. *Journal of Abnormal and Social Psychology, 62*, 35–40.

Baron, R. S., Baron, P. H., & Miller, N. (1973). The relation between distraction and persuasion. *Psychological Bulletin, 80*, 310–323.

Berlyne, D. E. (1960). *Conflict, arousal, and curiosity*. New York: McGraw-Hill.

Bettinghaus, E. P., & Cody, M. J. (1987). *Persuasive communication*. New York: Holt, Rinehart & Winston.

Bostrom, R. (1981). The interaction of sources, receivers, and objects: RSO theory. In M. Burgoon (Ed.), *Communication yearbook V* (pp. 833–855). New Brunswick, NJ: Transaction Books.

Bradac, J. J., Bowers, J. W., & Courtright, J. A. (1979). Three language variables in communication research: Intensity, immediacy, and diversity. *Human Communication Research, 5*, 257–269.

Brainerd, C. J., & Reyna, V. F. (1990). Gist if the grist: Fuzzy-trace theory and the new institutionism. *Developmental Review, 10*, 3–47.

Buller, D. (1986). Distraction during persuasive communication: A meta-analytic review. *Communication Monographs, 53*, 91–114.

Burgoon, J. K. (1978). A communication model of personal space violations: Explication and an initial test. *Human Communication Research, 4*, 129–142.

Burgoon, J. K., Buller, D. B., & Woodall, W. G. (1996). *Nonverbal communication: The unspoken dialogue* (2nd ed.). New York: McGraw-Hill.

Burgoon, J. K., & Hale, J. L. (1988). Non-verbal expectancy violations: Model elaboration and application to immediacy behaviors. *Communication Monographs, 55*, 58–79.

Burgoon, J. K., Stacks, D. W., & Burch, S. A. (1982). The role of interpersonal rewards and violations of distancing expectations in achieving influence in small groups. *Communication, 11*, 114–128.

Burgoon, M. (1989). Messages and persuasive effects. In J. Bradac (Ed.), *Message effects in communication science* (pp. 129–164). Newbury Park, CA: Sage.

Burgoon, M., Cohen, M., Miller, M. D., & Montgomery, C. L. (1978). An empirical test of a model of resistance to persuasion. *Human Communication Research, 5*, 27–39.

Burgoon, M., Fraedrich, L., & Bachman, S. (1979). Credibility of communicators and distraction as predictors of change in attitude. *Psychological Reports, 45*, 479–482.

Festinger, L. (1957). *A theory of cognitive dissonance*. Stanford, CA: Stanford University Press.

Festinger, L., & Maccoby, N. (1964). On resistance to persuasive communication. *Journal of Abnormal and Social Psychology, 1*, 359–366.

Freedman, J. L., & Sears, D. O. (1965). Warning, distraction, and resistance to influence. *Journal of Personality and Social Psychology, 1*, 262–266.

Glass, G. V., McGaw, B., & Smith, M. L. (1981). *Meta-analysis in social research*. Beverly Hills, CA: Sage.

Gruner, C. (1985). Advice to the beginning speaker on using humor: What the research tells us. *Communication Education, 34*, 142–147.

Haaland, G. A., & Venkatesen, M. (1968). Resistance to persuasive communications: An examination of the distraction hypotheses. *Journal of Personality and Social Psychology, 9*, 167–170.

Harkins, S. G., & Petty, R. E. (1981). The multiple source effect in persuasion: The effects of distraction. *Personality and Social Psychology Bulletin, 7*, 627–635.

Haslett, D. M. (1976). Distracting stimuli: Do they elicit or inhibit counterargumentation and attitude shift. *European Journal of Social Psychology, 6*, 81–94.

Hewgill, M., & Miller, G. R. (1965). Source credibility and response to fear-arousing communications. *Speech Monographs, 32*, 95–101.

Hunter, J. E., Schmidt, F. L., & Jackson, G. B. (1982). *Meta-analysis: Cumulating research finding across studies*. Beverly Hills, CA: Sage.

Insko, C. A., & Adewole, A. (1979). The role of assumed reciprocation and sentiment and assumed similarity in the production of attraction and agreement effects in p–o–x triads. *Journal of Personality and Social Psychology, 37*, 790–808.

Insko, C. A., Murashima, F., & Saiyadain, M. (1966). Communicator discrepancy, stimulus ambiguity, and influence. *Journal of Personality, 34*, 262–274.

Insko, C. A., Songer, E., & McGarvey, W. (1974). Balance, positivity, and agreement in the Jordan Paradigm: A defense of balance theory. *Journal of Experimental Social Psychology, 10*, 53–83.

Insko, C. A., Turnbull, W., & Yandell, B. (1974). Facilitative and inhibiting effects of distraction on attitude change. *Sociometry, 37*, 508–528.

Janis, I. L., Kaye, D., & Kirschner, P. (1965). Facilitating effects of "eating-while-reading" on responsiveness to persuasive communications. *Journal of Personality and Social Psychology, 1*, 181–186.

Kahneman, D. (1973). *Attention and effort*. Englewood Cliffs, NJ: Prentice-Hall.

Keating, J. P., & Brock, T. C. (1974). Acceptance of persuasion and the inhibition of counterargumentation under various distraction tasks. *Journal of Experimental Social Psychology, 10*, 301–309.

Kiesler, S. B., & Mathog, R. B. (1968). Distraction hypothesis in attitude change: Effects of effectiveness. *Psychological Reports, 23*, 1123–1133.

Kleinke, C. L. (1980). Interaction between gaze and legitimacy of request on compliance in a field setting. *Journal of Nonverbal Behavior, 5*, 3–12.

Lammers, H. B., & Becker, L. A. (1980). Distraction: Effects on the perceived extremity of a communication and on cognitive responses. *Personality and Social Psychology Bulletin, 6*, 261–266.

Langer, E. (1978). Rethinking the role of thought in social interaction. In J. H. Harvey, W. J. Ickes, & R. F. Kidd (Eds.), *New direction in attribution research* (Vol. 2, pp. 35–58). Hillsdale, NJ: Erlbaum.

Langer, E. J. (1985). Playing the middle against both ends: The usefulness of adult cognitive activity as a model for cognitive activity in childhood and old age. In S. R. Yussen (Ed.), *The growth of reflection in children* (pp. 262–286). New York: Academic Press.

Langer, E. J., & Imber, L. (1980). Role of mindlessness in the perception of deviance. *Journal of Personality and Social Psychology, 39*, 360–367.

Langer, E. J., & Piper, A. I. (1987). The prevention of mindlessness. *Journal of Personality and Social Psychology, 53*, 280–87.

McCroskey, J., & Mehrley, S. (1969). The effects of disorganization and nonfluencey on attitude change and source credibility. *Speech Monographs, 36*, 13–21.

McGuire, W. J. (1966). Attitude and opinions. *Annual Review of Psychology, 17*, 475–514.

McGuire, W. J. (1969). The nature of attitudes and attitude change. In G. Lindzey & E. Aronson (Eds.), *Handbook of social psychology* (Vol. 3, pp. 136–314). Reading, MA: Addison-Wesley.

Miller, G. R., & Basehart, J. (1969). Source trustworthiness, opinionated statements, and responses to persuasive communications. *Speech Monographs, 36*, 1–7.

Miller, G. R., & Lobe, J. (1967). Opinionated language, open- and closed-mindedness and response to persuasive communications. *Journal of Communication, 17*, 333–341.

Miller, N., & Baron, R. S. (1973). On measuring counterarguing. *Journal of the Theory of Social Behavior, 3*, 101–118.

Miller, N., & Levy, B. H. (1967). Defaming and agreeing with the communicator as a function of emotional arousal, communication extremity, and evaluative set. *Sociometry, 30*, 158–175.

Munch, J. M., & Swasy, J. L. (1988). Rhetorical question, summarization frequency, and argument strength effects on recall. *Journal of Consumer Research, 15*, 69–76.

Neisser, U. (1976). *Cognition and reality*. San Francisco: Freeman.

Osterhouse, R. A., & Brock, T. C. (1970). Distraction increases yielding to propaganda by inhibiting counterarguing. *Journal of Personality and Social Psychology, 13*, 344–358,

Petty, R. E., & Cacioppo, J. T. (1986). *Communication and persuasion: Central and peripheral routes to attitude change*. New York: Springer-Verlag.

Petty, R. E., Cacioppo, J. T., & Heesacker, M. (1981). The use of rhetorical questions in persuasion: A cognitive response analysis. *Journal of Personality and Social Psychology, 40*, 432–440.

Petty, R. E., Wells, G. L., & Brock, T. C. (1976). Distraction can enhance or reduce yielding to propaganda: Thought disruption versus effort justification. *Journal of Personality and Social Psychology, 34*, 874–884.

Posner, M. I., Nissen, M. J., & Klein, R. M. (1976). Visual dominance: An information-processing account of its origins and significance. *Psychological Review, 83*, 157–171.

Romer, D. (1979). Distraction, counterarguing and the internalization of attitude change. *European Journal of Social Psychology, 9*, 1–17.

Rosenblatt, P. C. (1966). Persuasion as a function of varying amounts of distraction. *Psychonomic Science, 5*, 85–86.

Rule, B. G., & Rehill, D. (1970). Distraction and self-esteem effects on attitude change. *Journal of Personality and Social Psychology, 15*, 359–365.

Schneider, W., & Shiffrin, R. M. (1977). Controlled and automatic human information processing: I. Detection, search, and attention. *Psychological Review, 84*, 1–66.

Shiffrin, R. M., & Schneider, W. (1977). Controlled and automatic human information processing: II. Perceptual learning, automatic attending, and a general theory. *Psychological Review, 84*, 127–190.

Silverman, I., & Regula, C. R. (1968). Evaluation apprehension, demand characteristics, and the effects of distraction on persuasibility. *The Journal of Social Psychology, 75*, 273–281.

Stacks, D. W., & Burgoon, J. K. (1981). The role of nonverbal behaviors as distractors in resistance to persuasion in interpersonal contexts. *Central States Speech Journal, 32*, 61–73.

Treisman, A. M. (1960). Contextual cues in selective listening. *Quarterly Journal of Experimental Psychology, 12*, 242–248.

Vohs, J. L., & Garrett, R. L. (1968). Resistance to persuasion: An integrative framework. *Public Opinion Quarterly, 32*, 445–452.

Watts, W. A., & Holt, L. E. (1979). Persistence of opinion change induced under conditions of forewarning and distraction. *Journal of Personality and Social Psychology, 37*, 778–789.

Wiener, M., & Mehrabian, A. (1968). *Language within language: Immediacy, a channel in verbal communication*. New York: Appleton-Century-Crofts.

Woodall, W. G., & Burgoon, J. K. (1981). The effects of nonverbal synchrony on message comprehension and persuasiveness. *Journal of Personality and Social Psychology, 37*, 778–789.

Zillman, D. (1972). Rhetorical elicitation of agreement in persuasion. *Journal of Personality and Social Psychology, 21*, 159–165.

Zimbardo, P. G., Snyder, M., Thomas, J., Gold, A., & Gurwitz, S. (1970). Modifying the impact of persuasive communications with external distraction. *Journal of Personality and Social Psychology, 16*, 669–680.

Zipf, G. K. (1949). *Human behavior and the principle of least effort*. Boston: Houghton Mifflin.

9

An Analysis of the Sleeper Effect

Mike Allen
University of Wisconsin-Milwaukee

James B. Stiff
Arizona State University

The impact the perception of source credibility by receivers of a message on attitude change remains a central issue in any theory of persuasion. The accepted advice given to communicators is to establish, in the minds of the receivers, those desirable characteristics associated with high credibility (trust, expertise, reliability, etc.). This, the logic goes, increases the probability of message receivers accepting the persuasive intent of the communicator. A communicator judged as highly credible would only present and argue for those things that offer benefit to the message receiver. Believing and acting on the basis of information from a highly credible source would be rational and prudent.

The normal expectation about the impact of a single persuasive message is that the immediate effect of the message is the maximal effect.

The persuasive effect of a single message diminishes or decays over time. Persuasion, especially when due a single message exposure, is usually temporary. For example, Petty and Cacioppo (1986) in their Elaboration Likelihood Model (ELM) explicitly made this an assumption of their general curves for both routes of information processing (central and peripheral). These assumptions about the difficulty of achieving permanent change from a single message assume that attitudes are permanent or enduring affective states. Permanent change requires more than exposure to single bit of information. Change probably requires an exposure to message that is reinforced and can eventually become permanent. However, it should be noted that some messages probably only require one exposure for permanent change. The distinction between these two areas of change is relatively unresearched.

The "sleeper" effect represents a phenomena whose existence runs counter to the general logic of persuasion theories. The sleeper effect (regardless of the particular definition of the model; see Allen & Stiff, 1989, for extended discussion of the models) is some violation of the theoretical logic that predicts a decay in the effect of a persuasive message over time. The term *sleeper* derives from an expectation that the long-term effect is larger than the short-term effect in some manner (the effect is asleep but awakes to be effective later). This review of the literature considers the definitional, theoretical, empirical, and practical concerns of the research surrounding the sleeper effect.

DEFINING THE SLEEPER EFFECT

The sleeper effect is defined by three different models. The first model defines the sleeper effect as an absolute increase over time in attitude change by the receivers of a low credible message (Cook, Gruder, Hennigan, & Flay, 1979, Matice, 1978). The attitude change immediately after message exposure is not as large as it is at a later time. The second model defines the sleeper effect as a relative diminution in the difference in attitude change comparing the high and low credible message source. The high credible message source receivers exhibit greater attitude decay than a message attributed to a low credible message source (Gillig & Greenwald, 1974; Gruder et al., 1978). The final model demonstrates a change of the relationships between the high and low credible message sources such that over time the low credible message source induces more attitude change in receivers than the high credible message source of change order citations (Gillig & Greenwald, 1974; Matice, 1978).

Defining the sleeper effect is an elusive but important endeavor. From the three definitions for the sleeper effect come their respective models: (a) discounting model, (b) forgetting model, and (c) traditional model. A more detailed mathematical explanation is available elsewhere (Allen & Stiff, 1989). The following paragraphs give a narrative explanation of each of the models.

The discounting model assumes that persuasion is caused by either message source credibility or message content. It posits that initial attitude change is a combination of message content and message source credibility. The long-term or permanent attitude change is based on message content. The existence of the sleeper effect is based on the convergence of the message receivers attitudes toward that final point based on the disassociation of message source and message content.

The credibility of the message source only temporarily impacts the level of attitude change, after disassociation between message source and message content, the long-term attitude change is determined by message content. Regardless of the level of message source credibility, the final attitudes of the receivers are determined by the message content. Message source credibility only temporarily effects the persuasiveness of the message. The highly credible message source generates greater attitude change than a low credible message source over the short term (methodologically, this would equate to the immediate posttest). Eventually, over time, the mean attitudes of each experimental group (high and low credible message source) converge as disassociation takes place between message content and message source (methodologically, this would amount to using a delayed posttest).

Methodologically, the key feature is to demonstrate that at the immediate posttest a group of message receivers were unpersuaded by a message attributed to a low credible message source. Over time, the processing of information, storage in memory, and subsequent recall has persons initially unpersuaded come to accept the conclusions of the message. The reason for this is that the association between message content and message source is forgotten. The message receiver remembers the message content but forgets the source of the information and therefore comes to accept the conclusions drawn from the information. The person should recall the information and the recommendations but not remember the source of the information. The initial exposure to the information occurred under conditions (low credible message source) that caused the receiver to discount the conclusions.

However, after the passing of time, the justification for discounting the message content is no longer associated with that content. This creates the conditions for the sleeper effect with the low credible message source. The theory, however, also explains the persuasion occurring with the message attributed to the high credible message source. Initially the person accepts the conclusions because both the message content is believable and the source is trusted, expert, and so on. However, over time the same process of disassociation between message content and message source occurs. Unlike the low credible source, which inhibits initial persuasion, the high credible message source enhances the persuasiveness of the content. The result of the disassociation of a highly credible message source from message content would be to reduce the long-term persuasiveness of the message.

The traditional model assumes that immediately after message exposure the high credible message source demonstrates a higher level of adherence in the message receivers than the low credible message source. However, after delay the low credible message source has more attitude change than the high credible message source. The model claims that high credibility for a message source is a benefit in the short run and a liability in the long run. The decision to seek a particular level of credibility should be based on the desire for long-term or short-term attitude adherence. Unfortunately, the empirical research to date as well as the theoretical writings on this issue do not define what is meant by "short" and "long" term.

The theoretical rationale for the model assumes that the judgement by a message receiver that the message source is highly credible acts to inhibit attention and retention of the information of the speech. The audience is less motivated to process and store the message content. Therefore, after a period of time the attitude change produced by the message is lost. The message receiver has nothing in memory that was retained to justify the continuation of the position.

Conversely, the audience hearing a message from a low credible source pays attention to the message content but does not agree with it. The message receivers are unpersuaded. The judgement that the message source is not credible acts as in inhibition against agreeing with information in the message. However, over time, a disassociation occurs between the message source and the message content. At a later time the audience uses the information stored in memory to evaluate and justify a position on a topic. Because the source of the information is forgotten, the position can now be accepted.

Although the traditional model and discounting models are similar in many aspects, there is an important difference. The discounting model views message content and message source as separate effects that are additive. The long-term impact of disassociation means that whatever effect the message source has will be removed, leaving only message content as a factor in persuasion. The traditional model assumes the same process for the low credible source as a discounting model. However, the traditional model assumes that a high credible message source actually inhibits any significant attention or retention of message content. The result is that according to the traditional model logic, the message attributed to the low credible message source will be eventually more persuasive than the message attributed to the highly credible source.

The forgetting model assumes that the high message source obtains greater adherence than the low credible message source. After a delay, the high and low credible sources *both* show diminished effectiveness. However, the difference in persuasiveness of message attributed to the high and low credible sources diminishes over time until there is no difference between high and low sources. This model argues that observed differences in persuasiveness between a message attributed to a high or low credible message source is only temporary. However, the amount of measured attitude change be message receivers always favors the highly credible message source.

The sleeper effect is therefore a relative effect. The effect of time is to diminish the advantage for a high credible message source. The sleeper effect does not have an increase in attitude change for either the high or low credible message source. The effect is simply a closing of the gap created by the differing levels of credibility assigned by the receivers to the source of the message. What appears as a great advantage for the highly credible message source slowly vanishes until no advantage remains.

CONTROVERSIAL STATUS OF THE SLEEPER

The status of the sleeper is at best controversial. The research presents a mixed and uncertain picture of the nature and even the existence of the effect. Published articles carry titles like "Is it Time to Lay the Sleeper Effect to Rest?" (Gillig & Greenwald, 1974), "History of the Sleeper Effect: Some Logical Pitfalls in Accepting the Null Hypothesis" (Cook et al., 1979), "The Sleeper Effect—An Awakening" (Capon & Hulbert, 1973), and "Under What Conditions does Theory Obstruct Research Progress?" (Greenwald, Pratkanis, Leippe, & Baumgardner, 1986). The titles of the articles suggest a sense of inconsistency and uncertainty regarding the evidence and context for the generation and interpretation of the effect. The result has been a confusing and complicated set of characterizations of the research.

Textbooks in particular find it difficult to incorporate the material in a consistent and comprehensive manner. The advanced textbooks have found the effect an anomaly not easily included within theoretical discussions. For example, Petty and Cacioppo (1986) in their book *Communication and Persuasion*, dismissed the sleeper effect because,

"Although the sleeper effect is of considerable conceptual significance, obtaining it may require conditions that are infrequently present in the 'real world' or in persuasion research" (p. 183). The sleeper effect, as is argued later, represents a problem for the ELM and therefore the characterization by Petty and Cacioppo is hardly surprising.

Other treatments by textbooks vary depending on the underlying theoretical assumptions of the author or desire to apply the findings of the sleeper effect to available theoretical positions or practical application. Reardon (1981) argued that the salience of the source to the message is the critical determining factor when analyzing data on the sleeper effect. Osborn and Osborn (1988) argued for an often occurring delayed effect for a message (which they call the sleeper effect). This explanation is not linked to source credibility. Hanna and Gibson (1989) argued that the sleeper effect is related to the credibility of the source of evidence in a speech. The message receivers will remember the source of evidence in the speech without remembering the evidence itself.

Reviewers of the literature on the sleeper effect seem in disarray when it comes to any kind of consensus about the nature and/or existence of the sleeper effect. The ability to use the present compilations of the literature to assess this position appear to not inspire great confidence. Although later research seems to support the discounting and disassociation assumptions (Gruder et al., 1978) the status of the sleeper effect is still controversial. The implications of this effect for both theory and practice justify the need for an examination and resolution of this conflict. Theoretically, the sleeper effect represents something contrary to the standard wisdom that the most positive effect of a message occurs immediately after exposure. This assumption underpins many theoretical perspectives in persuasion (e.g., the ELM). From a practical application perspective, the current advice offered communicators is to seek as high a level of credibility as possible. If this is not always advantageous over the longer term or even counterproductive (as the traditional model suggests) then advice given communicators may require a consideration of the effect the communicator desires. After determining the goal of the communicator a decision about what kind of source credibility can be implemented. The sleeper effect, if proven to exist, would represent a drastic departure from most general prescriptive advice.

META-ANALYTIC EVIDENCE

The full reporting and discussion of the methods and data is available elsewhere (Allen & Stiff, 1989). Only a short summary of the information contained in that report is reported here. The analysis in that report is not the typical meta-analytic summary of data, providing an average estimate of the effect and associated tests of homogeneity. The investigation provided an analysis of the observed patter of effects associated with each study, comparing them to the pattern of effects consistent with each model of the sleeper effect. The problem with averaging an effect is that most studies contained no credibility manipulation information. This was needed because the difference between the high and low credible source descriptions between experiments was not standardized. This meant that averaging the effects were problematic because the curves over time would be related to the size of the original manipulation as well as the length of the delay. However, the size of the credibility manipulation according to the three available theories should not effect the direction of any of the effects, only their magnitude. Because it is possible to differentiate between the three models on the basis of the direction of the effect, the inability to accurately compare the size of the effect while desirable is unnecessary.

Essentially, each model makes a series of predictions about the nature of the effects. The critical feature of the traditional model is that at the delayed posttest the low credible message source receivers show more effect than the high credible message source receivers. For the forgetting model the two critical features are: (a) that the effectiveness between the immediate posttest and delayed posttest between high and low credible message sources be diminished, and (b) there is for both the high and low credible sources a diminishing effectiveness over time. For the discounting model, the methodological requirement for a pretest to immediate posttest showing no change in attitude for the low credible group was only met by five studies. This requirement is necessary because if there is any change from pretest to immediate posttest in the low credible group the delayed posttest will not show an increase. This is because although there is the increase due to disassociation of message source and message content there is also the loss of the effect due to the original positive effect of the source. When the change is zero from pretest to immediate posttest, theoretically the change to delayed posttest should only be due to message content after disassociation from message source. Table 9.1 reproduces the data from the meta-analysis (Allen & Stiff, 1989).

The method still resembles a vote-counting procedure but uses a systematic and replicable standard. In the future as data sets become available, this finding can be tested and compared with available credibility information. At that point the data should become available to test this model using more sophisticated and exact procedures.

The results show that the traditional model fits only 5 of the data sets and the forgetting model only 10 of the data sets. There were only 5

Table 9.1. Summary of Available Data.

Study	Consistency of Data With the Model[a]		
	Discounting[b]	Forgetting	Traditional
Gillig & Greenwald		-	-
Gruder et al. (1)		+	-
(2)	+	-	+
2nd exp (1)	+	-	+
(2)	+	-	-
Hovland & Weiss		-	-
Johnson & Watkins (1)		+	-
(2)		-	-
Kelman & Hovland		+	-
Matice		-	-
McCroskey (1)		+	-
(2)		+	-
2nd exp (1)		+	-
(2)		+	-
Pratkanis et al.[c]		-	-
Schulman & Worrall		+	-
Watts & Holt		-	-
Watts & McGuire (1)	+	-	+
(2)	+	-	+
Weiss		+	-
Whittaker & Meade		+	-

Note. [a]A "-" means inconsistent with the model, whereas a "+" indicates consistency. [b]Only five studies met the precondition of a pretest demonstrating no immediate attitude change for the low credibility source. [c]This study is the only one that fits none of the available models. The findings suggest a different model for the sleeper effect, one that cannot be computed to other data sets. Also, the lack of statistical information in the report makes it impossible to accurately represent the results.

data sets that met the preconditions of the discounting model and essentially all 5 meet the basic model. The only deviation stems from a significant correlation in one of the comparisons between the delayed high and delayed low credible message source conditions.

The findings suggest that a sleeper effect does exist and it conforms to a model that predicts convergence over time of receiver's attitudes on a final point. The effect is that hypothesized by the discounting model consistent with the expectations that message content and message source become disassociated over time. The effect suggests only a temporary impact of credibility. The highly credible message source creates additional attitude change that is lost as disassociation occurs. The low credible message source inhibits processing and results in less positive persuasion. Over time the same disassociation that reduces the persuasiveness of the high credible message source increases the persuasive effect of the low credible message source. The long-term result becomes a convergence of the low and high credible attitude change curves around a final common point. This final point should be related to the content of the information after disassociation with message source. However, the available data that contribute directly weakly supports this point. Additional testing should be conducted to directly test the conclusions drawn from this data. The testing should clearly test the conclusions drawn from this reanalysis of the data.

THEORETICAL IMPLICATIONS

Theoretically, the sleeper effect must be something considered within the context of the associations between message source effects and message content effects. The need exists to establish a model that explains both message processing combined with a theory of memory for information retrieval. Shapiro (1990) commented that general theories of persuasion need to develop cognitive models to explain both processing and memory. It is probably precisely those areas where the available theories and data are weakest and most ambiguous.

The theories in persuasion need to distinguish between those elements in a cognitive system that change permanently and those that subject to forgetting or, with lack of reinforcement, simply fading. Consider an argument about some event, such as who won baseball's Cy Young award in a particular year. Appealing to some historical document or authoritative text will more than likely change the mind of a listener. If learning occurs, this particular fact will be stored in memory and the next time the issue comes up the person would retrieve this fact. Failure to correctly find the information would be due to some inability to locate this in memory rather than any real change in the belief of the person. This cognitive "bit" of information is probably different than some affective state like an attitude on some topic like abortion or the S & L defaults.

Even an effective belief may be different from a person believing themselves persuaded to go on a diet, exercise, give up smoking, and so forth. Such decisions and reactions to a message require more permanent behavioral changes and the need for almost daily reinforcement exists that does not usually exist in arguments about the quality of particular baseball pitcher or an expression of how a person feels about a social issue. When relatively stable behavioral patterns or perhaps changes to fundamental belief systems are involved, even if the intentions of the person are honest and fully committed, change may not be easy. The longevity of New Year's resolutions are a classic example of resolve and a decision that usually does not last. Any complete theory of persuasion should be able to consider and account for this because the sleeper effect may only involve a portion of those persuadable elements inside a person's cognitive system.

The sleeper effect assumes changes over time in the attitudes of the receivers. The evidence suggests that there exists a connection between the source of the message and the content of a message that either enhances or retards message acceptance. The Elaboration Likelihood Model (ELM) or persuasion (Petty & Cacioppo, 1981, 1986) was developed to deal with relationships among elements. The ELM categorizes the distinction between long-term and short-term effects as the difference between peripheral and central processing routes and neatly offers an explanation of the effect. Essentially, message source credibility is a peripheral cue that has only temporary persuasive effects. The effect of credibility is to provide a temporary association between the message source and message content that effects the processing of the information. After a time, there occurs a disassociation between the message source and message content such that the long-term effect of the message determined by message content (as processed by the central processing route) is the final resting place.

The existence of the sleeper effect, however, poses problems for the ELM. Petty and Cacioppo (1986) pointed out that the expectation for the long-term and short-term effects of both the central and peripheral route are decay. Nothing within the model allows for an increase over time within either the central or the peripheral route. The result is a finding that contradicts the basic premises of the model. A more extensive critique of the ELM related to the sleeper effect is available elsewhere (Allen & Reynolds, 1993). The existence of a sleeper effect poses a fundamental challenge to the basic tenets of the ELM.

Few other theories provide a detailed account of processing. For example, social judgement theory, congruity, and cognitive dissonance are persuasive theories that would simply accept the disassociation between message source and message content and then reinterpret the findings as consistent with the theory. The information after disassociation from the source would simply work within the parameters of the theory to persuade the individual by establishing dissonance, changing attitudes, and so on. However, the theories do not provide within them an expectation that the process of disassociation is natural and to be normally expected. The theories would be examples of post hoc explanations for observed effects rather than necessarily predicting those effects.

A theoretical issue unexplored by the data is the nature of the relationship of the message source to the message. Suppose a legislator gives a speech on abortion—there is nothing necessary about the relationship between the person and the topic. However, consider Nixon's famous "Checkers" speech. To recall the speech is to recall the source. Under those conditions it would appear unlikely that the source could be disassociated from the message. The very message and the conclusions of the message require an inextricable link between source and message that would seem to be recalled every time with the message. This may or may not be true, but current persuasion theories and writing have not fully established the relationship between message content and message source. Essentially, the sleeper effect is a finding about the relationship but unfortunately current theories do not fully construct an account of this relationship.

PRACTICAL IMPLICATIONS

The most immediate implication for the teaching and practice of communication is whether a message source should strive for high credibility in the minds of the receivers. The advice based on the evidence of this summary suggests that highly credible sources are more effective in the short term without any question. It is only in the longer term that any question of effect can be raised.

A review of textbooks in public speaking and persuasion (Allen & Preiss, 1990) demonstrated, however, that over 50% of the information was consistent with the available evidence. The controversy seems to exist more at the theoretical and experimental level rather than at the level of pedagogy. However, it should be noted that the meta-analysis was only able to establish existence of the effect rather than provide an adequate explanation or test competing explanations for the observed effect.

In many situations, the desire for long-term adherence is unnecessary. For example, a politician's persuasive efforts are either successful by election day or they are a failure. If the electorate are persuaded 5 months later (after election day), the victory is only moral, the decision and die is already cast.

PEDAGOGICAL IMPLICATIONS

The implications of the research findings for those teaching persuasion and public speaking are fairly straightforward. At the current time, the data suggests that for the short term the perception of high credibility is one to be sought by the message sender. The long-term implications are less clear and the information more difficult to summarize. However, the bulk of evidence indicates that a highly credible source will generally fare no worse and usually better over the longer term than the low credible message source. What should be noted is that no current complete theory of persuasion has been advanced which suggests the opposite. If the low credible message source is more persuasive over the long term than the high credible message source, the current theories do not explicitly endorse or explain this finding. The combination of a lack of empirical evidence and theoretical framework suggests that the age-old advice of seeking to establish high credibility is sound and should be followed. The only change in this advice is the caveat that the advantage of high credibility may only be short term. All the models and available data suggest that this advantage is time bound and any initial advantage will eventually diminish. The unresolved issue is how fast and how much diminution of the advantage occurs.

For the classroom, the instructor will have to make a decision about the level of theoretical discussion that this issue warrants. In an introductory public speaking class this issue will probably merit a different level of treatment than a graduate seminar on persuasive methodology and theory.

Fortunately, a review of public speaking and persuasion textbooks on this issue (Allen & Preiss, 1990) demonstrated that most instructors have available materials that correctly conclude that the sleeper effect exists. Until more sophisticated experimental evidence is generated and summarized much latitude should be given when explaining this effect. Although explanations are available, they are tentative and involve untested theoretical assumptions. Despite these problems, the traditional advice of a source wishing to be highly credible is maintained. The only issue is the long-term permanence and stability that source credibility has on attitude change.

REFERENCES

Allen, M., & Preiss, R. (1990). Using meta-analysis to evaluate curriculum: An examination of selected college textbooks. *Communication Education, 39*, 103–116.

Allen, M., & Reynolds, R. (1993). The elaboration likelihood model and the sleeper effect: An analysis of attitude change over time. *Communication Theory, 3*, 73–82.

Allen, M., & Stiff, J. (1989). Testing three models for the sleeper effect. *Western Journal of Speech Communication, 53*, 411–426.

Capon, N., & Hulbert, J. (1973). The sleeper effect—an awakening. *Public Opinion Quarterly, 37*, 333–358.

Cook, T., Gruder, C., Hennigan, K., & Flay, B. (1979). History of the sleeper effect: Some logical pitfalls in accepting the null hypothesis. *Psychological Bulletin, 86*, 662–679.

Gillig, P., & Greenwald, A. (1974). Is it time to lay the sleeper effect to rest? *Journal of Personality and Social Psychology, 29*, 132–139.

Greenwald, A., Pratkanis, J., Leippe, M., & Baumgardner, M. (1986). Under what conditions does theory obstruct research progress? *Psychological Review, 93*, 216–229.

Gruder, C., Cook, T., Hennigan, F., Flay, B., Alessis, C., & Halamaj, J. (1978). Empirical tests of the absolute sleeper effect predicted from the discounting cue hypothesis. *Journal of Personality and Social Psychology, 36*, 1061–1074.

Hanna, M., & Gibson, J. (1989). *Public speaking for personal success* (2nd ed.). Dubuque, IA: Brown.

Hovland, C., & Weiss, W. (1951). The influence of source credibility on communication effectiveness. *Public Opinion Quarterly, 15*, 635–650.

Johnson, H., & Watkins, L. (1971). The effects of message repetitions on immediate and delayed attitude change. *Bulletin of Psychonomic Science, 22*, 101–103.

Kelman, H., & Hovland, C. (1953). "Reinstatement" of the communicator in delayed measurement of opinion change. *Journal of Abnormal and Social Psychology, 48*, 327–335.

Matice, K. (1978). *The effect of source, class, dogmatism, and time on attitude change of police academy recruits*. Unpublished doctoral dissertation, University of Missouri–St. Louis, MO.

McCroskey, J. (1966). *Experimental studies of the effects of ethos and evidence in persuasive communication.* Unpublished doctoral dissertation, Pennsylvania State University, State College.

Osborn, M., & Osborn, S. (1988). *Public speaking*. Boston, MA: Houghton Mifflin.

Petty, R., & Cacioppo. J. (1981). *Attitudes and persuasion: Classic and contemporary approaches*. Dubuque, IA: Brown.

Petty, R., & Cacioppo. J. (1986). *Communication and persuasion: Central and peripheral routes to attitude change*. New York: Springer-Verlag.

Pratkanis, A., Greenwald, A., Leippe, M., & Baumgardner, M. (1988). In search of reliable persuasion effects: III. The sleeper effect is dead. Long live the sleeper effect. *Journal of Personality and Social Psychology, 54*, 203–218.

Reardon, K. (1981). *Persuasion*. Beverly Hills CA: Sage.
Schulman, G., & Worrall, C. (1970). Salience patterns, source credibility, and the sleeper effect. *Public Opinion Quarterly, 34*, 371–382.
Shapiro, M. (1990). *Models of memory and the ELM*. Unpublished manuscript, Cornell University, Ithaca, NY.
Watts, W., & Holt, L. (1979). Persistence of opinion change induced under conditions for forewarning and distraction. *Journal of Abnormal and Social Psychology, 83*, 778–789.
Watts, W., & McGuire, W. (1964). Persistence of induced opinion change and retention of the inducing message contents. *Journal of Abnormal and Social Psychology, 68*, 223–241.
Weiss, W. (1953). A "sleeper" effect in opinion change. *Journal of Abnormal and Social Psychology, 48*, 173–180.
Whittaker, J., & Meade, R. (1968). Retention of opinion change as a function of differential source credibility. *International Journal of Psychology, 3*, 103–108.

10

Another Look at the Use of Rhetorical Questions

Barbara Mae Gayle
University of Portland

Raymond W. Preiss
University of Puget Sound

Mike Allen
University of Wisconsin

The widely accepted persuasive technique of asking, then answering the question posed, is deeply rooted in Western rhetorical tradition. Demetrius advised rhetors to build force by asking audiences questions without giving answers (Benson & Prosser, 1969). Quintilian defined this type of question as an *interrogare* (Butler, 1921) and ancient Greeks called this rhetorical device *erotesis* (Lanham, 1968). Consistent with this rhetorical legacy, modern persuaders receive advice to use rhetorical questions to affirm or deny a point by asking an emphatic question to which no overt answer is expected (Devito, 1990; Hanna & Gibson, 1987; Heun & Heun, 1986; Hunt, 1987; Koch, 1988; Lucas, 1989; Osborn & Osborn, 1988; Verderber, 1988).

However, the conditions under which rhetorical questions function persuasively remains poorly articulated and not clearly understood. Research results reveal a bewildering array of definitions and conceptualizations, inconsistent theoretical interpretations, and contradictory results that obscure conclusions about the persuasive efficacy of rhetorical questions. This meta-analytic review statistically synthesizes the existing studies to elicit a unified perspective on the persuasibility of rhetorical questions questions.

DEFINITIONS AND CONCEPTUALIZATIONS PROBLEMS

The first set of contradictory issues involves the status of rhetorical questions: Are they one category of questions or are there several forms of rhetorical questions? Kertzer (1987) defined rhetorical questions as questions understood as indirect assertions; questions posed in such a way to suggest its own reply or to create an effect. Tracey (1989) argued that there are six broad categories of questions and rhetorical questions are but one kind of question. Brown (1982), on the other hand, suggested there are three types of rhetorical questions: agreement, concession, and informative, whereas Moore (1983) classified rhetorical questions into seven categories. However, a review of the empirical research (Brown, 1982; Burnkrant & Howard, 1984; Cantor, 1979; Enzle & Harvey, 1982; Howard, 1990; Munch, 1983) reveals a concentration on grammatical forms: indirect negated forms such as "You will help me won't you," and positive assertion or direct grammatical forms such as "Won't you write down an example?"

Disagreements over the categorization schema leads to controversies related to the components of rhetorical questions. Schmidt-Radefeldt (1977) suggested that rhetorical questions be classified by their components: (a) intention of the persuader; (b) common knowledge shared by persuader and receiver; (c) receiver's acceptance of the utterance; and (d) persuader's avoidance of false presuppositions. However, Kertzer (1987) classified rhetorical questions using three affective components: (a) consensus, (b) authority, and/or (c) enigma. He suggested that rhetorical questions impose consensus by: (a) forcefully excluding disagreement as they persuade or dissuade, (b) playing with the notion of authority by locating, shifting, asserting, defying, or testing it in various ways, and (c) intensifying the effect of asking questions by becoming puzzling or enigmatic. Unfortunately, no single comprehensive perspective on rhetorical questions emerges. The problem stems from the indecision about the multiforms of rhetorical questions If there are two or three different types of rhetorical questions, then the classification schema proposed should reflect the differences between the various forms, and as of now these schema do not.

The second area of controversy revolves around the communicative nature of rhetorical questions Researchers do not agree whether rhetorical questions demand an obvious response from the receiver. The disagreement centers on the process of generating an answer: (a) by the source of the message implicitly, (b) by the receiver either implicitly or explicitly, or (c) whether the receiver's response is immediate or latent. Several researchers suggest that rhetorical questions act to emphasize an important issue, and require both an intellectual and emotional involvement to elicit agreement (Enzle & Harvey, 1982; Zillmann & Cantor, 1973). Ervin-Tripp (1976) suggested that rhetorical questions comprise an indirect speech act that expects covert responses. Fisher (1985) believes that rhetorical questions serve as persuasive devices that operate mentally on receivers so that the receivers adopt the predetermined view of the speaker. Similarly, Nir (1988) claimed that rhetorical questions incorporate an often sarcastic or enigmatic answer. However, Schmidt-Radefeldt (1977) argued that rhetorical questions require no answers because they are pseudo statements, not questions. Leonard and Lowery (1984) claimed that rhetorical questions never require receivers to do anything mentally or otherwise. Thus, how rhetorical questions function as speech acts could cause differences in receiver's actions and expectations. The lack of agreement on this issue lays the foundation for the theoretical discrepancies in studying the persuasive efficacy of rhetorical questions.

Conceptual disagreements involve whether rhetorical questions function persuasively. Brown (1982) believes that rhetorical questions frustrate receivers and do not enhance persuasion. He argued, as Munch and Swasey (1983) did, if listeners ruminate over the questions they are distracted from the persuasive appeal. He also claimed, as did Otto and Schuck (1983), that receivers have difficulty retaining the message content when they are distracted or frustrated by the use of rhetorical questions. Cantor (1979) concurred and argued that rhetorical questions are ineffective and suggest avoiding them in favor of other persuasive techniques.

However, other researchers argue that the grammatical form of the rhetorical question determines its effectiveness (Enzle & Harvey, 1982) or that the effectiveness of rhetorical questions are dependent on: (a) the involvement of the receiver, (b) the strength of the argument, or (c) the frequency and placement of rhetorical questions (Burnkrant & Howard, 1984; Howard, 1990; Petty, Cacioppo, & Heesacker, 1981; Swasey & Munch, 1985). Both Ervin-Tripp (1976) and Kertzer (1987) argued that the way rhetorical questions persuade is dependent on the degree of familiarity between the parties, the size of the status discrepancy between them, and the way rhetorical questions are presented and received. Ervin-Tripp (1976) suggested that rhetorical questions are normally interpreted as commands and that noncompliance with these embedded imperatives requires some response by the receiver due to the social dynamics of the situation introduced by the extraverbal content of the rhetorical question. Thus, there is no consensus on either the way rhetorical questions function to elicit responses or persuade.

The lack of consensus about the categorization, components, and communicative nature of rhetorical questions is readily apparent. Disagreement about the nature and effectiveness of rhetorical questions also obscures the theoretical accounts of the variable.

THEORETICAL ISSUES

Explanations for the persuasive effects of rhetorical questions fall into four broad categories (Munch, 1983): operant conditioning, distraction theory, social interaction, and elicitation of agreement.

These categories provide useful rubrics for exploring the way rhetorical questions persuade, but they are not exhaustive or mutually exclusive. Also, the research results stemming from each theoretical stance are inconsistent and contradictory.

Operant Conditioning

Zillmann (1972) argued that by continually pairing rhetorical questions with good arguments, a predisposition is created where rhetorical questions are associated with powerful arguments. He found that rhetorical questions, whether they were positive assertions or indirectly negated, created the impression of a minimal intent to persuade.

Using operant conditioning theory, Brown (1982) found that student ratings of teachers using rhetorical questions were negatively associated with the use of all three types of rhetorical questions. Only teachers using interrogative questions were positively evaluated. Brown reasoned that rhetorical questions frustrate students by denying them the opportunity to act in ways most consistent with their prior learning experiences. In other words, he argued that students expect questions that encourage overt and immediate responses.

These findings remain perplexing, as they support the efficacy of operant conditioning while denying the efficacy of rhetorical questions. Apparently, the social context specifies an appropriate conditioning history that mediates the effects of message variables. Thus, educational contexts allow responses to questions that may cause frustration with rhetorical questions and favorable acceptance of interrogatives. In situations appropriate for oratory, expectations may inhibit audience participation and motivate receivers to search for markers of powerful arguments instead.

Distraction Hypothesis

The distraction hypothesis suggests that rhetorical questions disrupt the production of thoughts that would naturally be occurring while listening (Petty et al., 1981). Focusing on the attention issue, Petty et al. found that direct forms of rhetorical questions enhanced thinking when the message was of low relevance to the receiver but caused messages with strong arguments to become more persuasive than messages with weak arguments. When the message was of high relevance and receivers were motivated to process that message, the use of rhetorical questions disrupted or distracted thinking about the message.

Swasey and Munch (1985) replicated Petty et al.'s (1981) study and found that direct forms of rhetorical questions increased the persuasive effects of strong arguments and reduced persuasive effects of weak arguments. They also found that listeners were distracted by rhetorical questions in situations of high involvement using weak arguments. Munch and Swasey (1988) found that rhetorical questions with strong arguments decreased recall, and rhetorical questions with weak arguments did not. Thus, it appears that involvement and argument strength affects the amount of distraction created by rhetoricals and the positive or negative impact of distraction on attitude change. However, it is unclear which variable has the most impact on the persuasibility of rhetorical questions.

Social Interaction Perspective

The social interaction view suggests that, when compared to declarative statements, both direct and indirect forms of rhetorical questions exert more pressure on the receiver to conform (Munch, 1983). Cantor (1979) studied rhetorical requests for help and found that using rhetorical questions in a persuasive message did not have an effect on behavioral compliance. Munch (1983), on the other hand, found that rhetorical questions exert more force or interpersonal pressure to accept an argument because they convey a sense of immediacy between the speaker and listener. Enzle and Harvey (1982) extended Zillmann's (1972) and Cantor's (1979) research and found that receivers were more likely to help in response to indirect rhetorical question requests and that the indirectly negated rhetorical questions (but not the directly negated rhetorical questions) created both heightened perceptions of recipient need and increased help giving. These findings suggest that the grammatical form of rhetoricals alters the perception and affect receiver conformity to requests.

Elicitation of Agreement

The fourth approach accounts for the effects of rhetoricals by focusing on message potency apart from interpersonal pressure by the source. The basic premise assumes that rhetorical questions invoke receiver agreement by directing the receiver's attention to opposing issues that undercuts the arguments.

In a mock jury setting, Zillmann and Cantor's (1974) results indicated that using rhetorical questions on jurors with unfavorable attitudes resulted in harsher verdicts than those subjects with favorable attitudes. Consistent with the elicitation of agreement approach, these feelings withstood counterarguments from the prosecution.

Using rhetorical question introductions, Burnkrant and Howard (1984) found more favorable thoughts occurred when involvement was low and more unfavorable thoughts and less attitude change occurred when involvement was high. This is consistent with the elicitation perspective because rhetorical questions are thought to arouse receivers' uncertainty, heighten their curiosity, and motivate more intensive processing of the message content than normal statements.

On the other hand, Howard's (1990) research reveals that rhetorical questions function best as an elicitator of judgment that facilitate persuasion when they are presented after arguments. He suggested that "message processing is incidental to how rhetorical questions operate" (p. 237) and, thus, discounts the distraction model in favor of a more judgment elaboration paradigm. He argued that the availability of relevant information preceding the rhetorical question implies the answer and lays a foundation for a reasoned judgment.

Other research examining message processing contradicts the elicitation of agreement explanation for the effectiveness of rhetoricals more directly. Munch (1983) found more cognitive responses generated and less favorable attitudes observed when the message style contained both direct and indirect forms of rhetorical questions than when using declarative statements. In a later study, Munch (1987) found that rhetorical questions disrupted the receiver's elaboration in a strong argument version and that the disruption increased as the summarization frequency increased. In weak messages, Munch (1987) found that rhetorical questions disrupt receiver's message argument elaboration and increase the pressure on the receiver. In these instances, rhetoricals did not draw attention to or undercut counterarguments. Instead, distraction tended to reduce message processing.

Overall, no clear theoretical explanation of the persuasive effects (or lack of persuasiveness) of rhetoricals emerges. These results reveal a confusing array of theoretical interpretations and no clear criteria for discriminating between competing perspectives.

METHOD

To explore the persuasive effects of rhetorical questions, existing studies relevant to this phenomena were aggregated. By coding and transforming outcomes into a common metric, it is possible to combine results across these studies, estimate an average effect size, and detect moderator variables. Although meta-analysis is often used to resolve conflicting research findings, the technique is also useful in quantifying the empirical features of a body of literature (Cooper, 1981; Glass, McGaw, & Smith, 1981; Light & Pillemer, 1984) such as rhetorical questions.

Search Procedures

For this investigation, an extensive search of the literature was initiated using manual and computer searches of *Social Sciences Citation Index*, *Psychological Abstracts*, *Resources in Education*, *Dissertation Abstracts International*, and *Index to Journals in Speech Communication*.

Each study was subjected to inclusion rules for aggregation. A report was included if it: (a) was an experimental investigation providing enough statistical information to allow calculation of an effect size; (b) reported a relationship relevant to the persuasiveness of rhetorical questions.

Coding Procedures

The search procedures and coding procedures resulted in the location of 12 manuscripts relevant to the variable of interest. Seventeen separate experiments in 10 manuscripts were amenable to meta-analysis or dealt with the variable of interest. Basic information is contained in Table 10.1. Two studies—Munch (1983) and Munch (1987)—used the same data set as Munch and Swasey (1988) and thus were not included in the meta-analysis.

Studies were also coded for grammatical forms. Comparing studies relying on one type of grammatical form with studies that use a different grammatical form seemed problematic because the form of the rhetorical question may elicit more personal cognitive involvement and increase or

Table 10.1. Rhetorical Question Studies: Data and Effect Sizes.

Study author	Study date	Situation	Sample size	Form code	Effect size
Brown	1982	Classroom	230	3	.000
Burnkrant & Howard	1984	Editorials	160	2	-.099
Cantor	1979	Soliciting	56	2	.055
Enzle & Harvey	1982	Request for help			
		Exp One	100	1	.280
		Exp Two	70	2	-.143
		Exp Two	70	1	.240
		Exp Three	40	2	-.005
		Exp Three	40	1	.308
Howard	1990	Advertisement			
		Exp One	120	1	.067
		Exp Two	80	1	.115
		Exp Three	60	2	.095
		Exp Three	60	1	.095
		Exp Four	160	1	.000
Munch[a]	1988	Sales presentation	240	3	.110
Petty et al.	1981	Editorials	160	2	.000
Swasy & Munch	1985	Editorials	160	2	.000
Zillmann	1972	Courtroom scenario	90	3	.251
Zillmann & Cantor	1974	Courtroom scenario	54	2	-.166

Note. [a]This study uses data from Munch, 1983 and Munch, 1987. # Form Code: 1 = indirect, 2 = direct, 3 = mixed forms

decrease persuasiveness. Mixing rhetorical grammatical forms within one experiment also seemed problematic, because it is not easy to identify whether the success or failure of the persuasive effect is the result of anyone particular form. Therefore, we attempted to determine if the grammatical form of the rhetorical question change the nature of the persuasive outcomes.

Statistical Procedures

The summary statistics of each study were converted to correlations so that the magnitude of outcomes attributable to the persuasive effects of rhetorical questions could be quantified. The benchmark for evaluating effect sizes is found in Cohen (1977): $r = .10$ is a small effect; $r = .30$ is a medium effect; $r = .50$ is a large effect.

The correlations were weighted for sample size and then averaged. Each average correlation was assessed to determine if the variance in the observed sample correlation was larger than that expected by random sampling error (Hedges & Olkin, 1985).

This variance centered meta-analysis was selected because of its high power for detecting moderator variables. A finding that significantly more variance exists in the sample of observed correlations than can be attributed to random sampling error indicates that the effect sizes are heterogenous. Heterogenous variance suggests that the average correlation does not represent the average of a single sample of correlations, in which case a moderator variable probably exists. To detect a moderator, the sum of the squared error is tested using a chi-square test. A nonsignificant chi-square indicates that the amount of variability is probably the result of chance, whereas a significant chi-square indicates that the amount of variability is the result of some type of moderating variable.

RESULTS

The results of 10 manuscripts (18 separate studies) using 1,948 subjects were converted into common metrics using attitude change as the variable of interest to judge the persuasive effectiveness of rhetorical questions. The results for most studies reveal small, positive effect sizes (see Table 10.1). Four studies approached medium effect sizes and four studies had small, negative effect sizes.

The aggregated effect size for all studies (see Table 10.2) combined was small ($r = .053$). The formal significance test did not indicated the presence of a moderator variable ($\chi^2 = 25.09$, $p > .05$). When studies were separated into direct, indirect, or mixed grammatical forms, the average effect size for indirect and mixed rhetoricals was positive and small (indirect: $r = .127$; mixed: $r = .110$) whereas the direct rhetorical question effect size was negative and small ($r = -.034$). Formal significance tests revealed no indication of moderator variables (indirect: $\chi^2 = 7.36$, $p > .05$; direct: $\chi^2 = 4.08$, $p > .05$).

These results suggest that there are no positive persuasive advantages to be accrued by using rhetorical questions. There was no evidence for increased persuasive impact with a direct form of rhetoricals, and only minor increases in persuasive efficacy were observed in studies using indirect grammatical forms.

Table 10.2 Meta-Analysis Results.

	Overall	Indirect	Direct	Mixed
Number of studies	18	7	8	3
Sample size	1950	630	760	560
Average *r*	.053	.127	-.034	.090
χ^2	26.30	7.88	4.08	4.36
df	17	6	7	2

DISCUSSION

The results of this meta-analysis indicate that overall, rhetorical questions do not appear to generate persuasive thoughts in the mind of receivers. Our results are tempered, however, by practical and conceptual limitations. The extant literature does not address consistently the placement of rhetoricals, the frequency of use, or the application of rhetoricals in various settings with strong and weak arguments. Additionally, the research does not differentiate between the various types of rhetoricals suggested by Brown (1982) and Moore (1983), let alone the grammatical forms suggested by Enzle and Harvey (1982). Our findings are troubling, however, in the face of existing theoretical accounts for rhetoricals. Aggregated effect sizes indicate that rhetorical questions are not potent persuasive tools. However, the host of related message features preclude us from asserting that rhetorical questions disrupt the production of thoughts to distract the receiver, exert social pressure on the receiver to conform, direct the receiver's attention to opposing arguments, or do not create a minimal intent to persuade.

However, the meta-analytic findings are most consistent with Brown's (1982) conclusion that rhetoricals are not stylistically viable. Of course, these findings also indicate that there are no clear disadvantages associated with the use of rhetorical questions. A persuader might, for example, desire to increase recall of an argument or alter the emphasis of a certain statistic. Because existing research does not systematically address these issues, our meta-analysis provides no insights into the ability rhetoricals to achieve these goals. Nevertheless, rhetoricals were not consistently or substantially associated with attitude change, and this finding must be discouraging to theorists arguing for social pressure, attention, or persuasive intent accounts for the variable.

This investigation of the grammatical forms of rhetorical questions suggests that direct forms of rhetorical questions thwart attitude change, whereas indirect rhetoricals elicit a slight attitude change by requiring intellectual involvement. Thus, persuaders using indirect forms of rhetorical questions may be able to generate some message involvement through the interaction between receiver and sender. Enzle and Harvey (1982) suggested that this may occur by imposing consensus and excluding the opportunity to disagree with an obvious answer. This finding may indicate that indirect rhetorical questions are not powerless forms of language, but techniques that can be used to direct perceptions to produce limited persuasive outcomes. Unfortunately, only two researchers (Enzle & Harvey, 1982; Howard, 1990) using seven separate experiments have explored this type of rhetorical. Thus, given the overall findings that rhetorical questions do not promote persuasion, caution should be exercised in recommending indirect rhetoricals as a viable persuasive technique.

The results of this study provide a framework for further investigation of the persuasive efficacy of indirect rhetorical questions. Particular emphasis should be focused on conceptualizing, defining, and categorizing rhetoricals as well as placement, pairing, and frequency of this message feature. Additional research on these issues may clarify the theoretical explanations for, and the outcomes of, rhetorical questions. Concurring with Brown (1982), we see no compelling evidence that rhetoricals promote message acceptance.

REFERENCES

Benson, T. W., & Prosser, M. H. (1969). *Readings in classical rhetoric.* Boston, MA: Allyn and Bacon.

Brown, D. A. (1982). *Effects of use of different types of rhetorical questions on students' perceptions of college teachers.* Ann Arbor, MI: University Microfilms International.

Burnkrant, R. E., & Howard, D. J. (1984). Effects of the use of introductory rhetorical questions versus statements on information processing. *Journal of Personality and Social Psychology, 47*, 1218–1230.

Butler, H. E. (1921). *The intitutio oratoria of quintilian.* Cambridge, MA: Harvard University Press.

Cantor, J. R. (1979). Grammatical variations in persuasion: Effectiveness of four forms of request in door to door solicitations for funds. *Communication Monographs, 46*, 296–305.

Cohen, J. (1977). *Statistical power analysis for the behavioral sciences.* New York: Academic Press.

Cooper, H. (1981). *The integrative literature review.* Beverly Hills, CA: Sage.

Devito, J. A. (1990). *Elements of public speaking.* New York: Harper & Row.

Ervin-Tripp, S. (1976). Speech acts and social learning. In K. H. Basso and H. A. Selby (Eds.), *Meaning in anthropology* (pp. 123–153) Albuquerque: University of New Mexico Press.

Enzle, M. E., & Harvey, M. D. (1982). Rhetorical requests for help. *Social Psychology Quarterly, 45*, 172–175.

Fisher, B. F. (1985). *Questions in lecture.* (Teaching and Learning at Indiana University Series). (ERIC Document Reproduction Service No. ED 303 840)

Glass, G. V., McGaw, B., & Smith, M. L. (1981). *Meta-analysis in social research.* Beverly Hills, CA: Sage.

Hanna, M. S., & Gibson, J. W. (1987). *Public speaking for personal success.* Dubuque, IA: Brown.

Hedges, L. V., & Olkin, I. (1985). *Statistical methods for meta-analysis.* Orlando, FL: Academic Press.

Heun, L., & Heun, D. (1986). *Public speaking.* New York: West.

Howard, D. J. (1990). Rhetorical question effects on message processing and persuasion: The role of information availability and the elicitation of judgment. *Journal of Experimental Social Psychology, 26*, 217–239.

Hunt, G. T. (1987). *Public speaking* (2nd ed.). Englewood Cliffs, NJ: Prentice-Hall.

Kertzer, J. M. (1987). Rhetorical questions: Consensus, authority, enigma. *Language and Style: An International Journal, 20*, 242–256.

Koch, A. (1988). *Speaking with a purpose.* Englewood Cliffs, NJ: Prentice-Hall.

Lanham, R. A. (1968). *A handlist of rhetorical terms.* Berkeley: University of California Press.

Leonard, W. H., & Lowery, L. F. (1984). The effects of question types in textual reading upon retention of biology concepts. *Journal of Research in Science Teaching, 21*, 377–384.

Light, R. L., & Pillemer, D. B. (1984). *Summing up: The science of reviewing research.* Cambridge, MA: Harvard University Press.

Lucas, S. E. (1989). *Art of public speaking* (2nd. ed.). New York: Random House.

Moore, B. R. (1983). Rhetorical questions in Second Corinthians and in Ephesians through Revelation. *Notes on Translation, 97*, 3–33.

Munch, J. M. (1983). *The effects of rhetorical questions on cognitive elaboration and persuasion in dyadic exchange processes.* Ann Arbor, MI: University Microfilms International.

Munch, J. M. (1987). *An investigation of communication factors in a sales presentation: The effects of rhetorical questions, summarization frequency, and argument strength.* University Park, PA: College of Business Administration.

Munch, J. M., & Swasey, J. L. (1983). A conceptual view of questions and questioning in marketing communications. In A. Tybout & R. Bagozzi

(Eds.), *Advances in consumer research* (Vol. 10, pp. 209–214). Ann Arbor, MI: Association for Consumer Research.

Munch, J. M., & Swasey, J. L. (1988). Rhetorical question, summarization frequency, and argument strength effects on recall. *Journal of Consumer Research, 15*, 69–76.

Nir, R. (1988). Electoral rhetoric in Israel—The televised debates. A study in political discourse. *Language Learning, 38*, 187–208.

Osborn, M., & Osborn, S. (1988). *Public speaking.* Princeton, NJ: Houghton Mifflin.

Otto, P. B., & Schuck, R. F. (1983). The effect of a teacher questioning strategy training program on teaching behavior, student achievement, and retention. *Journal of Research in Science Teaching, 20*, 521–528.

Petty, R. E., Cacioppo, J. T., & Heesacker, M. (1981). Effects of rhetorical questions persuasion: A cognitive response analysis. *Journal of Personality & Social Psychology, 40*, 432–440.

Schmidt-Radefeldt, J. (1977). On so-called 'rhetorical' questions. *Journal of Pragmatics, 1*, 375–392.

Swasey, J. L., & Munch, J. M. (1985). Examining the target of receiver elaborations: Rhetorical question effects on source processing and persuasion. *Journal of Consumer Research, 11*, 877–886.

Tracey, R. M. (1989). *The rhetoric of questions in text.* Ann Arbor, MI: University Microfilm International.

Verderber, R. E. (1988). *The challenge of effective speaking* (7th ed.). Belmont, CA: Wadsworth.

Zillmann, D. (1972). Rhetorical elicitation of agreement in persuasion. *Journal of Personality and Social Psychology, 21*, 159–165.

Zillmann, D., & Cantor, J. R. (1973). Instruction of curiosity via rhetorical questions and its effect on the learning of factual materials. *British Journal of Educational Psychology, 43*, 172–180.

Zillmann, D., & Cantor, J. R. (1974). Rhetorical elicitation of concession in persuasion. *Journal of Social Psychology, 94*, 223–236.

11

The Efficacy of Powerful/Powerless Language on Attitudes and Source Credibility

Nancy A. Burrell
University of Wisconsin-Milwaukee

Randal J. Koper
University of the Pacific

> Language uses us as much as we use language.
> —Robin Lakoff (1975b, p. 3)

A substantial amount of published material was motivated by Lakoff's (1975b) *Language and Women's Place.* Lakoff's goals centered on (a) discovering what language use could tell us about inequality, (b) determining whether something could be done, and (c) indicating directions for future research. In this persuasive treatise, she argues that "women experience linguistic discrimination in two ways: in the way that they are taught to use language, and in the way general language use treats them." (1975b, p. 4). The acquisition of this special speech style becomes an excuse that others use to keep women in demeaning positions refusing to take them seriously as human beings (e.g., women cannot speak precisely nor forcefully). Through introspection, Lakoff identified specific linguistic features that characterized women's language.

These linguistic features differentiating men's and women's speech included (a) *vocabulary items* (e.g., women have a larger repertoire of colors); (b) *empty adjectives* (e.g., women use more adjectives like "cute," "sweet," "divine"); (c) *question forms* (e.g., women use tag questions and question forms in context that men use declaratives); (d) *polite forms* (e.g., women use "please" and "thank you" more frequently than men); (e) *hedges* and/or *forms of uncertainty* (e.g., forms like "I guess," "I think," "well," "kinda," and "you know"); (f) *intensives* (e.g., women use "so," "very," and "really" more than men;.and (g) *hypercorrect grammar* (e.g., women are less likely to use "ain't" or drop off ends of words like "doin' " and "goin' "). Although Lakoff discussed a few other features, those features that have been cited have been examined by other researchers in this area. In short, although Lakoff pointed out that men can use all of these forms, women are more likely to use the features in a wider range of linguistic, psychological, and social environments and that women lack assertiveness in more contexts than men.

Lakoff's model of *w*omen's *l*anguage (WL) provided a baseline for investigating gender related speech patterns in the courtroom for O'Barr and his associates (Lind & O'Barr, 1979; O'Barr & Atkins, 1980). While observing courtroom speakers (for 150 hours), O'Barr and his colleagues concluded that women's language is neither characteristic of all women nor limited only to women. In short, a similar continuum of WL features was observed among speakers of both sexes. The courtroom data indicated that the variation in WL feature was related more to social power than to gender. Thus, O'Barr and associates renamed WL *powerless language*—a term that better characterized the specific linguistic features that varied as a function of the apparent social power/status of speakers. "The tendency for more women to speak powerless language and for men to speak it less is due, at least in part, to the greater tendency of women to occupy relatively powerless social positions" (O'Barr, 1982, pp. 70–71).

Since the renaming of WL, researchers have conceptualized a powerless style as the frequent use of words and expressions that convey a lack of forcefulness in speaking. In other words, a powerless style reflects an abundance of hedges, hesitation forms, polite forms, and questioning intonations. Language that does not demonstrate frequent use of these features was thought to be more straightforward and characterized as "powerful" style (Stutman, 1987). The point is that scholars in various disciplines have been intrigued with the effects of powerful and powerless speech styles. The purpose of the following investigation is to summarize the effects of powerful and powerless speech styles through meta-analytic techniques.

REVIEW OF PAST RESEARCH

Because Lakoff provided no empirical evidence, numerous researchers became interested in the potential impact that powerful versus powerless speech styles might have on listeners (e.g., jurors) in such applied context as the courtroom (Bradac, Hemphill, & Tardy, 1981; Stutman, 1987; Wright & Hosman, 1983). Clearly, communication is the heart of a civil or criminal law case. That is, the positions of participants (defendant versus plaintiff) in a legal dispute are presented by their attorneys and subsequently orchestrated/supported by the testimony of carefully chosen witnesses. In a jury trial, the judge explains the statement of the law through instructions to the jury. In view of the importance of communication in legal trials, it is of interest to investigate empirically the manner in which those involved in a legal trial express themselves. In short, social scientists wondered about the perceived convincingness truthfulness, competence, intelligence, and trustworthiness of witnesses' testimony in relation to their use of powerful and/or powerless language. Unfortunately, the contradictory findings are difficult to sort through at best.

For example, O'Barr and associates asked subjects to evaluate witness' testimony by listening to tape recordings or reading transcripts ostensibly produced by a male or female witness demonstrating a powerful or powerless speech style (Erickson, Lind, Johnson, & O'Barr, 1978). Participants rated the powerful style as relatively competent and attractive. However, speakers' femininity/masculinity were not affected by speech style differences. In addition, subjects recommended a higher reward for damages when the speaker utilized a powerful speaking style. However, another investigation asking participants to make assessments of witness testimony found no evidence of a connection between speaker style and award for damages (Bradac et al.,1981) yet these results did support the claim that a powerful style was directed related to judgments of competence, and attractiveness in a hypothetical court case. Similarly, Bradac and associates found no relationship between a powerful/powerless style and masculinity/femininity respectively.

By contrast, Warfel (1984) examined gender schema theory and its relationship to communicator style. That is, participants were asked to evaluate transcripts involving interpersonal exchanges using either powerful or powerless speech styles. Results indicated that powerless speakers were rated as less dominant than powerful styles; however, powerless styles were deemed as more competent than powerful speakers. One possible interpretation of the contradictory results centers on the possibility of powerless speech forms representing deferential or polite speech forms. "This would explain many of the findings in the courtroom settings where powerless speech is used by the lower status discourse partner, regardless of speaker sex" (p. 265). Because there were no measures of deference or politeness in this study, future research should address these speculations.

Similarly, Bradac and Mulac (1984) asked participants to rate segments of job interviews evaluating interviewees' communicator styles (e.g., perceived power/powerlessness) and extent to which interviewees created the kind of desired impression. Results of study 1 suggested a multilevel model of linguistic power and effectiveness that was independent of communicator gender. Findings from study 2 showed that a powerful speech style interacted with communicator intention (e.g., appearing social or authoritative), qualifying the five-level model from the first study. Although participants made discriminations among powerful and powerless speech styles, several of the ostensibly powerless features were rated as relatively powerful. According to Bradac and Mulac (1984), "The outcomes for polite messages and for intensifiers suggest that the findings of previous research on consequences of powerful and powerless styles are potentially spurious" (p. 315).

In two investigations by Berryman and Wilcox (1980) hoped to clarify the relationships between objective communicative behavior differentiations and culturally based expectations of male and female speakers. Participants read one of two messages concerning grading policies in education. The content of the messages was comparable but linguistic features were manipulated to create sex-typed versions (e.g., the male version demonstrated more powerful features, whereas the female message exhibited more powerless linguistic features). In both investigations participants were asked about their attitudes toward the message, evaluation of the speaker, and the sex-role stereotype of the speaker. Participants identified the sources of the sex-anonymous messages accurately. The source of the male message was judged significantly more commanding than the source of the female message. However, the source of the female message was rated as significantly more self-oriented than the source of the male message. In the second study, the male speaker was rated as significantly less accommodating, whereas the female speaker was judged as more flexible. In short, the two factors of gender and command emerged in both investigations. However, Berryman and Wilcox (1980) pointed out that "it is often difficult to separate actual sex differences in communication from stereotypical beliefs, expectations, and perceptions of the communication of males and females" (p. 50).

Along the same line, Wright and Hosman (1983) investigated whether the gender of participants and witnesses were related to assessments of credibility, attractiveness, and blameworthiness by manipulating two linguistic features (e.g., hedges and intensifiers). Participants read transcripts of courtroom testimony describing a traffic accident. Results indicated that the gender of a witness relates to the participants' assessment of credibility and attractiveness when using hedges and intensifiers. In addition, participants' genders failed to produce any significant effects.

One implication of these results suggests that the gender of a juror is less of a determinant of impressions than gender of a witness. Essentially, when women used stereotypical language, they gained perceived credibility but lost attractiveness. A second implication is that intensifiers and hedges did not contribute equally to the impression formation process based on the results that hedges influenced perceptions of both attractiveness and credibility whereas intensifiers influenced only attractiveness impressions. According to Wright and Hosman (1983), "Intensifiers may be an excess subcomponent of powerful speech style" (p. 151). A third implication is that communicative behaviors were judged in conjunction with the gender of those individuals exhibiting them. These researchers conclude that particularly in a courtroom setting, the who and how testimony is presented may be equally as important as the what of the presentation.

Because of the contradictory and sometimes confusing results, the authors were interested in the efficacy of the persuasiveness on powerful versus powerless language and whether or not gender and communicative context mediated various research findings. Thus, the following research questions are forwarded:

RQ 1: To what degree are speakers using powerful linguistic features perceived as more persuasive/credible than speakers utilizing powerless features?

RQ 2: To what degree does communicative context function as a moderator variable on the persuasiveness of powerful and/or powerless language?

RQ 3: Considers two aspects:

a. To what extent does a source's gender serve as a moderating influence on the persuasion process when using powerful and/or powerless language?

b. To what extent does a receiver's gender serve as a moderating influence on the persuasion process when listening to powerful and/or powerless language?

The following discussion outlines the advantages of using meta-analysis as a literature summary. By contrasting this relatively new method of literature summary with the traditional narrative summary, the reader is asked to evaluate the advantages of each technique.

META-ANALYSIS AS LITERATURE SUMMARY

To synthesize various lines of research, two types of literature reviews are used: narrative or meta-analytic. Narrative reviews are usually qualitative, whereas meta-analytic reviews are quantitative. However, both review techniques analyze methodological and theoretical issues and give weight to "good" studies over "bad" studies (Allen & Preiss, 1990). The major difference between the two types of literature summaries is that narrative reviews rely on some type of vote counting of significant versus insignificant results from single studies whereas meta-analytic reviews base claims on quantitative summaries of observed effect sizes.

Pillemer (1984) characterized the traditional method of literature review as the narrative review. Essentially, the narrative review is a qualitative method of assessing the research on a given topic (Rosenthal, 1984). A researcher conducting a narrative review examines the literature in a specific area counting results of significant versus nonsignificant findings. The researcher's conclusions evaluate whether or not studies included in the review consistently find or did not find an effect. In short, if a large amount of inconsistency is found regarding effects, the likely conclusion is a need for additional research or that the results of "good" studies are preferable to the findings of "bad" studies.

By contrast, the researcher using meta-analysis quantifies the size of an effect across a line of research. Rather than vote counting, the meta-analytic reviewer (a) computes the effect size associated with significant tests, (b) determines the consistency of various effects, and (c) searches for potential features that could moderate specific outcomes (Harris, 1989; Hunter, Schmidt, & Jackson, 1982).

Unfortunately, narrative reviews possess several qualities that limit a reviewer's ability to isolate generalizations about communication research (Allen & Preiss, 1990). In short, narrative reviews treat significance tests as 100% accurate ignoring both Type I (false positives) and Type II (false negatives) error. A second problem for most narrative reviews is that information on the literature search methods has been excluded. In specific, a literature search should include: (a) a description of methods employed to locate information, (b) the method that author(s) utilized in determining the relevance of specific studies to their analysis, and (c) the criteria that were used to determine whether or not an effect existed. Typically, researchers survey a "representative sample" of investigations and, subsequently, reach a conclusion on a specific issue. Unless a description of the methodology for the literature search is included, the reader does not know the adequacy of the reviewer's "representative sample" nor the accuracy of the reviewer's conclusions.

On the other hand, most meta-analytic reviews provide a detailed description of the system used to gather relevant studies that can be replicated by additional reviewers and/or extended to additional areas/manuscripts excluded in the initial review. "The meta-analyst typically uses very public and objective rules of aggregating and analyzing coded data; the narrative reviewer often uses private and subjective rules in his or her integrations" (Mintz, 1983, p. 74).

To summarize, a good literature review should be systematic not only in its methods of literature search/relevance but also systematic in the calculation and interpretation of results from the studies obtained by that search. As Allen and Preiss (1990) pointed out, "While disagreements and issues still remain when evaluating a meta-analysis, these center on the proper method of performing a meta-analysis is NOT whether or not a meta-analysis is superior to a traditional narrative review" (p. 105). In short, the arguments for conducting a meta-analytic review include: (a) It prevents reviewers from typically concluding for additional research, (b) It limits reviewers from taking Type I and Type II errors, and (c) It encourages replication.

The meta-analysis described in the following addresses three research questions to determine the efficacy of persuasiveness/credibility when features of powerful versus powerless language are used. Gender and communicative context have been discussed as potential moderating variables.

METHOD

Sample

A thorough search of the research literature examining the perceptions of powerful/powerless speech was conducted. Three criteria were developed to determine whether a study would be included: (a) the major purpose of the study must have been to examine the perceptions of powerful versus powerless language on persuasion/credibility, (b) the manipulation of powerful/powerless language had to be some combination of Lakoff's WL features, and (c) the study provided some quantifiable estimate of the impact of powerful/powerless language on persuasion/credibility.

A review of relevant research on the effects of powerful/powerless language on persuasion/credibility included a census of relevant journals in communication, social psychology,and linguistics, as well as examination of several social science indexes. The unavailability of unpublished dissertations, theses, and convention papers restricted the literature search to published articles and book chapters.

Twenty-four studies were initially identified by the manual search. Of these, 8 were unusable due to unavailability, perceived impact was not reported, or a lack of summary data. Sixteen studies were included in the meta-analysis yielding 20 experimental manipulations of persuasiveness and/or credibility as illustrated in Table 11.1.

META-ANALYSIS PROCEDURES

The technique of meta-analysis was a procedure recommended by Hunter et al. (1982). The procedure involved converting available summary statistics (in such form of means, standard deviations, correlations, F-statistics) to

Table 11.1 Description of Overall Analysis.

Author		Date	Context[a]	*N*	Credibility	Persuasion
Berryman & Wilcox	(1)	1980	Educ.	108	+.189	.000
	(2)	1980	Educ.	101	+.306	
Bradac et al.	(1)	1981	Court	11	+.671	
	(2)	1981	Court	15	+.513	
Bradac & Mulac	(1)	1984	Court	31	+.610	
	(2)	1984	Court	29	+.560	
Erickson et al.		1978	Court	152	+.339	+.287
Hosman & Wright	(1)	1987	Court	131	+.150	
	(2)	1987	Court	197	+.154	
Lind & O'Barr		1979	Court	96	+.318	+.327
Scherer	(1)	1979	Court	28		+.317
	(2)	1979	Court	29		+.340
Siegler & Siegler		1976	Relat.	96	+.219	
Stutman		1987	Court	50	.000	
Warfel		1984	Mixed	207	+.074	
Wright & Hosman		1983	Court	166	+.175	

Note. [a]The context for Warfel's study was described as "mixed" because results were reported by averaging across three contexts.

standardized effect size estimates (*d*). The effect size estimates were then converted to correlational estimates for summarizing purposes.

The correlation coefficient permits identification of possible sources of variance in the estimate of average *r*. Hunter et al. (1982) discuss techniques for separating the variance in the *r* due to such statistical artifacts as sampling error, measurement error, and restriction in range. Once these statistical artifacts have been identified, the estimate of the true variance in *r* provides an estimate of the stability of the estimated effect size.

After calculation of correlations from each study, a sample size weighted average correlation was determined. This average correlation is considered an estimate of the true relationship between two variables because it is the average of the sampling distribution as opposed to the sample distribution in a single study. Using the procedures suggested by Hedges and Olkin (1986), the sampling error was compared to the sampling error for the average correlation. If the chi-square test was nonsignificant, the variance was considered trivial and the average correlation was assumed to be an accurate true score estimate. If the chi-square test was significant, the observed variance was considered nontrivial and alternative methods of examining average correlation were undertaken.

RESULTS

To address the first research question regarding the effectiveness of powerful versus powerless language on persuasion and credibility, a separate analysis was conducted for each variable. For the relationship between powerful/powerless language and perceived persuasiveness, five estimates were analyzed. The average effect of powerful/powerless language persuasiveness was $r = .23$ ($N = 413$). Results of the chi-square test ($X2(4) = 8.51$, $p > .05$), showed that the variance was trivial and that the average correlation was an accurate score estimate. The average correlation indicates that powerful language is more persuasive than less powerful language.

The next average correlation considers the impact of using powerful language. Powerful language increased the credibility of the message sender ($r = .21$, $k = 14$, $N = 1299$) across a homogeneous set of correlations ($X2(13) = 19.32$, $p < .05$). These findings indicate that powerful language is perceived as more credible than powerless language.

The second research question focused on the degree to which context functioned as a moderating variable on the persuasiveness of powerful/powerless language. Unfortunately, after the initial coding, 13 of the 16 students used courtroom/trial settings. Warfel's (1984) investigation used three different settings (courtroom, business, and social); however, the results were averaged across settings. Although Berryman and Wilcox (1980) used educational settings, and Siegler and Siegler (1976) used an interpersonal context, these researchers did not report sufficient summary statistics to test for a moderating variable. Essentially, there was no real variability between the studies to determine the effect of communicative context.

Along the same line, the third research question centered on the degree to which gender as both source and receiver moderated the effect of powerful/powerless language on the persuasion process. Only four of the investigations tested for a receiver's gender (Berryman & Wilcox, 1980; Bradac et al., 1981; Seigler & Seigler, 1976). Similarly, four studies tested for the source's gender (Bradac & Mulac, 1984; O'Barr & Atkins, 1980; Stutman, 1987; Wright & Hosman, 1983). The majority of these investigations did not include the necessary summary statistics to test for gender as a moderating variable.

DISCUSSION

Research on the impact of powerful versus powerless language on perceived persuasiveness and credibility has produced conflicting results. In this investigation, results from 16 studies examining powerful and powerless linguistic features were subjected to meta-analysis. Results showed that powerful language was perceived not only as more persuasive but also as more credible than powerless language. Because descriptive statistics were not included in many of the studies and the majority of investigations were framed in a legal context, testing for potential moderating variables (e.g., gender and context) was not possible.

Although these results seem quite obvious, there are some pragmatic issues to consider. First, this investigation focused on the perceptions of persuasion/credibility rather than evaluating actual behaviors/production of powerful/powerless language. From our perspective, we have additional work to do on the efficacy of powerful versus powerless language. Second, of the 20 manipulations of powerful/powerless language, 13 were framed in a legal setting. Because there is no variability in the communicative context, researchers cannot determine how context might attentuate various perceptions of powerful/powerless language.

Clearly, there are additional contexts to examine the impact of powerful/powerless language. For example, in an educational setting (i.e., teacher training), researchers could compare teaching styles of student teachers, first year faculty, and tenured faculty examining use of powerful/powerless language. It may be that teachers experiencing discipline problems use more powerless linguistic features and are perceived as uncertain, inexperienced, and less credible than those teachers demonstrating a more powerful style.

Another context to examine the effects of powerful/powerless speech styles is mediation. For example, audiotapes of divorce mediations, landlord/tenant conflicts, consumer versus retailer disputes, and so on could be examined for powerful/powerless language. Of interest in the mediation context would be to determine the impact of various combinations/sequences of powerful and/or powerless language. To what degree do participants intimidate each other? Are there instances when powerless language is more influential than powerful language? Recent mediation models suggest that mediators control/structure the process (Burrell, Donohue, & Allen, 1990). The question becomes which linguistic features and/or combination of features are perceived as more controlling/noncontrolling (e.g., powerful/powerless).

In a recent study examining the influence of initial use of hesitations and hedges on evaluations of witnesses and their persuasiveness in a budget hearing, results show that negative attributions triggered by the use of powerless language (Johnson & Vinson, 1990). Generalizing these results to the mediation context might be disastrous for the mediator. In other words, if a mediator opens the session using powerless language, he or she will undoubtedly lose control of the session. That is, the mediator would spend much of the session trying to reestablish his or her role as controller/leader of the interaction.

A final context to examine the impact of powerful/powerless language would be in an organizational setting. Observing different types of meetings (intraorganizational versus interorganizational) involving various levels of management/nonmanagement may be fruitful ground for examining the impact of powerful and powerless language. It may be that individuals have a threshold for powerless language. That is, organizational members may be tolerant and/or intolerant of specific linguistic features as the communicative context becomes more or less formal. Another interesting question might be to what degree can management manipulate organizational members by using powerless rather than powerful language?

To summarize, we recommend that researchers go beyond the courtroom setting when examining the impact of powerful and powerless speech. Second, we hope that researchers will report descriptive statistics such as means and standard deviations so that meta-analytic reviewers can test for moderating variables rather than to speculate about what might have been. Third, researchers could explore the various combinations of powerful and powerless features to determine our potential threshold for powerless language prior to forming negative attributions of another. Results of this meta-analytic review clearly suggest that powerful language is perceived as more persuasive and credible than powerless language. Finally, we recommend the following to communicators seeking to influence others: Use powerless language with great discretion/caution!

REFERENCES

Allen, M., & Preiss, R. (1990). Using meta-analysis to evaluated curriculum: An examination of selected college textbooks. *Communication Education, 38*, 103–116.

Berryman, C. L., & Wilcox, J. R. (1980). Attitudes toward male and female speech: Experiments on the effects of sex-typical language. *Western Journal of Speech Communication, 44*, 50–59.

Bradac, J. J., Hemphill, M. R., & Tardy, C. H. (1981). Language style on trial: Effects of "powerful" and "powerless" speech upon judgements of victims and villains. *Western Journal of Speech Communication, 45*, 327–341.

Bradac, J. J., & Mulac, A. (1984). A molecular view of powerful and powerless speech styles: Attributional consequences of specific language features and communicator intentions. *Communication Monographs, 51*, 307–319.

Burrell, N., Donohue, W. A., & Allen, M. (1990). The impact of disputants' expectations on mediation: Testing an interventionist model. *Human Communication Research, 17*, 104–139.

Erickson, B., Lind, E. A., Johnson, B. C., & O'Barr, W. M. (1978). Speech style and impression formation in a court setting: The effects of "powerful" and "powerless" speech. *Journal of Experimental Social Psychology, 14*, 266–279.

Harris, M. (1989, June). *Research and statistical methods in negotiation and bargaining*. Paper presented at the Second Biannual Conference of the International Association for Conflict Management, Athens, GA.

Hedges, L., & Olkin, I. (1986). *Statistical methods for meta-analysis*. Orlando, FL: Academic Press.

Hosman, L. A., & Wright, J. W., II, (1987). The effects of hedges and hesitations on impression formation in a simulated courtroom context. *Western Journal of Speech Communication , 51*, 173–188.

Hunter, J., Schmidt, F., & Jackson, G. (1982). *Meta-analysis*. Beverly Hills, CA: Sage.

Johnson, C., & Vinson, L. (1990). Placement and frequency of powerless talk and impression formation. *Communication Quarterly, 38*, 325–333.

Lakoff, R. (1975a). Language and woman's place. *Language and Society, 2*, 45–80.

Lakoff, R. (1975b). *Language and woman's place.* New York: Harper & Row.

Lind, E. A., & O'Barr, W. (1979). The social significance of speech in the courtroom. In H. Giles & R. N. St. Claire (Eds.), *Language and social psychology* (pp. 65–87). Oxford, England: Basil Blackwell.

Mintz, J. (1983). Integrating research evidence: A commentary on meta-analysis. *Journal of Consulting and Clinical Psychology, 51*, 71–75.

O'Barr, W. M. (1982). *Linguistic evidence: Language, power, and strategy in the courtroom.* New York: Academic Press.

O'Barr, W. M., & Atkins, B. K. (1980). "Women's language" or "powerless language"? In S. McConnell-Ginet, R. Borker, & N. Furman (Eds.), *Women and language in literature and society* (pp. 170–185) New York: Praeger.

Pillemer, D. (1984). Conceptual issues in research synthesis. *Journal of Special Education, 18*, 27–40.

Rosenthal, R. (1984). *Meta-analytic procedures for social research.* Beverly Hills, CA: Sage.

Scherer, K. R. (1979). Voice and speech correlates of perceived social influence in simulated juries. In H. Giles & R. N. St. Clair (Eds.), *Language and social psychology* (pp. 88–120). Oxford, England: Basil Blackwell.

Siegler, D. M., & Siegler, R. S. (1976). Stereotypes of males' and females' speech. *Psychological Reports, 39*, 167–170.

Stutman, R. K. (1987). Witness disclaiming during examination. *Journal of the American Forensic Association, 23*, 96–101.

Warfel, K. A. (1984). Gender schemas and perceptions of speech style. *Communication Monographs, 51*, 253–267.

Wright, J. W. II, & Hosman, L. A. (1983). Language style and sex bias in the courtroom: The effects of male and female use of hedges and intensifiers on impression formation. *Southern Speech Communication Journal, 48*, 137–152.

12

Explicit and Implicit Conclusions in Persuasive Messages

Michael G. Cruz
University of Wisconsin-Madison

When designing a persuasive message, a persuader may rely on an implicit conclusion rather than explicitly state his or her position. The question then arises: Is the implication of a conclusion more convincing than the conclusion itself? Arguments exist for the persuasive superiority of both explicit and implicit messages, but evidence to settle the issue is relatively scarce. In addition, a number of mediating and moderating variables have been proposed to be relevant to the conclusion-drawing–attitude-change relationship, but only one, involvement (Kardes, 1988; Sawyer & Howard, 1991) has been observed to have an impact. This chapter reviews the theories and research relevant to conclusion drawing and attitude change, and proposes a causal model to explain the extant findings (Cruz, 1991).

IMPACT OF CONCLUSION DRAWING ON ATTITUDES

Hovland and Mandell (1952) first studied the impact of conclusion drawing on attitude change. These authors noted that the nondirective school of psychotherapy (Rogers, 1947) indicates that implicit messages should be more persuasive. Rogers stated:

> When an individual has been authoritatively told that he is governed by certain factors or conditions beyond his control, it makes therapy more difficult, and it is only when the individual discovers for himself that he can organize his perceptions that change is possible. (p. 361)

In the present context, Roger's observation suggests that the targets of a persuasive message would be influenced more if they arrived at their own conclusions than if a conclusion were given to them.

Brehm's reactance theory has also been used to predict the superiority of implicit messages (Linder & Worchel, 1970). Psychological reactance is said to occur as a response to the restriction or elimination of a person's perceived freedom of action. Consequently, the person attempts to restore his or her freedom, and comes to value the restricted behaviors more highly. For reactance theory to be relevant in a persuasion context requires that individuals view persuasive attempts as attempts to restrict their freedom. In particular, implicit messages must be seen as unrestrictive. Put another way, the targets of explicit messages should be aware that a persuasive attempt has been made, whereas the targets of implicit messages should be unaware of the attempt.

Linder and Worchel (1970) offered a third reason to expect that implicit messages are more persuasive than explicit messages. They argued that stating the message conclusion reduces source credibility. An explicit communicator may appear to have a vested interest in persuading the audience and hence be less credible. An implicit communicator, however, was argued to be more objective or nonpartisan, and therefore more credible.

Contrary to the previous arguments, a number of reasons also have been offered for the superiority of explicit messages. In contrast to Linder and Worchel (1970), Hovland and Mandell (1952) argued that explicit messages would increase source credibility. Specifically, a communicator who offers an implicit conclusion is seen as having something to conceal, but a communicator who states a conclusion explicitly is seen as frank and forthright.

Hovland and Mandell (1952) further proposed that audience members may require an explicit conclusion to understand a persuasive message. Through insufficient intelligence, motivation, or lack of prior knowledge, audience members may not comprehend an implied conclusion. If the recipients of an implicit message reach no conclusion, reach a conclusion unrelated to that intended, or reach an opposite conclusion, then less attitude change would occur in the advocated direction than for a corresponding explicit message. Conclusion comprehension was seen as a critical mediating variable in the relationship between conclusion drawing and attitude change. Audience intelligence was advanced as a moderating variable such that less intelligent audience members require an explicit conclusion for comprehension, whereas more intelligent audience members can comprehend implicit conclusions (Hovland & Mandell, 1952).

Another variable thought to interact with conclusion drawing is involvement (Kardes, 1988; Sawyer & Howard, 1991; Tubbs, 1968). Kardes argued that persons high in outcome-relevant involvement (Johnson & Eagly, 1989) would reach the correct conclusion spontaneously after hearing an implicit message more frequently than would weakly involved persons. The self-generated conclusions of more involved persons were expected to produce greater attitude change than the incomplete information available to less involved persons. Thus, Kardes predicted that for highly involved persons, implicit messages would produce as much attitude change as explicit messages, but for less involved persons implicit messages would produce less attitude change than explicit messages.

Sawyer and Howard (1991) argued for a similar interaction between outcome-relevant involvement and conclusion drawing. They predicted that involved persons would generate conclusions to implicit messages more frequently than uninvolved persons, and that self-generated conclusions would be more persuasive. Contrary to Kardes (1988) however, Sawyer and Howard predicted that for involved persons, implicit messages would be *more* persuasive than explicit messages.

Unlike Kardes (1988) and Sawyer and Howard (1991), Tubbs (1968) did not include conclusion comprehension as a mediating variable. Instead, Tubbs hypothesized that commitment, or what Johnson and Eagly (1989) termed *value-relevant involvement,* would interact with conclusion drawing to affect attitude change. Although not specific, Tubbs implied that highly committed persons are more receptive to implicit messages, whereas less committed persons are persuaded by explicit messages.

A third variable proposed to interact with conclusion drawing was initial position (Fine, 1957; Weiss & Steenbock, 1965). Initial position was defined as a person's opinion on an issue prior to hearing a relevant persuasive message. Weiss and Steenbock (1965) argued that the principles of the nondirective school of psychotherapy apply only when the intended conclusion is disagreeable to the audience. When audience members hold initially negative opinions toward a source's position, they would resist an explicit message but accept an implicit message. On the other hand, when the conclusion being advocated was agreeable to the audience, Weiss and Steenbock (as well as Fine, 1957) predicted that explicit messages would be effective.

The validity of extant arguments is difficult to assess because of ambiguity about the definitions and operationalizations of implicit and explicit messages. Researchers describe their messages as stating a final conclusion explicitly or omitting the final conclusion, but have not been specific about conclusions other than the final one that may have been included in the message. That is, the messages used in past research may have contained subordinate conclusions that were used as premises for the overall conclusion, producing variation in the degree of implicitness in the message. In this context, the exact nature of the persuasive messages is critical because: (a) the application of nondirective psychotherapy (Rogers, 1947) and reactance theory (Brehm, 1966) dictates that implicit messages contain no explicit conclusions, (b) comprehension of the conclusion may depend strongly on the degree of implicitness in messages, and (c) Linder and Worchel's (1970) and Hovland and Mandell's (1952) speculations about the impact of conclusion drawing on source credibility may depend on the clarity, and hence the degree of implicitness, in the message.

META-ANALYSIS

To assess the viability of the preceding explanations, a meta-analysis (first presented in Cruz, 1991) was conducted on seven studies (see Table 12.1). These were the only studies found that examined the impact of conclusion type on attitude change.[1] The seven studies included a total of 1,675 participants. Participates in Thistlethwaite, de Haan, and Kamenetzky (1955) were Air Force recruits, the other six studies used college undergraduates.

The correlation was chosen as the measure of effect size. A positive correlation indicates that explicit messages produce greater attitude change than implicit messages. In each case, the effect size was calculated by taking the square root of η^2 with one degree of freedom.[2] Effect sizes then were weighted by sample size and cumulated.

---

[1]Linder and Worchel (1970) examined the impact of conclusion drawing, but did not include an implicit message condition in their design.

[2]For Tubbs (1968) and Fine (1957), this calculation was not straightforward. Tubbs reported an incorrect analysis of variance, but included his data in their entirety so the author could redo the analysis.

Table 12.1. Studies in the Meta-Analysis.

Authors	Correlation	Sample size	95% confidence interval
Fine (1957)	.092	375	$-.01 < p < .19$
Hovland & Mandell (1952)	.236	235	$.12 < p < .36$
Kardes (1988)[a]	.038	192	$-.03 < p < .11$
Sawyer & Howard (1991)[a]	-.167	252	$-.29 < p < -.05$
Thistlewaite et al. (1955)	.011	428	$-.08 < p < .10$
Tubbs (1968)	.376	52	$.14 < p < .61$
Weiss & Steenbock (1965)	.000	141	$-.17 < p < .17$
Total	.047	1675	$-.05 < p < .14$

[a]Indicates studies in which conclusion drawing was observed to interact with involvement.

Messages with explicit conclusions were more persuasive than messages with implicit conclusions ($r = .047$), but the observed variance in the correlations was significantly greater than expected due to a sampling error (which was 25.7% of the observed variance, $\chi^2(6) = 27.21, p < .05$), indicating the presence of additional statistical artifacts or moderating variables. Because insufficient data were reported, the impact of statistical artifacts, particularly measurement error and restriction in range of the independent variable, could not be assessed. Moreover, the impact of moderating variables was difficult to assess quantitatively because so few studies existed and the relevant data not reported. Nevertheless, findings relevant to source credibility, conclusion comprehension, involvement, and initial position are discussed in turn.

Source Credibility

Hovland and Mandell (1952) and Fine (1957) controlled the credibility of the source in their studies by using a high and low credible source. Neither study used a manipulation check to determine the effectiveness of the difference. The other five studies neither controlled nor measured source credibility. Furthermore, the credibility of the source used in the other four studies could not be assessed. Therefore, the data for only the two studies incorporating source credibility could be included in this analysis.

The two studies produced an average correlation of $r = .156$, $N = 574$. For the high credible source, $r = .170$, n = 282 and for the less credible source, $r = .116$, n = 292. The difference between the low and high credible correlations was not significant. These data suggest that source credibility does not moderate the relationship between conclusion type and attitude change, although this hypothesis cannot be eliminated given the limited sample size. Also, these data do not address the hypothesis that source credibility mediated the relationship between conclusion drawing and attitude change as postulated by Linder and Worchel (1970) and Hovland and Mandell (1952). That hypothesis has yet to be tested.

Involvement

Kardes (1988) and Sawyer and Howard (1991) each studied the role of outcome-relevant involvement (Johnson & Eagly, 1989) in the relationship between conclusion drawing and attitude change. These studies differed from the others reviewed in two ways. First, these were the only studies to use advertisements as persuasive stimuli. Second, both found a significant persuasive advantage for implicit messages under conditions of high involvement. The significant advantage of implicit messages for highly involved persons resulted from greater conclusion comprehension, and greater persuasiveness for self-generated conclusions compared to conclusions supplied by the messages.

These results may be unique to advertisements, and not applicable to other forms of persuasive messages. The advertisements by Kardes (1988) and Sawyer and Howard (1991) contained less information than the messages used by other researchers, and hence were likely easier to comprehend. In addition, although specific conclusions in an advertisement may fail to be comprehended, one conclusion is readily understood in all advertisements: Buy the product. In the context of conclusion drawing and message comprehension, these qualities of advertisements are critical, and cast doubt on the generalizability of the results.

Unfortunately, separating the results of Kardes (1988) and Sawyer and Howard (1991) does not eliminate the heterogeneity in effect sizes in the remaining studies. For the other five studies, the mean correlation was positive (r = .093, N = 1231), and the variance expected due to sampling error remained heterogeneous (χ^2= 12.24, $p < .01$).

In addition to outcome-relevant involvement, value-relevant involvement has received attention (Tubbs, 1968) under the term *commitment.* Tubbs reported an interaction between between commitment and conclusion drawing, but the analysis of variance presented by Tubbs is incorrect. Analyzing the data from Table 1 of Tubbs, one finds a main effect for conclusion drawing such that explicit conclusions were more persuasive than implicit conclusions. Commitment had no main effect and did not participate in an interaction with conclusion drawing.

Initial Position

Three studies (Fine, 1957; Thistlewaite et. al., 1955; Weiss & Steenbock, 1965) examined the interaction between conclusion type and initial position. Fine found that for persons initially favorable to the message, explicit conclusions were more persuasive than implicit conclusions, but for those initially unfavorable no differences between explicit and implicit conclusions were observed. Weiss and Steenbock reported the opposite. For persons initially favorable, no differences were found; for persons initially unfavorable, explicit conclusions were superior to implicit conclusions. Finally, Thistlethwaite et. al. reported no interaction between initial position and conclusion type.

The results for initial position could not be cumulated because neither Fine (1957) nor Thistlethwaite et. al. (1955) reported cell means. The data were not available on the initial attitudes of participants in Hovland and Mandell (1952), Kardes (1988), and Tubbs (1968). The topics used were such that no determination could be made of participants' initial attitudes. Results appear to conflict, but these may or may not be within sampling error of each other.

Summary

The preceding meta-analysis indicates that few conclusions can be drawn from the previous research.[3] Although explicit messages were found to be slightly more persuasive than implicit messages, the heterogeneity of effect sizes precludes any confidence in that result. Also, the role of specific moderating variables has been investigated, but only involvement has been observed to have an impact (Kardes, 1988; Sawyer & Howard, 1991). Moreover, separating Kardes and Sawyer and Howard's results does not eliminate the heterogeneity in effect sizes.

Perhaps the most critical difficulty in interpreting the previous research stems from ambiguity about the messages used in previous research. Variation in the construction of the persuasive messages may be the source of the heterogeneity of effect sizes. Variation in the implicitness of the messages used from study to study may have obscured the roles of source credibility, conclusion comprehension, and involvement as mediating and moderating variables. Linder and Worchel (1970) provided indirect evi-

---

[3]Kardes (1988) and Petty and Cacioppo (1981) interpreted the literature differently. Both came to fairly decisive conclusions based on the extant literature, but offered little direct empirical evidence for their interpretations.

dence for this point. They observed the greatest attitude change when target's were allowed to ponder implicit messages, and then later supplied with the correct conclusion. Unfortunately, the study conducted by Linder and Worchel did not include an implicit message condition, so their results cannot be directly compared to the others reviewed.

Modeling of the Impact of Conclusion Drawing

Although the role of variation in message implicitness could not be assessed in past research, Cruz (1991) addressed the issue. Cruz argued that conclusion comprehension has a causal impact on targets' perceptions of the position advocated by the message. Consider that a persuasive message typically takes a stand on an issue rather than arguing for a neutral position. When message recipients understand the conclusions to such messages, they naturally perceive that the source of the message holds a nonneutral opinion. However, when message recipients do not understand the conclusions, they have no reason for attributing a nonneutral opinion to the source. Audiences failing to discern the intended conclusion may be unaware that a persuasive attempt has been made, and may view the persuasive message as merely an informative one. Hence, lack of conclusion comprehension would produce an overall more moderate perception of the source's position.

If the targets of a persuasive message perceive the source's position as less extreme, then, on average, the discrepancy between the targets' attitudes and the sources should be perceived as less extreme. Linear discrepancy theory (see Hunter, Danes, & Cohen, 1984) predicts that the greater the discrepancy between one's position and the position advocated in a message, the greater the attitude change.

Cruz (1991) examined the impact of outcome-relevant involvement on conclusion comprehension. The goal was to test the interactions observed by Kardes (1988) and Sawyer and Howard (1991) in a context other than advertising. If the results from Kardes and Sawyer and Howard generalize, then the regression of conclusion comprehension onto involvement should have: (a) a steep positive slope for the strongly implicit message, (b) a moderately positive slope for the moderately implicit message, and (c) a zero slope for the explicit message. In addition, outcome-relevant involvement was predicted to have a positive association with attitude change (Johnson & Eagly, 1989).

Finally, Cruz (1991) examined the role of source credibility as a mediating variable (Hovland & Mandell, 1952; Linder & Worchel, 1970). Compared to explicit messages, implicit messages are postulated to either reduce or increase source credibility.

To test the above hypotheses, a 3 x 2 independent-groups design with random assignment to treatments was used. The independent variables were conclusion type (explicit, moderately implicit, and strongly implicit) and involvement (high and low), and the dependent variable was posttest attitude. In addition, the following variables were assessed: (a) pretest attitudes, (b) perceived position advocated by the source, (c) pre- and posttest source credibility, (d) outcome-relevant involvement with the topic, and (e) conclusion comprehension.

Persuasive Message

A pretest was conducted to find a topic on which initial attitudes varied widely and represented a wide range of opinions. The topic chosen was the legalization of marijuana. An explicit message was constructed that contained three of the common arguments for legalization without any mention of the topic. After each argument, a statement was made connecting those arguments to the topic of marijuana legalization. Finally, an explicit conclusion was stated after each argument, and the same conclusion was stated at the end of the message. A moderately implicit message was produced by removing all four statements of the conclusion from the explicit message. A strongly implicit message was constructed by removing each explicit statement of the topic from the moderately implicit message. The three messages were described as editorials in the newspaper *USA Today*. In the low-involvement condition the editorials were said to concern a political debate in California in 1986. In the high-involvement condition the editorials were said to concern a current local political debate.

Results

A manipulation check indicated that perceived involvement was not affected by the involvement induction ($r = -.05$, $p > .10$). Because the induction failed, perceived involvement was used in all subsequent analyses. Table 12.2 lists the means, standard deviations, and Cronbach's αs for each of the scales in the study, and Table 12.3 contains the zero-order correlations.[4]

To test the interaction between conclusion drawing and involvement, conclusion comprehension was regressed onto involvement at each level of explicitness. In the explicit, moderately implicit, and strongly

---

[4]Each scale was first subjected to confirmatory factor analysis and found to be unidimensional.

Table 12.2. Descriptive Statistics for All Scales.

Scale	# of items	Mean	SD	α
Perceived involvement	6	5.15	1.12	.85
Pretest attitude	6	3.77	1.68	.87
Posttest attitude	6	3.93	1.67	.90
Conclusion comprehension	3	0.67	0.33	.57
Perceived position of source	6	5.43	1.47	.86
Pretest source credibility	7	5.75	1.03	.89
Posttest source credibility	7	4.90	0.94	.89

Note. Higher scores indicate greater involvement, comprehension, and credibility, and more favorable attitude (1 to 7 scale)

Table 12.3. Observed Correlations.

Variable	1	2	3	4	5	6
1. Perceived involvement						
2. Pretest attitude	.26					
3. Conclusion drawing	-.05	.08				
4. Conclusion comprehension	.04	.10	.55			
5. Perceived position of source	.17	.23	.46	.66		
6. Posttest attitude	.22	.94	.10	.13	.27	

N = 169

implicit conditions, the regressions had slopes of $b = .020$, $b = -.002$, and $b = .025$, respectively. These slopes did not differ significantly from zero or from each other ($p > .10$), and hence were not consistent with the hypothesized interaction between involvement and conclusion drawing.

Causal modeling was employed to test the remaining hypotheses. To reiterate, it was hypothesized that conclusion drawing affects conclusion comprehension, which affects the perceived position of the source, which affects attitudes. Pretest attitude was also included as a predictor of posttest attitude, and, because involvement and conclusion comprehension were found to be unrelated in the previous analysis, the interaction of involvement and conclusion drawing on comprehension was not included in the model, although involvement was kept as a predictor of posttest attitudes. Based on a goodness of fit index ($\chi^2_{(7)} = 8.06$, $p > .10$) the model fit the data. All path coefficients, displayed in Figure 12.1, were significant at $p <$ .05, except the path from involvement to posttest attitude, and none of the correlations predicted by the model differed significantly from those observed in the data.

Because involvement did not have the anticipated impact on attitude, the data were reanalyzed with involvement removed, as shown in Figure 12.2. Again, the model fit the data ($\chi^2_{(5)} = 2.66, p > .10$). No correlation predicted by the model differed significantly from the observed correlation (the largest discrepancy, for the link between pretest attitude and perceived position of the source, was .16, $z = 1.31, p > .10$).

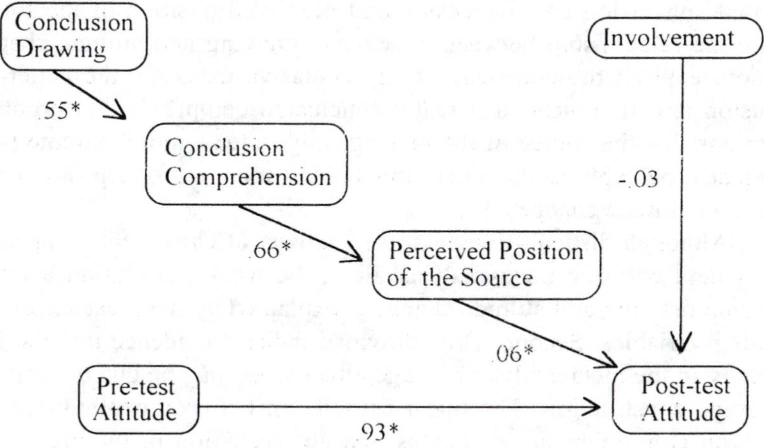

Figure 12.1. Original causal model

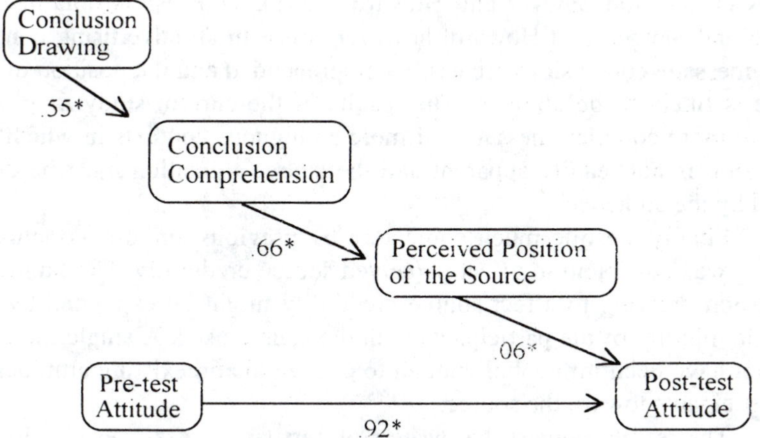

Figure 12.2. Revised causal model

The role of source credibility was observed to have no association with conclusion drawing ($r = -.01, p > .10$). The impact of conclusion drawing on posttest source credibility also was examined with pretest source credibility as a covariate but no significant relationship was found.

CONCLUSION

The goal of this chapter was to clarify the relationship between conclusion drawing and attitude change. A causal model consistent with the data indicates that conclusion comprehension and perceived position of the source mediate the relationship between conclusion drawing and attitude change. The more explicit the conclusion to a persuasive message, the better the conclusion is comprehended. Greater conclusion comprehension produces perceptions that the source of the message advocates a more extreme position. Finally, perceptions that the source holds a more extreme position produces more attitude change.

Although difficult to assess, the findings of Cruz (1991) appear to be consistent with the meta-analysis. First, the weak association between conclusion drawing and attitude change is explained by the presence of two mediating variables. Second, Cruz provided indirect evidence that the heterogeneity in the meta-analysis average effect sizes may be due to variation in message construction. The linear association between explicitness and conclusion comprehension indicates that any variation in the previously used messages could create variation in effect sizes.

The hypothesized effects of involvement did not appear, contrary to Kardes (1988) and Sawyer and Howard (1991). The results obtained by Kardes and Sawyer and Howard, however, arose in an advertising context where message conclusions are easily comprehended and the position of the source is likely to be obvious. The results of the current study may only apply to more complex messages or more ambiguous contexts in which the conclusion is not readily apparent and the source's position must be deciphered by the audience.

Finally, despite much conjecture by previous authors, conclusion drawing was not found to affect perceived source credibility. The failure of conclusion drawing to affect source credibility might be explained by the likely familiarity of the participants with the source used. A single message may not have been influential enough to change the preexisting attitudes of the participants toward the source.

The results suggest that writers of persuasive messages should use explicit conclusions in messages whenever their position is unknown to the audience. If an audience fails to understand the communicator's position, then the audience will fail to accept it. However, when a source's position is clear, there may be a use for implicit message conclusions. As observed by Kardes (1988) and Sawyer and Howard (1991), advertisers may prefer implicit messages because their audiences understand their position. Another potentially effective strategy is suggested by Linder and Worchel's (1970) study in which participants were informed of the intended conclusions to implicit persuasive messages after attempting to discern the conclusion for themselves. Under these conditions, initially implicit but ultimately explicit messages were more persuasive than initially explicit messages.

REFERENCES

Brehm, J. (1966). *A theory of psychological reactance*. New York: Academic Press.

Cruz, M. (1991, May). *Explicit and implicit conclusions in persuasive messages*. Paper presented at the International Communication Association Convention, Miami, FL.

Fine, B. (1957). Conclusion-drawing, communicator credibility, and anxiety as factors in opinion change. *Journal of Abnormal and Social Psychology, 54*, 369–374.

Hovland, C., & Mandell, W. (1952). An experimental comparison of conclusion-drawing by the communicator and by the audience. *Journal of Abnormal and Social Psychology, 47*, 581–588.

Hunter, J., Danes, J., & Cohen, S. (1984). *Mathematical models of attitude change* (Vol. 1). Orlando, FL: Academic Press.

Johnson, B., & Eagly, A. (1989). Effects of involvement on persuasion: A meta-analysis. *Psychological Bulletin, 106*, 290–314.

Kardes, F. (1988). Spontaneous inference processes in advertising: The effects of conclusion omission and involvement on persuasion. *Journal of Consumer Research, 15*, 225–233.

Linder, D., & Worchel, S. (1970). Opinion change as a result of effortfully drawing a counterattitudinal conclusion. *Journal of Experimental Social Psychology, 6*, 432–448.

Petty, R., & Cacioppo, J. (1981). *Attitudes and persuasion: Classic and contemporary approaches*. Dubuque, IA: Brown.

Rogers, C. (1947). Some observations on the organization of personality. *American Psychologist, 2*, 358–368.

Sawyer, A., & Howard, D. (1991). Effects of omitting conclusions in advertisements to involved and uninvolved audiences. *Journal of Marketing Research, 28*, 467–474.

Thistlethwaite, D., de Haan, H., & Kamenetzky, J. (1955). The effects of "directive" and "nondirective" communication procedures on attitudes. *Journal of Abnormal and Social Psychology, 51*, 107–113.

Tubbs, S. (1968). Explicit versus implicit conclusions and audience commitment. *Speech Monographs, 35*, 14–19.

Weiss, W., & Steenbock, S. (1965). The influence on communication effectiveness of explicitly urging action and policy consequences. *Journal of Experimental Social Psychology, 1*, 396–406.

13

Performing Counterattitudinal Advocacy: The Persuasive Impact of Incentives

Raymond W. Preiss
University of Puget Sound

Mike Allen
University of Wisconsin-Milwaukee

Theorists and practitioners wishing to understand and/or implement programs of attitude change may employ receiver- or source-based techniques. Receiver-based persuasion focuses on how some stylistic feature (language intensity, evidence, etc.) affects an audience consuming a message. An alternative to receiver-based persuasion involves the encoding (source-based) function of communication. The goal of the procedure is to change the attitudes of a person by using the cognitive processing associated with generating a persuasive message. Termed counterattitudinal advocacy (CAA), the participant serves as the source encoding the message (written, spoken, or written) that changes the attitude. Necessarily, this technique is Source-based because persuasion results from the production rather than reception of a message.

Counterattitudinal advocacy procedures have generated a substantial body of literature on message encoding. Narrative reviews suggest that belief-discrepant advocacy causes the source to adjust his or her attitudes in the direction of the encoded message. However, explanations for this outcome are equivocal. At issue is the magnitude of attitude change associated with CAA and the variables mediating the encoding—persuasion relationship. This chapter focuses on incentives, the most frequent debated issue when evaluating theoretical explanations for CAA-induced attitude change. Empirically summarizing this literature to assess the viability of message encoding as a persuasive technique and revealing fundamental cognitive mechanisms associated with persuasion is in order.

INCENTIVES AND CAA OUTCOMES

Research on the effects of incentives to perform belief-discrepant advocacy trace back to Kelman's (1953) investigation of encoding freedom and reward contingency. He found that voluntary participation and encoding reward (payable to a small percentage of the encoders) produced the greatest attitude change. This basic finding served as the genesis of scores of studies attempting to account for CAA-related persuasion by experimentally manipulating the incentive to advocate. Incentives become the variable of choice to many researchers because these inducements mediate perceptions of justification, effort, and choice for encoding. These variables remain central to devising "critical tests" of evaluating rival theories for CAA effects.

Theoretical Background of Incentives and Self-Persuasion

Since Kelman's (1953) observation theat offering a small reward under conditions of free choice resulted in attitude change, an array of theoretical accounts have existed to explain the effect. Our summary of these approaches is offered as a sketch of the major predictions regarding to incentives to encode. Subtle features of the theories are not considered and nuances of the class between theories are less important than assessing the overall impact of incentives on encoding-induced persuasion.

Dissonance Interpretation. Festinger (1957) provided the dissonance interpretation for the effects of incentives. He claimed that persuasion was positively related to publicly encoding a position inconsistent with privately held beliefs. The conflicting cognitions are theorized to produce dissonance (a noxious psychological state akin to anxiety) that mediates self-persuasion. Because the magnitude of dissonance should be proportionally related to the degree of inconsistency between beliefs and the position advocated, providing incentives for CAA should reduce observed self-persuasion. In most experiments, incentives are operationalized as monetary inducements for encoding, and dissonance theory asserts that self-persuasion negatively correlates to the size of payments.

Self-Perception Interpretation. The self-perception approach to CAA advances similar predictions to dissonance theory, but posits an alternative mechanism. Instead of speculating about a cognitive change resulting from inconsistent attitudes and behaviors, Bem (1965; Bem & McConnell, 1970) suggested that attitudes positively correlate to self-observations of behavior when weak or ambiguous external grounds for inferring internal states exist. In situations where justification for CAA is low, the encoder infers that the message reflects a privately held belief. When justification is high, the encoder discards the message an indicator of internal states (Bem & McConnell, 1970). Although the dispute between dissonance and self-perception theory was lively in the 1970s, researchers appear to agree on the low-justification/high-self-persuasion relationship. It is possible that dissonance and self-perception theory are operating in difference encoding contexts and that a critical test that discriminates between the two explanations is not feasible. (Greenwald, 1975).

Incentive Interpretation. Incentive theory advances different mechanisms and makes competing predictions compared to dissonance theory and self-perception theory. From the incentive perspective, CAA-related persuasion results from the accentuated information processing linked to the counterattitudinal task. Asked to generate belief-discrepant arguments, the motivation to suspend judgements and "brainstorm" issues contrary to privately held beliefs induces change. Incentive theorists posit that this process skews appraisal of positive and antagonistic thoughts related to the topic. As a result of "biased scanning" (Janis & Gilmore, 1965), antagonistic thoughts will be suppressed when the encoder searches for reasons to support a belief-discrepant position. From this view, the incentive (justification) to encode positively correlates with self-persuasion.

Impression Management Interpretation. Impression management theorists recast evidence for CAA-induced cognitive change as a mechanism for appearing moderate in situations potentially embarrassing or compromising (Tedeschi & Rosenfield, 1981). The emphasis focuses on strategies used to appear rational and consistent, especially in situations where the encoder performs tasks that undermine personal integrity. One strategy to maintain consistency involves the display of short-term cognitive change following CAA. After the encoding situation, however, pressure to maintain consistent declines and self-persuasion reverts to the preencoding position.

Functional Interpretation. A functional approach to CAA (Baron, 1968) is conceptually similar to impression management explanations. This account stresses the varieties of encoding situations that a counterattitudinal advocate encounters. In situations where the encoder must justify a poor or foolish decision (a hedonistic dilemma), the functional perspective makes predictions consistent with dissonance theory. A hedonistic dilemma is less significant than a moral dilemma, where an individual may violate societal values and codes of conduct. In situation where moral imperatives operate and an encoder performs a socially repugnant task, self-persuasion is not expected because of the power of the social norm. A final dilemma is posed on consensual issues. If encoding causes an individual to reconsider or doubt prior attitudes, the situation may cause the encoder to strive to validate the prior opinion or to assess the correctness of the new opinion. Stated another way, the functional approach predicts self-persuasion in hedonistic situations, no changes in moral situations, and some or no change if the situation results in a need for consensual validation.

Summary of Theoretical Accounts

It is clear that explanations for CAA overlap, yet take different approaches to message encoding. With regard to the effects of incentives to encode, only dissonance, self-perception, and the incentive theories make directional hypotheses. Impression management theory may make dissonance or incentive predictions depending on the nature of the encoding situation. Functional approaches make either dissonance of incentive predictions depending on the nature of the dilemmas the encoder faces. These predictions are summarized in Table 13.1.

The variety of predictions points to the controversies involved at every level in the CAA literature. The disagreement over cognitive processes, situational cues, impression management tactics, and situated dilemmas has frustrated virtually every reviewer of the CAA literature (see, for example, Miller, 1973; Rosenberg, 1968). On a second level, advocates of each theory select from an array of conflicting and specialized experimental conditions to gather evidence supporting their theoretical approach. We elected to standardize methods around the classic incentive-essay-writing experiment in an attempt to determine the overall effect of incentives on self-persuasion following CAA.

Table 13.1. Incentive-Induced Persuasion for Various Theories of CAA.

	Incentive level	
	Low	High
Dissonance	+	-
Self-perception	+	-
Incentive	-	+
Impression management	?	?
Functional approach	?	?

META-ANALYSIS

Overview

The meta-analysis was performed on a set of 32 studies reporting 41 experimental manipulations of written CAA under conditions of an incentive provided for compliance with the request. Written CAA was selected over other encoding modes (spoken or written then delivered) in an effort to limit the number of context-based moderator variables. Even with this restriction, a variety of experimental manipulations were included (Choice, Commitment, Incentive).

Method

Consistent with other chapters in this book, procedures by Hunter, Schmidt, and Jackson (1982) were employed. Summary statistics were converted to standardized effect estimates (see Table 13.2). The average correlation was examined for stability and a weighted average correlation computed. Finally, a moderator search was conducted to determine if other variables affected the average relationship.

RESULTS

Incentive to Encode

The 41 effects located in the literature search produced an average correlation of -.106. The negative relationship indicates that higher incentives are

Table 13.2. Effect Sizes for Incentive Conditions.

Study	Correlation	N
Ashmore & Collins (1968)	.000	89
Benware & Deci (1975)	+.301	50
Berger (1969)	+.087	129
Bodaken & Miller (1971)	+.109	86
Carlsmith et al. (1966)	+.192	85
	+.288	85
Chiu (1982)	-.409	77
Cohen (1962)	-.300	40
Collins & Helmreich (1970)	-.158	32
Collins & Hoyt (1972)	-.262	103
Cooper & Duncan (1971)	-.440	60
Cooper et al. (1972)	-.469	56
Crano & Messé (1970)	+.345	88
Crano & Sivacek (1984)	-.234	88
Darley & Cooper (1972)	-.699	30
Gerard (1967)	-.181	48
Gerodo (1970)	-.039	128
Harris & Tamler (1971)	-.300	21
Helmreich & Collins (1968)	-.328	66
Holmes & Strickland (1970)	-.399	30
	+.399	30
Hornbeck (1971)	-.267	173
Janis & Gilmore (1965)	-.140	64
Jones (1966)	-.271	23
Kahle (1978)	-.391	235
Kiesler & Sakamura (1966)	+.283	68
Linder et al. (1967)	-.417	20
	+.230	20
	-.363	25
	+.313	25
Nel et al. (1969)	-.289	42
Pilliavin et al. (1969)	-.098	207
Rosenberg (1965)	+.296	51
Rossamondo & Weiss (1970)	-.342	20
Schlenker et al. (1980)	-.132	60
	+.132	60
Sherman (1970a)	-.378	20
	+.423	20
Sherman (1970b)	-.324	35
	+.360	35
Touhey (1973)	-.336	58

associated with lower levels of attitude change. An examination of the distribution of effect sizes revealed that the effect was unstable, accounting for only 22% of the variance.

This caused a search for moderating variables. The first decision was to eliminate those studies using proattitudinal messages. A second decision was to separate studies based on the choice provided the participants (see Table 13.3). Twenty three studies used procedures that permitted participants a choice to participate. The average effect for those studies was negative (r = -.295). This average effect size was homogeneous and account for 87% of the actual variance. The correlation indicates that higher incentives generate less attitude change in participants.

Examining only those studies that did not allow participants to decline participation (k = 5), the average correlation for the "no choice" was .330. This means that when forced to encode there is a positive relationship between incentives and attitude change. This finding should be contrasted with the overall effect when persons are permitted to make a choice of -.295 (for the set of 23 studies discussed earlier).

DISCUSSION

The meta-analysis reveals that incentives are negatively related to self-persuasion following written CAA only under the conditions of no choice to participate. When studies permit persons to choose to participate, the impact for incentives is positive. These results provide important information for theoretical and practical reasons.

Table 13.3.Moderator Search.

	Overall	No choice
K	41	23
Total *N*	2,682	1,515
Average *N*	65	66
Average *r*	-.106	-.295
Expected variance	.015	.013
Actual variance	.067	.015
Percent	22%	87%

On a theoretical level, the meta-analysis has implications for several theories. The negative-incentive-self-persuasion relationship can be interpreted as an outcome of dissonance, self-perception, impression management, or functional accounts for CAA. The incentive interpretation becomes clearly inconsistent with the summary of the studies. The impression management account may be feasible because features of the experimental situation might produce a desire to convey consistency and/or the essay writing might pose a hedonistic or moral dilemma. In spite of this possibility, the moderator variables were not detected. This indicates a stable effect, not one associated with different types of dilemmas or different features of situations.

Of the remaining theories, the results tend to favor a dissonance interpretation. In the studies allowing participants no choice to encode, an average correlation for the effects of incentives was .330 (high incentives more persuasive). However, the 23 effect sizes allowing free encoding choice show a correlation of -.295 (low incentives more persuasive). Dissonance theory postulates the superiority of free-choice-low-incentive situation, the encoder must consider the counterattitudinal nature of the task and the motive for performing. To resolve the inconsistency, the encoder changes his or her attitude. In the no-encoding-choice condition, a different process maybe operating. Faced with coercion to encode, inducements or payments may create the dissonance for counterattitudinal behavior. For those given no choice, the incentive becomes a bribe. This means that the person does not confront a crisis with their own personal attitudes, they are only doing it for the money.

Of course, self-perception, impression management, or functional theorists can make an equally plausible case by abandoning dissonance theory's cognitive consistency approach and adopting behavioral consistency. If the behavior is self-observed, then low incentive-high choice may be interpreted as a sign of internal states and results in attitude change (self-perception theory). If the same low-incentive-high-choice condition is made, the encoder feels the need to appear rational to the person conducting the experiment (impression management), and the persuasion might be reported. If encoders feel they have appeared foolish by voluntarily encoding silly information, they may hide their embarrassment by indicating a change in opinion. This meta-analysis confirms the incentive-choice-to-encode relationship detected by Kelman (1953), but it does not identify a single explanation for the effect. Little progress seems to have made since Rosenberg (1968) noted that mediational processes for CAA outcomes were not well understood.

The meta-analysis suggests that advocacy in counterattitudinal situations will be most effective if individuals have the choice about whether to participate and if limited reward is offered for participation. This logic is also consistent with marketing practices that offer token incentives (coupons, rebates, and bonuses) to induce purchasing behavior and build brand loyalty. It remains to be determined if this offer involves counterattitudinal behavior or not.

Often institutions or other social groups require persons to articulate messages they do not fully accept. The findings of this meta-analysis indicate that such a procedure may be fruitful at inducing eventual acceptance of the message conclusion by persons. The authors are currently at work expanding this meta-analysis to include consideration of nonwritten messages and other features of the counterattitudinal situation that contributes to self-persuasion.

REFERENCES

Ashmore, R. D., & Collins, B. E. (1968). Studies in forced compliance: X. Attitude change and commitment to maintain publicly a counterattitudinal position. *Psychological Reports, 22,* 1229-1234.

Baron, R. M. (1968). Attitude change through discrepant action: A functional analysis. In T. C. Brock & T. M. Ostrom (Eds.), *Psychological foundation of attitudes* (pp. 297-326). New York: Academic Press.

Bem, D. J. (1965). An experimental analysis of self-persuasion. *Journal of Experimental Social Psychology, 1*, 199-218.

Bem, D. J., & McConnell, H. K. (1970). Testing the self-perception explanation of dissonance phenomena: On the salience of premanipulation attitudes. *Journal of Personality and Social Psychology, 14*, 23-31.

Benware, C., & Deci, E. L. (1975). Attitude change as a function of the inducement for espousing a proattitudinal communication. *Journal of Experimental Social Psychology, 11*, 271-278.

Berger, C. R. (1969). Need to influence and feedback regarding influence outcomes as determinants of the relationship between incentive magnitude and attitude change. *Speech Monographs, 36*, 435-442.

Bodaken, E. M., & Miller, G. R. (1971). Choice and prior audience attitude as determinants of attitude change following counterattitudinal advocacy. *Speech Monographs, 38*, 109-112.

Carlsmith, J. M., Collins, B. E., & Helmreich, R. L. (1966). Studies in forced compliance: I. The effect of Pressure for compliance on attitude change produced by face-to-face role playing and anonymous essay writing. *Journal of Personality and Social Psychology, 4*, 1-13.

Chiu, W. C. L. (1982). *Cognitive dissonance reduction: Attitude and behavior change in forced compliance*. Unpublished doctoral dissertation, University of Washington, Seattle, WA.

Cohen, A. R. (1962). A "forced compliance" experiment on repeated dissonances. In J. W. Brehm & A. R. Cohen (Eds.), *Explorations in cognitive dissonance* (pp. 97-104. New York: Wiley.

Collins, B. E., & Helmreich, R. L. (1970). Studies in forced compliance: II. Contrasting mechanism of attitude change produced by public-persuasive and private-true essays. *Journal of Social Psychology, 81*, 253-264.

Collins, B. E., & Hoyt, M. F. (1972). Personal responsibility-for-consequences: An integration and extension of the "forced compliance" literature. *Journal of Experimental Social Psychology, 8*, 558-593.

Cooper, J., & Duncan, B. L. (1971). Cognitive dissonance as a function of self-esteem and logical inconsistency. *Journal of Personality, 39*, 289-302.

Cooper J., Jones, E. E., & Tuller, S. M. (1972). Attribution dissonance, and the illusion of uniqueness. *Journal of Experimental Social Psychology, 8*, 45-57.

Crano, W. D., & Messé, L. A. (1970). When does dissonance fail? The time dimension in attitude measurement. *Journal of Psychology, 38*, 493-508.

Crano, W. D., & Sivacek, J. (1984). The influence of incentive-aroused ambivalence on overjustification effects in attitude change. *Journal of Experimental Social Psychology, 20*, 137-158.

Darley, S. A., & Cooper, J. (1972). Cognitive consequences of forced noncompliance. *Journal of Personality and Social Psychology, 24*, 321-326.

Festinger, L. (1957). *A theory of cognitive dissonance*. Stanford, CA: Stanford University Press.

Gerard, H. B. (1967). Compliance, expectation of reward, and opinion change. *Journal of Personality and Social Psychology, 6*, 360-364.

Girodo, M. (1970). *A conflict-theory approach to attitude change*. Unpublished doctoral dissertation, Carleton University, Northfield, MN.

Greenwald, A. G. (1975). On the inconclusiveness of "crucial" cognitive tests of dissonance versus self-perception theories. *Journal of Experimental Social Psychology, 11*, 490-499.

Harris, V. A., & Tamler, H. (1971). Reinstatement of initial attitude and forced-compliance attitude change. *Journal of Social Psychology, 84*, 127-134.

Helmreich, R. L., & Collins, B. E. (1968). Studies in forced compliance: Commitment and magnitude of inducement to comply as determinants of attitude change. *Journal of Personality and Social Psychology, 10*, 75-81.

Holmes, J. G., & Strickland, L. H. (1970). Choice freedom and confirmation of incentive expectancy as determinants of attitude change. *Journal of Personality and Social Psychology, 14*, 39-45.

Hornbeck, F. W. (1971). Studies in forced compliance: IX. The effects of deception, commitment, and incentive on attitude change produced by the writing of a counterattitudinal essay. *Journal of Social Psychology, 83*, 63-72.

Hunter, J., Schmidt, F., & Jackson, G. (1982). *Meta-analysis*. Beverly Hills, CA: Sage.

Janis, I. L., & Gilmore, J. B. (1965). The influence of incentive conditions on the success of role playing in modifying attitudes. *Journal of Personality and Social Psychology, 1*, 17-25.

Jones, S. E. (1966). Attitude change of public speakers during the investigative and expressive stages of advocacy. *Speech Monographs, 33*, 137-146.

Kahle, L. R. (1978). Dissonance and impression management as theories of attitude change. *Journal of Social Psychology, 105*, 53-64.

Kelman, H. C. (1953). Attitude change as a function of response restriction. *Human Relations, 6*, 185-214.

Kiesler, C. A., & Sakamura, J. A. (1966). A test of model for commitment. *Journal of Personality and Social Psychology, 3*, 349-353.

Linder, D. E., Cooper, J., & Jones, E. E. (1967). Decision freedom as a determinant of the role of incentive magnitude in attitude change. *Journal of Personality and Social Psychology, 6*, 245-254.

Miller, G. R. (1973). Counterattitudinal advocacy: A current appraisal. In C.D. Mortensen & K. K. Sereno (Eds.), *Advances in communication research* (pp. 105-152). New York: Harper & Row.

Nel, E., Helmreich, E., & Aronson, E. (1969). Opinion change in the advocate as a function of the persuasibility of his audience. *Journal of Personality and Social Psychology, 12*, 117-124.

Piliavin, J. A., Paliavin, I. M., Loewenton, E. P., McCauley, C., & Hammond, P. (1969). On observers' reproductions of dissonance effects: The right answers for the wrong reasons? *Journal of Personality and Social Psychology, 13*, 98-106.

Rosenberg, M. J. (1965). When dissonance fails: On eliminating evaluation apprehension from attitude measurement. *Journal of Personality and Social Psychology, 1*, 28-42.

Rosenberg, M. J. (1968). Discussion: On reducing the inconsistency between consistency theories. In R. P. Abelson, E. Aronson, W. J. McGuire, I. M. Newcomb, M. J. Rosenberg, & P. H. Tabin (Eds.), *Theories of cognitive consistency: A sourcebook* (pp. 827-833). Chicago: Rand-McNally.

Rossomando, N. P., & Weiss, W. (1970). Attitude change effects of timing and amount of payment for counterattitudinal behavior. *Journal of Personality and Social Psychology, 14*, 23-31.

Schlenker, B. R., Forsyth, D. R., Leary, M. R., & Miller, R. S. (1980). Self-presentational analysis of the effects of incentives on attitude change following counterattitudinal behavior. *Journal of Personality and Social Psychology, 39*, 553-577.

Sherman, S. J. (1970a). Effects of choice and incentive on attitude change in a discrepant action situation. *Journal of Personality and Social Psychology, 15*, 245-252.

Sherman, S. J. (1970b). Attitudinal effects of unforeseen consequences. *Journal of Personality and Social Psychology, 16*, 510-520.

Tedeschi, J. T., & Rosenfield, P. (1981). Impression management theory and the forced-compliance paradigm. In J. T. Tedeschi (Ed.), *Impression management theory and social psychological research* (pp. 149-180). New York: Academic Press.

Touhey, J.C. (1973). Individual differences in attitude change following two acts of forced compliance. *Journal of Personality and Social Psychology, 27*, 96-99.

14

Evaluating the Advice Offered by the Tool Users

Mike Allen
University of Wisconsin-Milwaukee

Raymond W. Preiss
University of Puget Sound

This chapter takes the meta-analyses in this book and compares the conclusions of those reviews to the prescriptions and conclusions offered by public speaking and persuasion textbooks. This comparison represents a more comprehensive extension of the earlier work of the present authors appearing in *Communication Education* (1990). Such a review provides a report card or status check of the field. The continued progression of the scientific study of communication requires and expects that as knowledge is obtained, there will be corrections and improvements in the textbooks in communication. The field of medicine uses meta-analysis to achieve similar advances as in persuasion (Altman, 1991). The meta-analytic findings create changes in practices of writing textbook summaries of available research. The change has authors relying on quantitative summaries of available research when drawing conclusions. The process of meta-analysis is common to all the sciences.

Physics, as a field, utilizes the same solution for the same challenges. For example, the gravitational constant represents a constant based on an average of estimates from studies. Each estimate is based on possible errors involves comparing various samples and each estimate could be in error. The check or correction for possible errors involves comparing various samples and experiments. The scientific study of communication addresses and resolves the same disputes as in other sciences by beginning to rely on systematic summary of results. The process of this change takes time,and is constantly an ongoing process; however, the prognosis looks favorable for the field.

Several important aspects of scientific knowledge exist that deserve consideration (Allen & Preiss, 1993): (a) stability, (b) lack of bias, (c) predictability, and (d) contextual generalizability. Scientific knowledge should provide a set of results that are stable over time and across conditions. The lack of bias aspect just indicates that the results do not represent the personal idiosyncrasies of the scientist but in fact are replicable across contexts and scientists. The predictability invites the idea that replications or predictions based on results demonstrate a necessary accuracy of results. The final aspect, contextual generalizability, argues that contextuality represents a theoretical issue. Context is relevant, but only within the framework of a particular theory, otherwise research should generalize across contextual parameters.

Meta-analysis, if it works, represents the distinct possibility of generating this type of knowledge. The chapters in this book represent attempts at generating those kinds of claims based on homogeneous findings across a variety of conditions. The claims then receive some empirical support in meeting the four conditions or aspects of scientific knowledge.

BOUNDARIES, LIMITATIONS, AND CONSIDERATIONS

The comparison between meta-analysis findings and textbooks requires the establishing of ground rules about what the comparison indicates. The scope of this review of textbooks, when compared to the entire scope of the works evaluated, remains extremely limited. Textbooks must take into consideration the prior knowledge and reading level of the students. The ability of introductory textbooks to introduce complicated or extended analyses of available data is not possible. This makes it difficult for authors to provide any full and in-depth evaluation of issues.

Public speaking and persuasion textbook authors comprehend and synthesize a vast and enormous literature spread across disciplines and over decades of published works. The identification, let alone compilation of such literature, represents a difficult and time consuming task for any single issue. No textbook author could perform a meta-analysis or anything resembling a comprehensive literature search in any general area, let along the vast and diverse areas necessary for an introductory textbook. The textbook author relies on advanced textbooks or competent reviewer's to provide syntheses and conclusions about issues. The disagreements between a textbook and a meta-analysis summary result not from any lack of competence or failure on the part of the textbook author(s), but rather from the weakness of the box score or narrative review techniques used by most other reviewers. The reliance on inadequate methods of summarizing experimental and survey research increases the probability that the representations within a textbook will not be entirely consistent with more thorough reviews.

In addition, meta-analysis is a relatively new technique and several of the particular meta-analyses included in this book are appearing for the first time. Any judgements made about textbooks stem from claims directed at the state of textbook writing about available research rather than particular books or authors. As pointed out, textbook authors generally rely on other experts for particular statements. The authors, in a very real sense, report a synopsis of the summaries made by others by a reading of a portion of the primary research on a topic. A comparison of the material footnoted to the actual textbook should demonstrate few errors or misrepresentations. The inconsistencies between textbook conclusions and the meta-analyses compare box score reviews to systematic quantitative summaries. This is not the case of the textbook author(s) reading the wrong primary material; the issue is that the nature of the task involved in handling the primary material is what is at stake. The analytic tool of the narrative review, without a supplementing systematic quantitative synthesis, contains a high potential for error. The resulting textbook summary simply reflects the errors of that analytic technique.

Reliance on narrative review techniques creates a confusing and contradictory set of literature in communication textbooks. If a person takes an individual textbook and compares the representation of the research in that textbook to another textbook, there would be no guarantee of consistency. Compare that situation to the Atomic chart of the elements in a chemistry book. If someone takes a collection of chemistry textbooks, the expectation would be that a large amount of agreement about the ordering and placement of elements on the chart would exist. Everything on the Atomic chart stems from the result of experimental and observational research. An examination of textbooks over a range of time would demonstrate differences as changes in scientific theory and findings accumulate. The additional information would increase the accuracy and completeness of the information in the table. A scientific endeavor requires at some point, an ability for the scientists to reach consensus about the existence of facts. Communication, until recently, developed little consensus about what conclusions to draw from research. There exists a reliance on complicated methodologies and theories to explicate the apparent inconsistency in research finding rather than simpler artifactual explanations.

The potential exists that some early set of results would become a standard for reviewers and textbook authors. This sort of research could create conditions of any early finding having immense credibility, despite all subsequent research failing to support hat finding. An example of this is provided by an article in the *Economist*, "Under the Metascope" (1991, May 18), which points out that the results of the Janis and Feshbach study on fear a appeals had never been replicated (the results were the basis of the claim of a curvilinear effect such that high and low fear appeals have little effect and only moderate fear appeals have great effect). The article points out that commercial users of such information (e.g., advertising firms) avoided fear appeals based on that "influential" study. The "influential" study possesses great impact, independent of the value or truth of the findings when compared to subsequent research.

The same can be said of the "cold" fusion research of the late 1980s. A first study promised fascinating findings, indicating the fusion could be a chemical rather than a thermal reaction, but now replications of this research lead to doubt. In the meantime, thousands of hours and effort have been devoted to this issue. However, physicists and chemists expect that as a result of this effort some conclusions will eventually emerge. The conclusions will be based on research and treated by textbooks "as facts." Although traditional science using rhetorical strategies to gain acceptance and adjudicate rival claims, the claims themselves are not rhetorical. The claims of the scientist involves no simple manipulation of symbolic references; the claims, if accepted, represent an empirical set of relations. Social science has found itself doubting the ability to be a "hard" science. There has been some question as to whether any set of "facts" will emerge from the available research. The basis of this problem largely stems from an inability to generate consistent conclusions from the research. This leads to speculation about the nature of the social sciences having variability and problems of specification different from that in the natural sciences. The argument was made that studying human behavior was a study of something complex and infinitely varied, defying systematic analysis. Given all the potential moderating conditions and intervening forces, and understanding of any phenomenon would be impossible. The failures or research in the 1960s and 1970s to generate lawlike statements and/or generalizable results created conditions of self-doubt and transformed the meaning of the term *scientific* study of communication. Scientific became difficult to define because all knowledge claims became bound by historical and cultural conditions.

Meta-analysis reintroduces and resurrects the possibility of generalizable results consistent with traditional scientific advancement. Cappella (1991) pointed out that science should produce knowledge claims that are "stable, pancultural, and ahistorical" (p. 6) with the goals of "prediction, causal explanation, control in principle, and understanding" (p. 28). This view of science is consistent with our position on the four aspects of scientific knowledge claims. The use of meta-analysis uniquely contributes to the possibility of the kinds of knowledge that Cappella sees as necessary for the development of a scientific study of communication.

The important aspect of Cappella's view is that the issue becomes defined as an empirical, rather than a philosophical, issue. The tendency in the social sciences is to sometimes substitute a philosophical position for what should be an empirical proposition. The test of a knowledge claim is the ability to fulfill the standards Cappella invoked. The failure of a scientific claim to meet those standards by definition indicates that the claim is not a scientific claim. The only challenge to the social scientists is to provide an example of one claim meeting that standard; once one claim is established, the possibility exists for establishing other such claims.

Sets of findings, like those in the chapters of this book, provide the basis of generalizable facts. The evaluation of theoretical statements becomes possible because there exists a series of acceptable statements consistent with available evidence. For example, the "language-as-fixed-effect" fallacy is inconsistent with the bulk of the empirical evidence in this volume. The ability of meta-analysis after meta-analysis to demonstrate homogeneous findings offers an empirical disproof for the arguments of this position. To continue to require particular types of experimental designs based on this argument would appear irrational.

Hedges (1987) reported that observed variability in experiments in particle physics resembles mathematically (virtually identical) the variability observed in several different areas of psychological research. If conclusions are possible in physics and chemistry despite the same problems of variability, the human communication issues should be resolvable. To put it another way, the variability of individual particles in physics experiments is the same as the variability of individual people in psychological experiments. Scholars have few objections to considering physics as a "hard" science; therefore, the case can be made that psychological studies may be a "hard" science in the same sense.

Meta-analysis, only in its infancy, has a long way to go before the generation of firm and definitive conclusions on issues. Some areas of agreement exist on issues like the attitude/behavior relationship (Kim &

Hunter, 1993a, 1993b) and fear appeals (Mongeau, Chapter 3, this volume). These areas start to establish "factoids" that can be eventually accumulated to establish or refute theoretical positions.

There exists a misunderstanding about the need to understand the complex forces at work to be able to make conclusions. Many scholars express the concern that the human mind and society are complex and the forces at work do not permit representation by theories. However, consider the human body: How can there exist medical science capable of prognosis and diagnosis and prescriptions for action (surgery and medicine)? Is not the DNA of each person different? Is not the blood chemistry and history such that no generalizable statements are possible? Medical science (as well as biology, ecology, and a host of other sciences) solved the same problems facing the communication scientist. The solutions involve rhetorical and persuasive acts typical to scientific endeavors. Commitment to a particular scientific product or to the process does not meant that science necessitates coherency or logicalness. Some views of science hold that all knowing as rhetorical and indicate that changes resemble "mob psychology." That is one interpretation of the Kuhnian view of scientific revolutions which are based on consensus to adopt changes. Consider however, Brown's (1977) view that the changes in science stem from the inherent desire for rationality and need to implement effective and useful solutions to problems prevents this "mob psychology" in the long term.

One important limitation of meta-analysis involves the nature of the original data. The original reports and operationalizations may not provide enough variability in situations to permit generalizable conclusions about the nature of "true" effects. A meta-analysis still produces correct conclusions about the state of the *current* research. That conclusion faces the boundary conditions of the *available* data. Meta-analysis permits the accumulation of data and therefore more certainty in the conclusions drawn from available data. Obviously, conclusions about effects of potential explanatory processes or moderating conclusions are not possible if they do not exist in the primary data. The limitations and definitions of the existing data for each of the meta-analyses should be read with extreme interest. The conclusions of the meta-analysis are bonded by those definitions and limitations described as well as those not described but present. However, these limitations do not uniquely effect meta-analysis. Any form of review contains the same limitations and those becomes exacerbated by an inability to systematically sort out *true* moderators from *possible* moderating influences. The difference between meta-analysis and other forms of review is the efficiency, explicitness, and replicability of the findings.

Despite the limitations of all forms of reviews, textbooks still must be written and advice must be offered to practitioners. Communication scientists must practice the art of muddling through the myriad of research findings from a variety of different fields to generate conclusions. Meta-analysis only represents a distinct form of improvement in the ability to generate conclusions from large bodies of research. Before relying on the scientific method, scholars relied on the brilliance of great thinkers. However, great thinkers can disagree about the effectiveness of particular choices. When great thinkers disagree about what advice to give, there exist few means of resolving those disputes. Eventually, social scientists sought to objectify knowledge claims within the framework of the scientific methodology. This claim of objectivity permits the resolution of disputes stemming from divergent set of claims.

The kind of objectivity stems from intersubjectivity, not objectivity in a logical or realistic sense. The acceptance of evidence eventually standardizes a set of beliefs. The claim advanced is not that the conclusions offered by an meta-analysis or set of empirical studies is correct, but rather that the eventual conclusion over a course of a body of work represents a consensus based on a consistent body of replicated findings. The subsequent conclusions can be incorrect and the theoretical interpretations and understandings erroneous. Science does not guarantee truth, science professes a search for truth using a preferred method.

ANALYSIS OF TEXTBOOKS

This section of the chapter takes the conclusions of the various meta-analyses and compares them to statements made by textbooks about those issues. If no statement was made about that issue in a textbook then no comparison can be made. A textbook could be scored as consistent (+), unclear (0), or inconsistent (-). This represents a crude but effective method of generally representing information in the textbooks. The purpose of this review is to demonstrate the advancement findings make, for pedagogy rather than a precise understanding of the field.

The full statistical summary and list of textbooks in this analysis is provided in Table 14.1. The choice of textbooks is a sample of convenience and represents no attempt to generate a random or representative sample. the purpose generates an illustrative example of the textbook treatment of the issues. This analysis gives an indication of what kinds on conclusions exist in textbooks rather than providing a definitive state of the art assessment.

The results demonstrate that only for the use of evidence is there overwhelming agreement among textbooks consistent with the available meta-analysis. The conclusion of the meta-analysis suggests that use of tes-

Table 14.1. Coding of Textbooks for Agreement with Meta-Analysis.

Textbook	Meta-Analysis[a]										
	1	2	3	4	5	6	7	8	9	10	11
Beebe & Beebe (1991)		+						+	-		
Bettinghaus & Cody (1987)	+	-	+	-				+	-		
Dance & Dance (1986)								+			
Glenn & Forman (1990)		-						+	-		
Larson (1989)	+	0						+	-		
Lee & Lee (1989)		+						+			
Lucas (1989)		+						+	0		
O'Keefe (1990)	-	+				+	0		+	+	+
Osborn & Osborn (1991)	0	-					+				
Petty & Cacioppo (1986)	-	-			0	+	+	0	0		
Powers (1987)								+			
Ross (1989)		0						+			
Simons (1986)		+						+	0		
Sprague & Stewart (1984)		-	0					+			
Stiff (1994)	+	+				+		+	+		-
Tedford (1991)		-						+	0		
Trenholm (1989)		-		0		+	-	+	0		
Vasile & Mintz (1989)								+			
Verderber (1991a)					+				+		
Verderber (1991b)		+				0			+		
Woodward & Denton (1988)	+		0								

[a]The numbers correspond to the following meta-analyses: (1) sleeper effect, (2) message sidedness, (3) powerful/powerless language, (4) language intensity, (5) rhetorical questions, (6) distraction, (7) forewarning, (8) evidence, (9) fear appeals, (10) counterattitudinal advocacy, (11) conclusion drawing.

timonial assertion evidence increases the persuasiveness of a message. This conclusion comes as little surprise to students of persuasion. The advantage of the meta-analysis is the consistency provided as well as an estimate of the effectiveness that the inclusion of evidence has on a message.

For the rest of the issues, the results are mixed. In general, the issues are not considered by large numbers of texts (only message sidedness is included in more than 50% of the textbooks). Generally, the research on these issues in persuasion/public speaking is not included. The particular issues seem to be considered only briefly and with little detail. This suggests that communication textbooks in persuasion and public speaking are operating outside of the research domain and more based on more traditional considerations as defined by rhetorical approaches. Generally, if one were to compare public speaking textbooks to Aristotle's *The Rhetoric* (trans. 1932) a person would find generally a great deal of correspondence. Either this indicates that the pedagogy of public speaking/persuasion has changed little or that textbook writers fail to capitalize on the wealth of available research. This need for integration is happening, but the expectation is that changes will occur slowly, while over the longer term the writing will improve.

Excluding the analysis of testimonial assertion evidence, the field averages about 50% on a hit-or-miss rate. The conclusions offered by textbooks often differ from that of the meta-analytic summary. One factor noted by the authors about the textbooks was the increasing use of meta-analytic summaries when making claims. This was responsible for a number of the accurate judgements. We expect this trend to continue and the accuracy and completeness of textbooks to increase. Although the current results do not demonstrate any immediate effect, the long term prospects should be positive.

Although the general outlook should be positive, there are a number of disturbing example encountered when reading the textbook representations. For example, one textbook review treated the meta-analysis as though it were a single study rather than an accumulation of studies. The text cited the meta-analysis as proving one point and than caveated the claim by pointing out that other studies disagreed. The authors of this chapter checked the bibliography of the meta-analysis and found that the "counterstudies" were included in the meta-analysis!

This illustrates the lack of understanding the textbook author had of what the meta-analysis indicated about the available literature. This is a concern because textbook authors must understand that such inconsistencies between primary research reports are often resolvable on the basis of sampling or artifactual error without recourse to more complex methodological or theoretical issues. There exists a real need to incorporate meta-analysis within the education of individuals both as undergraduate and graduate students. Meta-analysis represents a technique that continues to grow in importance and utilization. The application to practical issues requires that persons making such applications have some basic knowledge about the practices of the technique. The danger for misinformation and misleading claims is a real one.

A question might be asked about holding textbook authors accountable for the meta-analysis findings. The analysis treats the meta-analysis as an objective standard by which to compare the textbook. Such a standard implicitly (and in this case explicitly) assumes that the meta-analysis generates a correct answer. The textbook author is held accountable not to an objective appraisal but rather a particular standard of appraisal in the quantitative literature. A question not addressed by this review is whether and when such a standard should be used. Meta-analysis conclusions, when from a flawed analysis, can fail to accurately represent literature. The question becomes the timing of the acceptance of the conclusions and the implications of those conclusions for pedagogy and practical application. However, when compared to narrative review, meta-analysis offers a far better chance of making fewer errors.

This question goes to the heart of textbook writing and scientific inquiry. A textbook author can choose to ignore a particular meta-analysis or even the technique as a whole. However, when an author uses social scientific evidence as support for claims, this assumes the underlying principles of meta-analysis. Probability distributions and sampling error are the basis for inferential statistics, whether they are in the form of the t-test, correlation, F-test, or a meta-analytic summary. As the adage goes, "in for a penny, in for a pound." Once the decision is made to incorporate social science methods and results, the author should be prepared to complete the commitment to the method.

The other aspect is for textbooks that advance theoretical issues. When advancing a theory or evaluating various theories, textbook authors must demonstrate a willingness to evaluate theories based on available facts. Often textbook authors advance a theory, explain the theory, and provide some contradictions; however, the authors do not compare the theory to the available evidence. This is difficult in introductory textbooks in classes where the focus is skill improvement. The willingness to duck tough issues may be appropriate at that level and should be introduced at higher levels.

CONCLUSIONS AND OFFERINGS

The ability of research to provide some application to solving problems in the real world must become much more than a dream. Although not all research provides immediate solutions to practical problems, it is in the doing that the research bears fruit, not in the thinking. Persuasion research, in particular, is connected to practice. It is difficult to take the conclusions offered by the chapter authors and not quickly identify some context in which the conclusions could improve practice. The ability to incorporate research into the communicative practices of individuals provides the best opportunity for the test of true science.

Meta-analysis is not without drawbacks. One trend has been that reviewers and editors examine an empirical investigation and say that the relevant meta-analysis has been conducted and no more research needs to be conducted. Such a perspective misses much of what meta-analysis should offer. Meta-analysis provides a tool to clarify existing research for the conduct of future research. Meta-analysis offers a beginning point of departure for the scholar, not a destination. There is a need to replicate any particular meta-analysis using meta-analysis. Every meta-analysis is fraught with the potential for error at both a statistical, conceptual, and classification level. Every study, every statistic, every classification requires a decision on the part of some coder (typically the author of the meta-analysis).

The future of the quantitative approaches to the study of human behavior has never looked brighter. The ability to synthesize data existing across time and cultures and permit comparisons means that current investigations have lasting value and contribution to the development of theories and databases. The challenge of incorporating that knowledge into textbooks becomes an important one for both improving the textbooks and unifying knowledge claims. The result will reflect increasing homogenization of textbook content and the real importance of texts, the generation of forms that increase understanding of material become highlighted.

Meta-analysis represents opportunities to resolve disputes and improve the claimmaking of the scientific community. The tool users represent those persons that take the available knowledge (tools) and fashion something useful. Campaigns designed to reduce unsafe sex practices, diminish harmful drug use, and improve productivity of workers represent uses of the tools of persuasion. Meta-analysis makes possible the development of those tools that generate potential applications. Persuasion, because of the amount of research over the last 50 or so years stands to benefit uniquely from this approach.

REFERENCES

Allen, M., & Preiss, R. (1990). Using meta-analysis to evaluate curriculum: An examination of selected college textbooks. *Communication Education, 39,* 103–116.

Allen, M., & Preiss, R. (1993). Replication and meta-analysis: A necessary connection. *Journal of Social Behavior and Personality, 8*, 9–20.

Altman, L. (1991, May 7). Textbooks fall behind advance in medicine. *New York Times*, p. B6.

Aristotle. (1932). *The rhetoric of Aristotle* (L. Cooper, trans.). New York: Appleton–Crofts.

Beebe, S., & Beebe, S. (1991). *Public speaking: An audience-centered approach*. Englewood Cliffs, NJ: Prentice-Hall.

Bettinghaus, E., & Cody, M. (1987). *Persuasive communication* (4th ed.). New York: Holt, Rinehart & Winston.

Brown, H. (1977). *Perception, theory, and commitment*. Chicago: University of Chicago Press.

Cappella, J. (1991). The biological origins of automated patterns of human interaction. *Communication Theory, 1*, 4–35.

Dance, F., & Dance, G. (1986). *Public speaking*. New York: Harper & Row.

Glenn, E., & Forman, S. (1990). *Public speaking: Today and tomorrow*. Englewood Cliffs, NJ: Prentice-Hall

Hedges, L. (1987). How hard is hard science, and how soft is soft science? The empirical cumulativeness of research. *American Psychologist, 42*, 443–455.

Kim, M., & Hunter, J. (1993a). Attitude–behavior relations: A meta-analysis of attitudinal relevance and topic. *Journal of Communication, 43*, 101–142.

Kim, M., & Hunter, J. (1993b). Relationships among attitudes, behavioral intentions, and behavior. *Communication Research, 20*, 331–364.

Larson, C. (1989). *Persuasion: Reception and responsibility* (5th ed.). Belmont, CA: Wadsworth.

Lee, R., & Lee, K. (1989). *Arguing persuasively*. New York: Longman.

Lucas, S. (1989). *The art of public speaking* (3rd ed.). New York: Random House.

O'Keefe, D. (1990). *Persuasion: Theory and research*. Newbury Park, CA: Sage.

Osborn, M., & Osborn, S. (1991). *Public speaking* (2nd ed.). Boston: Houghton-Mifflin.

Petty, R., & Cacioppo, J. (1986). *Communication and persuasion: Central and peripheral routes to attitude change*. New York: Springer-Verlag.

Powers, J. (1987). *Public speaking: The lively art*. Belmont, CA: Wadsworth.

Ross, R. (1989). *Speech communication: The speechmaking system* (8th ed.). Englewood Cliffs, NJ: Prentice-Hall.

Simons, H. (1986). *Persuasion: Understanding practice and analysis* (2nd ed.). New York: Random House.

Sprague, J., & Stuart, D. (1984). *The speaker's handbook*. Orlando, FL: Harcourt Brace Jovanovich.

Stiff, J. (1994). *Persuasive communication*. New York: Guilford.

Tedford, T. (1991). *Public speaking in a free society*. New York: McGraw-Hill.

Trenholm, S. (1989). *Persuasion and social influence*. Englewood Cliffs, NJ: Prentice-Hall.

Under the metascope. (1991, May 18). *Economist*, 83, 91–92.

Vasile, A., & Mintz, H. (1989). *Speak with confidence: A practical guide* (5th ed.). Boston: Scott, Foresman.

Verderber, R. (1991a). *The challenge of effective speaking* (8th ed.). Belmont, CA: Wadsworth.

Verderber, R. (1991b). *Essentials of persuasive speaking: Theory and contexts*. Belmont, CA: Wadsworth.

Woodward, G., & Denton, R. (1988). *Persuasion & influence in American life*. Prospect Heights, IL: Waveland Press.

15

Evaluating and Using Meta-Analytic Knowledge Claims

James Price Dillard
University of Wisconsin-Madison

This is a heady time to be a student of persuasion. The application of meta-analytic methods to the persuasion literature promises to yield estimates of message effects that are more precise and more systematically derived than anything that we have seen before. That alone should be sufficient to make the heart of any quantitative persuasion researcher beat a bit more rapidly. However, the exhilarating fact is that we can expect the rate of knowledge generation to be faster in the near future than it ever has been or ever will be again. This is likely because of the time required to generate the number of primary studies suitable for meta-analysis versus the time required to carry out the meta-analyses themselves. Presently, we have the luxury of a great many investigations waiting to have their results integrated. As each meta-analysis consumes some portion of the existing primary studies, fewer data points remain for future analysts. At some future point, the generation of primary studies and meta-analyses will reach equilibrium. However, right now we are passing through a period in which the cumulation of knowledge may proceed at a more rapid pace than the generation of knowledge (at the level of primary studies).

Because this swift cumulation of knowledge should shape the future of persuasion research and determine which direction primary studies should take, it is important to give some consideration to the contents of this volume. What kinds of claims are the contributors making and on what basis do they make those claims? In the first portion of this chapter I discuss the process of statistical inference and the basis for making different types of knowledge claims. In the second portion I apply those ideas to the chapters that precede this one.

EVALUATING META-ANALYTIC KNOWLEDGE CLAIMS

The task of the researcher, whether involved with primary or meta-analytic data, is to assess the degree of support in the data for the claims made by the theory. In the ultra high-contrast world of Fisherian hypothesis testing, the significance test acts as arbiter. It determines in a black-and-white manner whether knowledge is present or absent.

As all beginning research methods textbooks explain, there are two kinds of mistakes that can be made in the course of significance testing. A Type I error occurs whenever the null hypothesis is incorrectly rejected. That is, a researcher concludes that a relationship exists between two variables when, in fact, this is not the case. Alpha error is the phrase used to describe the likelihood of Type I error. In communication, and in most allied disciplines, it is reified in that long-standing, but completely arbitrary, tradition of setting alpha at .05.

The obverse of a Type I error is said to be a Type II or beta error; the null hypothesis is incorrectly accepted. This can be defined as 1 - power, where the power of a statistical test is the likelihood that it will indicate the presence of a relationship provided that such a relationship exists.

Besides being two sides of the same coin, alpha and beta error have several things in common. One is their mutual dependence on two other parameters: sample size and effect size. It is well known that as sample size increases, the likelihood of making either sort of inferential error declines. Estimates become more accurate with larger samples because errors, which are random, have greater opportunity of cancel out one another. In addition, the likelihood of both error types decreases as a direct function of effect size. As the magnitude of the difference between two groups increases, the likelihood diminishes that the difference will be overwhelmed by error. Thus, bigger is better for both sample size and effect size.

Another thing that is shared by both types of error is their conditional nature. A Type I error is defined to be rejection of the null hypothesis *when in fact it is false*. Similarly, Type II error is acceptance of the null *when in fact it is false*. There is a certain paradoxical aspect to these definitions. Both errors are predicated on knowing the true status of the null hypothesis. Isn't that what we were trying to find out in the first place?

A Statistical Inference Problem

Although the logic of hypothesis testing appears sound enough, in practice it can be problematic. One difficulty is that investigations are frequently underpowered. To get a sense of the pervasiveness of this problem consider the following: Thirty years ago, Cohen (1962) published a review of articles in that had appeared in the *Journal of Abnormal and Social Psychology*. The median power of the investigations he examined was .46. In other words, assuming that the null hypothesis was false in every case, the investigators had less than a 50-50 chance of obtaining that finding using a significance test.

More recently, Sedlmeier and Gigerenzer (1989) conducted a similar study of a broader range of psychological journals. Out of their efforts came the disheartening conclusion that the median power under the same conditions had actually decreased over the years (to .44)! Lest you jump to the conclusion that such irrational behavior is limited to the field of psychology, the predilection for underpowered inquiry has also been documented in communication (Chase & Tucker, 1975) and mass communication (Chase & Baran, 1976).

It is generally thought that there is a bias against the publication of nonsignificant results (Greenwald, 1975). Individual authors suffer most directly from this bias because their underpowered studies are not likely to yield significant findings. However, the problem goes well beyond the consequences to individual. Consider a body of studies in which the null hypothesis is false, but the power to detect a relationship is .44. Most of the studies will not find a significant relationship and thus most will conclude that no reliable empirical relationship exists. As Hedges and Olkin (1980) noted, as more studies are conducted, confidence in the no-relationship conclusion will grow. The broad consequence is that an area of inquiry may wither and die simply because of underpowered studies. Although meta-analysis has the capacity to save the day by demonstrating an effect via cumulation, someone must be sufficiently interested in the area in question to apply meta-analytic methods to the literature.

A Logical Problem

In many instances, a significance test is conducted that yields a result that does not quite vault the $p < .05$ hurdle. The proper interpretation of such a finding is that there is no evidence of a reliable relationship. In plainer language, that conclusion amounts to the inference that "Nothing can be concluded." All too frequently, however, the conclusion shades over into something like "This study shows that the relationship does not exist." Armed with the absence of a positive relationship, the researcher asserts the existence of a negative relationship.

Clearly this is not logical, but it occurs with alarming frequency. Sedlmeier and Gigerenzer (1989) reported that in 11% of the studies they examined, research hypotheses were framed as null hypotheses and their nonsignificance was construed as confirmation.

Types of Knowledge Claims

As I hope the preceding discussion makes apparent, knowledge claims of the categorical sort can take two forms. A positive claim is made whenever a researcher asserts the existence of a relationship between two or more variables. When evidence is generated that is consistent with such claim, we speak of this result as having supported the research hypothesis. When no such evidence is forthcoming, we might hear the phrase "Failed to reject the null hypothesis."

A negative claim is made whenever a researcher asserts that there is no relationship between two or more variables. Although this language is no doubt familiar, it encourages some confusion because the terms positive and negative are used here to indicate the presence and absence respectively of a relationship and the same terms are frequently used to refer to characterize the sign of a relationship. Whereas I normally try to resist the urge to generate acronyms and neologisms, for the sake of clarity I refer here to positive knowledge claims as RP claims (for relationship present) and negative knowledge claims as RA claims (for relationship absent).

Both RP and RA claims are equally important to the study of persuasion and to the assessment of theory in any area of inquiry. As an illustration of this point, assume a theory that specifies a short causal chain; X causes Y causes Z. This theory contains two RP claims (X directly influences Y and Y directly influences Z) and one RA (X has no direct effect on Z). If empirical testing revealed that X had a direct effect on Z, this would indicate misspecification equal in importance to a failure to observe either of the associations predicted as XY or YZ. The absence of the X-Z relationship has the same logical status relative to the theory as the presence of the XY or YZ relationships (see Segrin & Dillard, 1992, for a meta-analytic application).

Moreover, the basis for inferring support for either type of claim is the same at the level of primary data or meta-analytic data. The degree of support for either an RP or an RA claim can be determined by attending to the four pillars of statistical inference: sample size; effect size; the likelihood of alpha error—that is a false positive; and the likelihood of beta error—that is a false negative. The interrelationships among these parameters are described in Table 15.1.

RP CLAIMS IN THIS VOLUME

With these relationships in mind it is useful to consider the findings of the meta-analyses in this volume. A sampling of RP claims appears in Table 15.2. The criteria used in selecting these findings were twofold. First, because the attitude concept is so fundamental to research in persuasion, I tried to cull

Table 15.1. The Relationships Among the Parameters of Statistical Inference.

	Sample size	Effect size	Likelihood of alpha error	Alpha level
Effect size	Independent	-------		
Likelihood of alpha error[a]	Negative	Negative	-------	
Alpha level[a]	Independent	Independent	Positive	-------
Likelihood of beta error[b]	Negative	Negative	Negative	Negative
Power[b]	Positive	Positive	Positive	Positive

[a]Alpha level is set by the researcher or by the research community. As it decreases (i.e., becomes more stringent), the likelihood of alpha error decreases correspondingly.

[b]Power is defined as 1 - β. Thus, the two rows are mirror images of one another.

Table 15.2. A Sampling of RP (Relationship Present) Knowledge Claims.

Chapter author	Claim	*k*	*N*	*r*
Mongeau	Manipulated fear increases agreement	13	1,914	.21
Allen	Refutational two-sided messages increase agreement	43	7,359	.07
Reinard	Testimonial assertions increase agreement	16	2,800	.19
Benoit	Forewarning decreases agreement	12	1,359	.18
Buller& Hall	Auditory, nonverbal distractors decrease agreement	11	476	-.05
Burrell & Koper	Powerful language increases agreement	6	463	.25
Hamilton & Hunter	Perceived language intensity increases agreement	5	1,567	.11
Gayle, Preiss, & Allen	Indirect rhetorical questions increase agreement	3	210	.27
Preiss & Allen	Incentives decrease agreement with counterattitudinal advocacy	23	1,515	-.29
Average		15	1,963	|.18|

Note. Because some of the findings require qualifications that could not be made explicit in this table, readers are encouraged to review the individual chapters. The estimate attributed to Buller and Hall is taken from Buller (1986).

one finding from each chapter that described the effect of some message variable on attitude; that is, agreement with the message. Second, only those relationships that were reported to represent statistically homogeneous distributions were included in the table. Chapters that did not find stable estimates do not appear in the table,such as Allen and Stiff's work in Chapter 9 on the sleeper effect and Cruz's work in Chapter 12 on explicitness.

The final row of the table provides a numerical summary of the findings. It shows the average number of estimates on which the findings are based to be 15, the average number of subjects to be 1,963, and the absolute average effect size to be .18. What are we to make of such numbers? First of all, consider average effect size; r = .18. By Cohen's (1987) standards, our average effect is small. In fact, by Cohen's standards, *all* of the effects in the table are small. Although convincing arguments have been advanced regarding the theoretical and practical importance of small effects (Prentice & Miller, 1992; Rosenthal, 1984), the fact remains that smaller effects are more difficult to detect than are larger effects (see Table 15.1). If, as Table 15.2 suggests, the field of persuasion is built on effects that are roughly .18 in magnitude, then we need correspondingly large *N*s in order to make sound knowledge claims. Taking the effect size of .18 as a guide for future work, researchers should plan on utilizing samples of almost 200 for two-cell designs to achieve Cohen's (1987) recommended power of .80.

Next, let's look at the average number of estimates; that is, 15. Assuming homogeneity of variance, 15 would seem to be a comfortable number of studies on which to draw a conclusion. However, conditions may obtain in a literature of that size that should limit our confidence in the resulting meta-analytic finding. One such condition occurs when the literature is dominated by a single researcher or set of researchers. For example, Gayle, Preiss, and Allen (Chapter 10, this volume) report a positive relationship between persuasion and the use of indirect rhetorical questions; a conclusion that is qualified by the fact that it is based on three studies conducted by the same authors. That should not be taken as an indictment of the primary researchers. However, every research project contains a myriad of details that may shape the findings in ways that are not obvious to the researchers or consumers of the research. These scope conditions or "operational contingencies" (Chaffee, 1991, p. 19) qualify the results. We can expect that effects of unstated or unrecognized operational contingencies should average out across researchers. When the literature is dominated by a single or small set of researchers, that desirable cancellation of scope conditions is much less likely.

Another problem, conceptually similar but distinct in practice, is that of multiple uses of the same message. The worst case scenario is a literature of 15 studies, all of which use the same message. The limitations of such a literature are so apparent that they need no elaboration.

Returning to Table 15.2, consider the column labeled "*N*." Here we see that the average number of subjects across findings is 1,963. Assuming an effect size of r = .18—the average effect in the table—the *N* of 1,963 yields a 95% confidence interval that runs from .14 to .22. These values encourage a cautious confidence toward the meta-analytic findings, but they are inflated by an outlier: Allen's *N* of 7,359. When Allen's sidedness *N* is excluded, the average becomes 1,288 and the 95% confidence interval grows to .13 to .23. The resulting average *N* is remarkably close to the average *N* of 1,197 reported by Hale and Dillard (1991) in their review of meta-analyses that appeared *Communication Monographs* and *Human Communication Research* prior to 1991. Although both average *N*s are clearly larger than samples of the vast majority of primary studies, neither permits confidence that our estimates do any more than establish the effect size of first value to the right of the decimal.

To review, the confidence with which a meta-analytic RP knowledge claim can be advanced depends very heavily on the number of studies reviewed (*k*), the number of subjects included in those studies (*N*), and the strength of the effect (*r*). Like inference at the level of primary studies, larger sample sizes and effect sizes encourage greater faith in the claim. The data reviewed in Table 15.1 suggest that we should adopt a somewhat humble attitude toward many of the knowledge RP claims found in this volume. Without question, they represent the best estimates currently available. However, the databases are not typically so large that we can suggest that the issues are settled.

RA CLAIMS IN THIS VOLUME

RA claims assert the absence of a relationship between two variables. When I attempted to construct a table of RA claims to parallel the table of RP claims, I found that I was unable to do so. In some cases, the problem arose from lack of data. Burrell and Koper (Chapter 11, this volume) indicated that they would have liked to make an RA claim regarding the role of gender as a moderator of the effects of powerful-powerless language, but their database lacked the necessary information to conduct the test.

For other chapters, however, the authors did make more or less explicit RA claims, but they used different strategies for doing so. One approach to advancing an RA claim is closely tied to the logic of the homogeneity of variance test. Benoit, for example, concludes in Chapter 7 of this volume that a delay, between forewarning and message, has no impact on the relationship between forewarning and persuasion. His conclusion flows from the observation that "the ratio of error variance to observed variance was .75. This indicates that no moderator variables influence the operation of forewarning in persuasion" (p. 145). Although Benoit does not do so, many researchers depend on a nonsignificant chi-square test to advance their RA claim (Johnson & Turco, 1992).

Other authors pursued a more focused strategy. For example, Hamilton and Hunter (Chapter 6, this volume) tested the effect of source gender on the relationship between perceived language intensity and attitude by first cumulating effects within groups defined by male (r = .05) and female (r = .02) sources, then conducting a formal significance test of the difference between two correlations. The resulting z value of .74 indicated that the correlations were not reliably different from one another. The Reinard chapter (4) offers additional examples of this approach.

A third group of meta-analysts prefer a different standard for making RA claims. Among them is Mongeau (Chapter 3, this volume). He argues that the quadratic effect of perceived fear on attitude change is inconsequential relative to the main effect. This approach privileges effect size and over the significance test.

A summary of the three approaches to making RA claims is given in Table 15.3. As the table shows, the first approach does not explicitly contrast any particular pair of effects, but rather depends on the overall test of homogeneity of variance (i.e., either the significance test or the 75% rule). Although the statistics are sound, there is a temptation to draw a stronger conclusion than the data might warrant. The seductive, but potentially dangerous, inference from a nonsignificant chi-square is that "There are no moderators that influence the magnitude of the relationship under scrutiny." Such a sweeping RA claim might be justified given a large number of primary studies conducted by different investigators who had identified and included all of the potential moderators. In reality, this strategy must yield more modest RA claims that (a) recognize the assumptions and weaknesses of the entire body of research studies and (b) explicitly identify the theoretically based moderators that actually appear in the primary studies. A nonsignificant result from a homogeneity of variance test does not confirm the absence of moderator variables. Rather, it asserts that such an account of the data may be plausible.

The second strategy is characterized in Table 15.3 as the focused, significance test. Purely in terms of conceptual inference, this method is superior to the previous approach insofar as it focuses the attention of the researcher on the limits of the RA claim. Focused tests are less likely to be seen as the basis for sweeping inferences. In addition, because there is the possibility that a group of studies could contain a significant contrast despite a nonsignificant homogeneity of variance statistic (Johnson & Turco, 1992), focused tests provide much more compelling evidence for RA claims than do unfocused tests.

The third strategy is a very practical one. It asks simply whether or not the effect is big enough to matter. A meaningful answer requires some standard against which to evaluate the effect. This is a desirable approach in

Table 15.3. Strategies for Making RA (Relationship-Absent) Knowledge Claims.

Information strategy	Comparison	Criterion	Relative desirability	Demand
1	Unfocused test or 75% rule	Significance	Low	Low
2	Focused test	Significance	Medium	Medium
3	Focused size	Effect	High	High

that it sidesteps the numerous problems associated with significance tests. As an illustration, consider Mongeau's assessment of the quadratic effect of perceived fear on attitude change. He dismissed an effect of $r = .09$ because it was small relative to the size of the main effect, $r = .19$. By contrast, Allen reports that "the two-sided message with refutation was superior to the one-sided message" (Chapter 5, this volume, p. 93) on the basis of an effect size or $r = .07$.

As the column labeled Relative Desirability shows, the three strategies are arrayed in terms of their comparative utility for making RA knowledge claims. The basis for this ordering is primarily the specificity of thought that corresponds to each strategy; more precise predictions result in more precise knowledge gains. However, each of the three strategies has different information demands. Strategy 1 requires no theory, but produces the weakest evidence in favor of an RA claim. To utilize a focused significance test, Strategy 2, the researcher must have, at minimum, some hunch that will guide the partitioning of the data set. The third strategy, which produces the most valuable sort of result, also requires the greatest amount of information. A context for implementing Strategy 3 might come from strong theory or a well-defined applied context.

USING META-ANALYTIC KNOWLEDGE CLAIMS

When a research literature is summarized, there is frequently an implication that the meta-analyst has wrestled The Final Answers out of that body of work. Anyone who is interested a particular area of inquiry has only to read the appropriate meta-analysis, then move on to research in other realms that are too new to have been quantitatively summarized. I believe that such a view is wrongheaded. In light of the relatively small sample sizes of entire literatures, the relatively small effect sizes, and the lack of consensus regarding how to evaluate RA claims, it will usually be better to treat meta-analytic findings as guidance for future research rather than problems that have been fully solved. Cooper and Hedges (1994) made this same point forcefully when they noted that a "synthesis that concludes that a problem is solved, that no future research is needed, should be deemed a failure" (p. 524). Several kinds of studies can usefully follow meta-analyses (Hale & Dillard, 1991):

1. *Replications of claims based on small samples.* As several of the chapters in this volume illustrate, meta-analytic claims are sometimes based on small numbers of studies, messages, or subjects. For example, Gayle, Preiss, and Allen (Chapter 10, this volume) advance the RP claim that indirect rhetorical questions increase agreement with the advocacy of the persuasive message. However, that conclusion is based on only three studies with a combined *N* of 210. Clearly, further primary research on rhetorical questions is needed. If, in fact, the field of persuasion is a field of relatively small effects, replications will be judged valuable to the extent that they are built on large samples of subjects and messages.
2. T*ests of proposed moderators.* Typically, the existing literature contains studies that have examined the influence of one or more moderators for the effect in question. Naturally, meta-analysts often explicitly test those same moderators. The chapter concerned with conclusion explicitness offers several examples. Cruz (Chapter 12, this volume) tests three potential moderators: source credibility, involvement, and initial position. Despite his vigorous efforts, none of the moderators proved adequate to the task of organizing the data into homogeneous groups. As he notes, the "meta-analysis indicates that few conclusions can be drawn from previous research" (p. 223). His pessimism is justified; there are not enough data in the research literature on explicitness to draw any firm inferences whatsoever. Additional primary research into all of the moderators proposed in the literature will have to be conducted before we can make any sort of theoretical claim with confidence.

3. *Primary studies based on post hoc ratings of moderators.* One of the strengths of meta-analysis is its capacity for testing hypotheses that were not tested by any one of the primary studies in the data base. This is achieved by grouping studies so as to reflect moderator variables not considered by the primary researchers. Buller and Hall (Chapter 8, this volume) illustrate this point nicely in their distinction between communication-relevant and -irrelevant distractors. Their post hoc grouping of studies, based on the communication relevance of the distractors, led them to argue for the existence of distinct theoretical processes arising from the two different types of distractors. The next step is primary research that examines the operation of the distractors in a single, factorial design.
4. *Direct tests of theoretical processes.* In his summary of the effects of two-sided messages, Allen (Chapter 5, this volume) is blessed with a substantial number of both studies (43) and subjects (7,359). This wealth of data yields some of the strongest generalizations to be found in this publication. Despite solid empirical generalizations about the effect of sidedness on persuasion, a clear understanding of the underlying process remains elusive. Does the effectiveness of two-sided messages come about because such messages short circuit the counterargumentation process that occurs with one-sided messages? Or do two-sided messages have greater impact than one-sided messages because they produce stronger inferences of source credibility which, in turn, produce more agreement with the advocacy? Primary studies that directly assess each stage of the proposed theoretical process would be extremely valuable (see also Benoit, Chapter 7, this volume).

CONCLUSION

Readers of this volume are probably already convinced of the value of meta-analysis. My aim has not been to reinforce that opinion, which I obviously share, but rather to make clear some of the criteria for judging meta-analytic claims as well as to specify how primary studies might usefully follow from meta-analyses. In large measure, that has meant simply reconsidering the statistical principles that all working social scientists use on a regular basis; that is the interrelationships among alpha, beta, *N*, and effect size. Appreciation of these basic ideas as they relate to meta-analysis allows for a sophisticated evaluation of the knowledge claims found in this volume. Just as importantly, careful consideration of the knowledge claims allow us to plan the next generation of persuasion studies. Some findings demand replication. Other results suggest ways in which theory can be sharpened so that the scope conditions of the effects are better specified or the mediating processes made more clear. Whatever the state of knowledge in a particular question, the chapters in this volume should reinvigorate the study of persuasion.

REFERENCES

Buller, D. B. (1986). Distraction during persuasive communication: A meta-analytic review. *Communication Monographs, 53*, 91-114.

Chaffee, S. H. (1991). *Explication*. Newbury Park, CA: Sage.

Chase, L. J., & Baran, S. J. (1976). A methodological assessment of quantitative research in mass communication: Statistical power, type II error, and data description. *Journalism Quarterly, 53*, 308-311.

Chase, L. J., & Tucker, R. K. (1975). A power-analytic examination of contemporary communication research. *Speech Monographs, 42*, 29-41.

Cohen, J. (1962). The statistical power of abnormal-social psychological research: A review. *Journal of Abnormal and Social Psychology, 65*, 145-153.

Cohen, J. (1987). *Statistical power analysis for the behavioral sciences* (2nd ed.). Hillsdale, NJ: Erlbaum.

Cooper, H., & Hedges, L. V. (1994). Potentials and limitations of research synthesis. In H. Cooper & L.V. Hedges (Eds.), *The handbook of research synthesis* (pp. 521-530). New York: Russell Sage Foundation.

Greenwald, A. G. (1975). Consequences of prejudice against the null hypothesis. *Psychological Bulletin, 82*, 1-20.

Hale, J. L., & Dillard, J. P. (1991). The uses of meta-analysis: Making knowledge claims and setting research agendas. *Communication Monographs, 58*, 463-471.

Hedges, L. V., & Olkin, I. (1980). Vote counting methods in research synthesis. *Psychological Bulletin, 88*, 359-369.

Johnson, B. T., & Turco, R. M. (1992). The value of goodness-of-fit indices in meta-analysis: A comment on Hall and Rosenthal. *Communication Monographs, 59*, 388-396.

Prentice, D., & Miller, D. T. (1992). When small effects are impressive. *Psychological Bulletin, 112*, 160-164.

Rosenthal, R. (1984). *Meta-analytic procedures for social research*. Beverly Hills, CA: Sage.

Sedlmeier, P., & Gigerenzer, G. (1989) Do studies of statistical power have an effect on the power of studies? *Psychological Bulletin, 105*, 309-316.

Segrin, C., & Dillard, J.P. (1992). The interactional theory of depression: A meta-analysis of the research literature. *Journal of Social and Clinical Psychology, 11*, 43-70.

Sedlmeier, P., & Gigerenzer, G. (1989) Do studies of statistical power have an effect on the power of studies? *Psychological Bulletin, 105*, 309-316.

Segrin, C., & Dillard, J.P. (1992). The interactional theory of depression: A meta-analysis of the research literature. *Journal of Social and Clinical Psychology, 11*, 43-70.

Author Index

Subject Index